The Canyon Wren

The Canyon Wren

Stories of My Horses: Volume III

Written and Illustrated by

Martín Prechtel

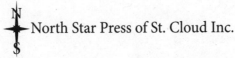North Star Press of St. Cloud Inc.

Library of Congress CIP data available upon request.

First Edition
ISBN: 978-1-68201-129-4

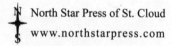 North Star Press of St. Cloud
www.northstarpress.com

Printed in Canada.

Cover painting: *Voice of the Giant*, by Martín Prechtel.
All text and interior line drawings by Martín Prechtel.
Cover design and interior layout by Liz Dwyer of North Star Press.

Type set in Times New Roman, headings set in Brioso, and Brioso Semibold Italic.

Table of Contents

Notice

All three volumes of the *Stories of My Horses* are meant as an overdue love letter and tribute to all the horses of my life and my beloved New Mexico for the spiritual nourishment and down-to-earth vitality that like a beautiful warm blanket has kept me warm and hopeful through the cold cynical blizzard of modernity's compromised sense of wonder.

While every adventure, misadventure, and episode found in these books took place precisely where and how they are described, I have taken the liberty of assigning alternative names for most but not all of the humans in my eternal faith that even mean people can change for the better, but also to protect the sweeter kind from any retribution from those that won't change and to respect the privacy of the shy. None of the horse's names have been changed so they can be remembered again by those who knew them.

Disclaimer

Neither the Publisher nor the Author accepts any liability for any mishaps, accidents, or any damages to people, property, or animals occurring from anyone who after reading the *Stories of My Horses* is erroneously led to act on any of the opinions expressed herein as advice of any type or who foolishly decides that they should try to re-enact any of the episodes described in these books in their own lives!

While We Were Riding, We Were Singing
A Horse Song:

(everyone sing)

For the never-ending wild land.
For the never-ending wild land.
For the never-ending wild land.
For the never-ending wild land.

For the wide-open ride.
For the wide-open ride.
For the wide-open ride.
For the wide-open ride.

For our horses' never-ending wild epic hearts, ridden by a
truly wide-open mind.
For our horses' never-ending wild epic hearts, ridden by a
truly wide-open mind.
For our horses' never-ending wild epic hearts, ridden by a
truly wide-open mind.
For our horses' never-ending wild epic hearts, ridden by a
truly wide-open mind.

Into every hoof print that we leave, may seeds of rich spiritual
substance fall.
Into every hoof print that we leave, may seeds of rich spiritual
substance fall.

Into every hoof print that we leave, may seeds of rich spiritual
substance fall.
Into every hoof print that we leave, may seeds of rich spiritual
substance fall.

To sprout a time of hope beyond our own.
To sprout a time of hope beyond our own.
To sprout a time of hope beyond our own.
To sprout a time of hope beyond our own.

Let the world jump back to life.
Let the world jump back to life.
Let the world jump back to life.
Let the world jump back to life.

(Please repeat — singing)

A Dedication

Because the undeniable presence of Pueblo people's early expertise with the old magnificent breed of horse on which their European oppressors arrived has been consciously and unfairly diminished, dismissed, or completely written out of the record of horse history by Euro-American academics, all three books of this series *Stories of My Horses*, are dedicated to the Tewa, Tiwa, Towa, Ashiwi, and especially the Keres speaking villages of the area now called New Mexico. These Pueblo people were indisputably the very first North American First Nation tribes to ever ride, drive, own, and raise horses. Despite four and a half centuries of colonial oppression, it was the original Native Pueblo people's continued proficiency with, reverence for, and adoption of the old Spanish *Mesta*-raised horses into the heart of their spiritual lives that actually converted these unique horses right out from under their own would-be religious converters, turning the colonialist's animals into the very different and fine Native horses they became. Either directly or indirectly it was from these Pueblo herds that *all* the great Native horse cultures—of the Plains, Prairies, and Northwest, of the entire American and Canadian west—received their first "indigified horses" upon whose backs their renowned mobility sky rocketed into the prominence their memory still maintains in the history of the North American Native West.

Introduction

Through their beauty, windy minds and zany souls, all the horses I have ever known have struggled to educate me. They have tried hard to teach me that true learning has less to do with what Life presents us than it does with how much of ourselves we put into learning from whatever Life hands us.

Nature has a million motives for all the twists and turns She takes, but Nature has no menu, for Nature is the soul of an infinite universe and in infinity there is no goal. However that infinite soul does have an unrelenting motive and that is to make infinite permutations of reality and existence, each one blossoming from the last.

These permutations are what people call Life. And since Life is Nature's precious offspring, then Her baby cannot be taken to task for any inappropriateness of the nature of that Life or whether or not our limited imaginations even accept the unexpected character of Life's lessons.

After all, Life is a lot bigger than we are and not really all that much about people when you get down to it. On the other hand, though each of us is only a fine particle of Life's bigger picture, our small human presence has always had the possibility of being a curiously wonderful part of that same whole. It is only our willingness as people to learn from whatever details of fate life throws at us that allows us to gestate into worthy people of true substance.

To repeat: real learning has less to do with what the shuffling lottery of Life's vast ever-morphing supply of intertwined circumstances present than it has to do with the degree of big-picture awareness we can muster out of the muddle of our scared self-centered steerage, so as to be willing to ride out all of Life's slopes, creative bucks, wriggles, doldrums, changes of direction and the unforeseen never-before-seen that forces us to really learn and turns us into people.

But most of all it is our inborn love for living, the thrill of seeing each sunrise returning, revealing the beauty of the world once again and the joy of seeing one another that drives any of us on and makes those who do determined and strong enough to stay in the struggle. The love of life is the grand muscle of our souls always straining to lift the water of our smaller destinies from Chance's infinite well of possibilities.

If even in our reckless embrace of life we are diligent enough to remember any of the details or sequences of our willingness to ride out what we have been given, then the memory of having done so is precious. For it is only from such in-your-face learning that we can build a mental personal reference library from our soul's actual experiences, a true knowing which others can revel in and rely on, now and in times to come, if only for the tale of having survived to *tell* the tale and pass it on to those who may feel too timid to live that purposefully. If our lives inspire in others what Nature has always commanded our lives to be—that a story-making life emerge from even the quietest citizen—then we have done well.

There are times when sitting on your butt for hours is necessary, but only when you're trying to mentally organize, remember and put together what you've learned when you weren't sitting on your bottom. There is worthy motion and worthy sitting, and evil motion and worthless sitting.

Even if we live artfully with the purpose of creating living beauty in our life's motion, it's still not enough, unless one's life is crafted to be a particle, a corpuscle, an actively useful part of Nature's evolving search to make more life. Contrary to what some unquestioningly tedious outdated "science" still teaches, evolution as present in Nature's proceedance cannot be characterized as truly competitive. In Nature there is no race, no goalpost and nothing to win. Nature evolves more and more intricate ways to keep alive a race-like flooding of effort toward beauty in order that all things "compete" to only make more and more interdependent forms that tangibly manifest more and more of the beauty and intricacy of each never-before-seen possibility of Nature's incurable imagination and Her need to tangibly manifest it. But there is no real race to win anything, just a race to constantly revive and renew all the racers. So if we must designate a winner, then only continued life is the winner.

It really is a bother to have to hide all the blanketing layers of my wild river-bottom-desert-learning behind the fake humility of human invented spiritualities and mores, so what's wrong with me unabashedly saying out loud that I'm pretty sure if you are reading or listening to this and have a body, you are nothing less than a walking miracle? No matter how unappreciative you might be of this fact and just go around jumping away from life, all the while muttering about how screwed up you and the world are: Open your eyes, get them off your idiot box, take a look around you and then a little farther. Then dig it. Think about it. What do you see?

No matter how you cut it, in the end you are an incomprehensibly complex arrangement of beautiful muscle, blood, organs, skin and bones which lives, moves, thinks, feels, sings, and fails. And then think about it: this fine assemblage at the molecular level, is... actually a heavy little pile of metallic ash, (mostly calcium, magnesium, iron, phosphorus, sodium, potassium, selenium) all magically convened to work together in a myriad of forms and functions by infinite configurations of the wind's breath: oxygen, nitrogen and hydrogen, and the strange presence of pubescent diamonds—carbon! Dig it. What's strange is you started with none of this mineral wealth. You weren't there. Then through the brilliant urge of the mildly electro-charged mind of a chromosomally organized bit of carbon and water, who knew how to gather all these metals into a growing, gestating initial form called "you", you were rhythmically wrapped into form, layer by layer into a food-eating, noisy, seeing, feeling, hearing, moving, ever complaining, never-satisfied animate person.

Wow! Is this not a miracle? That a pile of metallic ash, some water made of what was lightning-riven air, the whole beguiled by carbon's secret spell into something with an electro-nerve-flow can feel and live? How likely is this? Not very! How likely is it that this should happen over and over again? Not very! Are we not satisfied? Why? Whether you are or not, be happy anyway for the miracle that your unappreciative unlikely presence happens and keeps happening. Be happy whether you like it or not. I command you to be amazed and happy about it.

And the least we can do is to show our gratitude for the gift of this unlikely miracle by agreeing to allow the miracle we are to live fully with some panache, with at least enough imagination to give our small magic to Nature's mind, to give Her a place to play us like an instrument, whereby this miracle's unique sound can play her incredibly beautiful riffs in the never-ending music of life's biojazz.

It is not a given that any of this will continue but it keeps happening, this magically generated miracle of the improbability of having a feeling nervous system in our bodies and minds that can see, hear, touch, taste and grab all the circumstances of all that life as generated by Nature's tangibly manifesting mind. All the time, all the while.

So why not let the awe we feel for this unlikely, transient miracle of living make us grateful?

To me we have no other choice at all than to be utterly obligated to live with this amazing moving sack of metal ash, carbon, breath and water in such a way that the *way* we live becomes our initial gift to the Holy in Nature, adding still more to Nature's prime motive of making more and more details of beauty, instead of us spewing a mentality whose inventions leave toxicity and pollution in the wake of trying to escape life's wonder while locked into a citified sarcophagus of comfort, viewing virtual life on a screen.

We must realize that to live fully in love with Life's big hug of unforeseen circumstance, no matter how it comes, is an obligation of our appreciation for having been granted this form we've been given in this particular time with other humans, plants, animals and the entire world.

Because we need open minds, a clean body, eyes awake and our musical ears attuned, full living cannot be had with a drugged-out existence, legal or illegal. Living fully is living awake, not numbed out, not inebriated, not mood controlled with substances to give us the illusion we are really living when we are only drowning in shallowness. Pull out of that fake cyber swamp; natural organic life is psychedelic enough on its own, why miss it by allowing your moods, hormones, and nerves to be manipulated into a chute of pharmaceutical blindness by a culture that can't seem to love life much less see the deliciousness of Nature's natural ruckus? Make the change and I won't bother you any more about it.

As for me, at three years of age my mind was certainly wide awake and taking it all in. My heart was a whale's maw straining the world's experience like a luscious rich sea through the baleen of my fierce love for life. Though I was tiny and my soul clean, I was born a fully-fledged life-loving fool passionately curious and wind-blown; for the moment I could walk on my own, without any plan or map I sailed gleefully right into my earliest forays of full living courageously pushed by sheer instinct.

Probably my earliest significant addition to flamboyant living came about when on a lark I decided to swing from a horse's penis at the age of three and a half, not unlike a little monkey.

Unless you've been around lots of horses it's a little difficult to describe, but just to ask, how many of you have ever thought to swing from a live horse's penis like a rambunctious chimpanzee on a forest vine? Well I did.

You have to be really short to achieve such a joyful goal, and at three and a half I was just the right size for such an ill-advised activity.

Always singing, burbling and making music with every-thing that rattled, boomed, dinged or pinged, tooted or creaked, I was a noisy child of incurable curiosity and to my parents' great frustration, constantly worried about the welfare of every living thing (a definition which extended to a number of beings some people don't consider to be alive, like rocks, toys, tools, etc). At that early age my life was thoroughly immersed with my heroic efforts to save all the bugs, birds, mammals, turtles and snakes of the entire world from being crushed, drowned, lost, or eaten by other creatures. It was a lot of work, and I was very dedicated and workman-like at three.

Before we were on the Rez and while my little brother was still a baby in my mother's arms, we lived on a square chunk of flat bosque filled with giant limbed cottonwood trees, in an old two-story ranch house surrounded on three-and-a-half sides by grass hayfields, alfalfa, chicken coops, and another ranch house where an old woman reigned, the mother of three men who cared for the ranch and whose husband was the manager.

During the daytime this old white lady was alone in her house. She missed little children and was charmed by my candid weirdness and loved feeding me as much as I loved eating. An industrious rancher woman from those times before plastic and reliable TV reception, she was against wasting any fruit from all the plum, apricot, cherry and apple trees that both of our houses were surrounded by, or any of the tomatoes or vegetables she tended in her well-irrigated garden. So at any hour of the day from midsummer to November, pots bubbled and canning jars rattled, incessantly boiling away on her big stove.

In her lonely adamant industry she piled up walls and walls of preserved food, but most of the endless shelving was taken up by way over-sugared, over-pectinned fruit jellies. She always had a cake or two baked and frosted whose edges curled like her tightly curled little hairdo, and whenever I could escape my own mother's scrutiny I'd waddle over to her doorstep and sit down, trying to look as abandoned as possible hoping to be pitied and pulled in, sat up at her lace-tableclothed cake table and served hot chocolate in gold-rimmed, fluted green celadon cups and saucers with a big chunk of cake on a matching plate. But if I was not careful and she was cooking down some of her over-done jellies (jars of which she always sent me home with in a little bucket), we would get to tasting them and more than once I'd get my top teeth so firmly cemented to my bottom ones I couldn't open my mouth. Terrified, I'd run home to my mother's arms where, unable to properly scream and describe my situation, my beautiful mother would have to divine the cause of my distress. After she'd figured it out and had released the jelly's grip by running hot tea over my teeth and rubbing them with her fingers until my jaws came apart, I'd drown the world with my piteous wailing.

Though admonished repeatedly not to wander into that old lady's teeth-gluing domain, even at that age I knew not every sweet food she concocted was as industrial and dangerous as her jellies. So with the prompt surety of receiving a big wedge of cake and an endless cup of hot chocolate made with their own cow's milk, Mrs. Galbraith's spell was too strong, and regardless of any dressing down I might have to later bear I'd always end up seated at her lace-covered table. I can still smell the bubbles of chocolate coming out of the teapot into my green fluted cup at the table's edge (eye level for me).

The bigger reason I was forbidden to visit that sugar-filled house didn't stem so much from the low esteem my mother held for the kindly old lady's badly made mouth-gluing jellies, but from the trepidation both my parents bore about what might happen if I had been there when her three sweaty, blustery sons showed up after work.

My mother was especially afraid of them. She was home alone a lot with just my brother and me, and as a beautiful young mother, the old lady's unpredictable, pushy, grudge-bearing, cowboy-hat-wearing, unmarried sons in their twenties and thirties loomed as a threat.

At my eye level I loved the colored glass jewels set into the belts that held up these dangerous men's jeans because the magic delicious orange light, ruby sparks and lemon yellow rays they emanated, I could actually taste on the tongue of my mind. But all three of those men lived just to make people jump. Slamming their big fists into tables and walls wherever they went, bellowing and charging around, they were delighted when startled people flinched. The youngest one turned out to be especially mean. Every morning and every afternoon to my great horror, when that plaid shirt-wearing cowboy kid left for work or returned from mowing or baling the hay fields or chasing cows, his pointy boots found the ribs or head of any dog within range, kicking them hard, even his own family's dogs, sending them all squealing and yelping for cover.

One little rat-tailed cattle dog, a sleek yellow coated, ears up, pointy nosed creature, always ran towards our house for shelter, and eventually he learned to search for my little comforting lap where he'd sit shivering in my arms. After a while, as to be expected, this little cow dog decided not to return to the old lady's house. He was pretty licky-faced and an on-the-ball little nervous mutt, but like the fool I'd always be, I named him Smokey and told everybody he was my dog.

Though technically he belonged to the rough crew at the old lady's house, they had plenty of dogs and didn't miss him, so Smokey lived with me following alongside me everywhere, eating the leftover food from our family's meals. Sleeping outside right on our front step, he'd bark like hell and impressively snarl, guarding both me and my family against everything that wasn't us, even his former owners! Nobody on either side said much about it, but I think my mother liked the tiny dog's protective presence. Inasmuch as I was my mother's son, I figured Smokey was my son and I made sure nothing happened to him.

I stopped visiting the old lady for fear her bad kids would take Smokey away again, or worse hurt him. But, missing our friendship the old woman started bringing her cake, jellies and chocolate directly to our house. But my mother didn't let me eat as much cake.

To the north side of the big square of fruit trees, cotton-woods and the two houses, an *acequia* ran, an irrigation canal, from whose constant current water was diverted once a week into a big flat alfalfa hay field that extended for what I think must've been a half-a-mile.

For some reason both of my parents were irrationally terrified of snakes. I, who was in love with every creature I came across, had recently endeared myself to my parents when one afternoon my father, upon returning already grumpy from his work, came in the house to find my mother shivering and pale, marooned on top of our dining table while I held up an armload of writhing snakes of every species and description. I think my father would've joined her, but covering his cold sweat with a real-man vibe he began yelling at me, barking orders for me to release those snakes outdoors "where they belong, in nature."

I was little and I'd been barely strong enough to catch most of them, but I couldn't maintain my grip on so many sizes of wriggling creatures wrapping themselves around my arms trying to escape my grasp, and predictably I lost them, every one of them inside the house after one by one all "my" snakes squirmed loose, quickly disappearing in every direction into closets, behind appliances, under carpets, hidden everywhere all over the house.

Earlier the old lady's dogs (including "my" Smokey) had been harassing a mysterious congregation of snakes, barking and snapping at them until the snakes had all taken to the flowing waters of the irrigation ditch to escape. Being good swimmers a few of the snakes wriggled safely away disappearing into the current, but most of them were desert snakes not adapted to water, and looked to my little horrified self to be drowning. So I got down on my belly and pulled out as many wet snakes from the ditch's fast-flowing stream as I could grab. Intending to return for more after I'd deposited my first armload with my mother, who I was sure would keep them safe till I could come back with another armload, I struggled to my feet and waddled my burdened self into the house with a big chestful of wriggling snakes only to watch my mother leap up onto the table armed with a broom, pleading with me to take them outside. She was *not* going to keep them safe.

My father was only slightly braver and in the end, with the door wide open, he went around swearing to give himself courage, and weirdly hissing like a snake drove out as many snakes from the house as he could with a push broom. I pummeled my dad on the thighs with my little fists whining and weeping about how the dogs outside were going to kill all the little snakes, which actually came to pass for some of them.

At the clear-souled age of almost four, it was against all my instincts that I shouldn't share everything I prized with everyone. Over the years I would slowly learn to hide what I held most precious for myself, but at three and a half I hadn't yet learned guile or personal greed.

When for three days afterwards I brooded, refused to talk and wouldn't eat, my parents just thought my little kid's soul had been furious with them for getting "my" snakes killed. But my big heart was broken: not only had my parents failed to uphold the safety I'd promised the snakes, but they'd both gone on to give me a terrible dressing down about something for which I thought I'd been a hero. I felt like one of the unwanted snakes run out of the house.

After some distance from the event, when my parents began to see the funniness of it all they tried to humor me out of my gloom. They'd never been *that* angry at me before, and it had been a shock, but I don't think they were miffed at me so much for trying to bring snakes into *their* house, as for how my actions had caused a situation that showed both my parents in a light of extreme inability and reactionary cowardice. Though their weakness did create a snake massacre and broke a little boy's heart, I was more outraged that they thought I should apologize to them for making them look bad. Though I was only three and a half I somehow knew they were blaming me, a tiny kid, for their own inadequacies, and for that I wasn't so easily coaxed out of the den of my Irish-Native resentment by the false motive of their guilty cajoling.

But, like most people, the resolve of my burning indignation was eventually dampened by the pain of the loneliness of my self exile, and a couple of days later at the morning breakfast table, I cheerfully re-joined the family conversation. It was going pretty well until, intending to make friends again by sharing a secret, I unabashedly announced over our French toast and maple syrup (from our Canadian Native relatives) that I had been feeding a beautiful big skunk living under my bed for a month! My parents went silent, stared at me and were saddened. Assuming that I was trying to save face, by impressing them with an obvious fabrication engineered to get back at them for the rude lack of welcome they'd shown all the carefully gathered snakes I'd saved from drowning, to whom I'd promised a safe haven and with whom I'd planned to live in the house for the rest of our lives. So now I had a skunk?

They clucked at me, rolled their eyeballs and scoffing at the idea, they renewed their scolding, this time for lying, amazed at the precocious cupidity of me thinking I could make them believe that any animal of the size, aroma, wildness and reactionary nature of a Skunk could possibly be living openly right inside our house, having eluded the scrutiny of their eyes, ears and noses for weeks. I couldn't believe my life; the minute I tried to be friends again I was once again betrayed! My face burning, my feelings singed, I insisted: "There *is* a skunk under my bed!"

My father started to lose his stirrups. "Stop it, there is *no* Skunk and you know it; you're just making it up."

They wouldn't believe me.

It was scary; I felt so thrown away.

I began to sink again into a cloud of outraged self-pity and despair. There I was already at age three-and-a-half the unbelieved bearer of wild unsuspected truths that I would always be! Not only did nobody I love care about the animals, plants, rocks that I loved at my eye level, but they didn't even regard my word as trustworthy; my news was not legitimate information to them, my talk not relevant to the welfare of our family. I realized then that I wasn't part of the family counsel. All along they had only been patronizing me. They just wanted a small child with cute fluffy dismissible thoughts, but to them I was a liar with big ideas who acted on them.

But my eyes had seen my own hand repeatedly feeding a grateful Skunk bacon saved from our family breakfasts. My mind knew perfectly well what my mouth truthfully spoke. I was not believed, and what I believed in was not held as worthy.

Smokey (against whom I still carried a serious grudge for his part in the snake massacre with the other ranch dogs) had always known that a Skunk was in the house because he was the major reason I'd been feeding a wild Skunk under my bed: the Skunk had rushed into the house through the cat door to get away from Smokey one summer night, and knowing the little dog was diligently waiting for him to exit through the same door for an entire month, had accepted refuge beneath my bed.

But now Smokey, gallant Smokey, came to vindicate the honor of my word, saving me from being thought of as a lying, whiny little kid, lightening the load of my sad heart. For that very morning after having announced that I had a "pet" Skunk under my bed, Smokey began frantically yipping and moaning and scratching at the bottom of the big wooden screen door that opened into the very kitchen where we all sat at the Saturday breakfast table with my mother's fabulous French toast and my ancestor's maple syrup before us, my fat, spoiled little brother bouncing in his lean-to seat on the table being fawned, fed and fussed over by my mother, and me trying to eat between my tears.

My father, who had now kind of started liking the dog for his part in protecting us from snakes and bad cowboys, assuming that Smokey was making a fuss for some bacon of which he was so famously fond, rose from the table with two strips of the same intending to reward the sparky little mutt outside.

But before the screen door had barely even cracked, before my father could get his arm out the door to toss the bacon past the front stoop as he planned, Smokey, paying absolutely no attention to his prize forced his pointy head in, and shoving his shoulders into the crack, wedged the door wide open like a log splitter and bolted past all of us straight into the interior of the house.

Smokey had been waiting for that very moment and knew right where "my" skunk was keeping himself, and before anyone had even turned to look, a wheel of spinning fur came twirling through the house like a rolling car-wash brush, emitting a horrible stench, hair flying everywhere, accompanied with frantic wild unearthly screams, hisses, yelps and whines, with all the thunks, bumps, scuttling, and scraping sounds of lamps falling over and furniture moving, till in a flash this cyclone of furious gnashing animals turned and rushed right under our breakfast table, over our feet and out the other side, cannonballing straight out of the screen door into the big ranch world where Smokey, his nose bleeding from a skunk bite, rolled back to lick another big skunk gash under his tail, while the Skunk, his fur bristling, tail up, bolted for the ditch, jumped it and disappeared into the big hay field, whose progress you could track by the line of jiggling purple-flowered alfalfa plants above him as he beelined out and away.

I can't really remember if I was smiling when it all broke loose, but I know my parents certainly weren't, especially once we'd all blown out the door, intending to escape the Skunk's gas attack that now perfumed the entire house and our kitchen. We were all so saturated with the stench we had to cook out of doors for weeks, get new clothing and could only gradually move back inside a month later. Luckily it was summer. I loved eating outside.

After that people started believing me a little more, but my dad kind of avoided me. I think he was always a little suspicious of me for years until I'd grown to his eye level, at which point he knew what he'd always suspected was now a certainty: that I'd come out of a different drawer than the rest of the world, that I knew things nobody else knew and did things nobody else would do.

Well. There HAD been a Skunk under my bed! I was not a liar.

By the time we'd finally been able to tolerate the residual stench and took up residency once again inside the old house, the cowboys next door had gone in together on buying what looked to me like an enormous fancy stallion, for whom they built a corral just off the north side of their mother's chicken coop. I loved going with Mrs. Galbraith into the chicken house to get eggs; like her house it was very clean and organized, but still had that great go-get-the-eggs-chicken-smell chicken coops can have.

After the skunk scene my mother let me keep company with the old lady again. She knew I stood very little chance of being invited into that woman's neurotically organized house and getting my teeth glued shut because we were all still a little skunky smelling. But outside she let me meet up with her on my little kid rounds and we'd go get the eggs in her coop.

Little kids are very observant, and in the process of getting eggs together one morning, I noticed that the finely speckled stallion was not in his corral next to the chicken coop. His corral gate was down and he was gone, probably hauled away by his owners to be a stallion with a mare somewhere, but at my height and age I thought none of this, only that his usual presence was missing.

While we were exiting the coop, in the short instance that Mrs. Galbraith, her eggs cradled in a basket dangling from the crook of her elbow, took to relatch the chicken-wired frame door behind us, I surveyed the world and saw that the missing big horse had actually made his own way off to the north of our house, where square in the middle of the giant flooded alfalfa field he stood, grazing the tops of the green alfalfa poking out of the water.

He'd no doubt gotten there all by himself, as this would have killed any horse and no one would have intentionally allowed this fancy animal to graze on a solid field of green alfalfa, much less a hay field in the process of being irrigated, for fear of founder.

Though not yet that savvy about horse feeding, for me it was a bad sight anyway, because Smokey, who was back in my good graces for having saved my honor by exposing the house-bound skunk, had bellied under the low strand on the barbed wire fence enclosing the field and was bounding and splashing, yipping all the way out to the horse. When he got there he alternately charged and nipped at the big horse's legs as cattle dogs do to get herd animals moving, which in this case only caused this gigantic horse to kick back.

In my young mind all I saw was what I interpreted as a situation of extreme danger for "my" dog, who was taking care of himself perfectly well. But the horse did finally connect once on Smokey's ribs, sending him rolling and yelping into the drink. Terrified that the little dog might be trampled to death or drowned when he rolled under water, as the field was flooded a foot deep, without one thought to the contrary I ran as fast as my baggy corduroy overalls would let all three-and-a-half years of me, and miraculously, without hanging up on the barb wire, I successfully pushed through the fence and made my way sloshing straight across the field to "save" Smokey, intending to take him away from there in my arms.

But Smokey was a fierce little dinky dog and had already righted himself, and having been made more ferocious by the kick started leaping up out of the water like a bass, viciously yipping and snapping at every hop. As I dragged my worried soul toward the horse, incredibly hampered in my efforts by the underwater bushes of alfalfa, the water itself, and the fact that my clothes were saturated and now weighed more than I did, the stallion, weirdly enough, all of a sudden seemed utterly unperturbed by my presence or the dog's and stopped kicking, stretched out, and letting his penis out to dangle decided to take a nice long pee.

The acrid smell of his piss and steam foaming up in the water grew in strength as I, calling for Smokey, came right up to less than a couple of feet of both the dog and the horse.

Right at that point Smokey, to my great dismay, took it into his little skull to run right smack under the gigantic pissing beast whose belly stretched above the height of my head (some gigantic draft horse I guess).

Alarmed that the horse would now step on "my" dog and kill him, without thinking I too ran under the horse to fetch him. But by then the horse had stopped peeing and Smokey, who had calmed down too, was just standing there smiling, his head barely out of the drink tail wagging like a stick poking out of the water, and when the horse shifted a bit, his two-and-a-half-foot long dingus began to gently swing and it softly whomped me in the face, its weight almost knocking me over.

The sweet smell of the big horse, the calmness of "my" dog and the weird horse-piss aroma must've put a spell on me that has never left.

The soft tactility of the horse's thick penis was so inviting, and I'd always loved swinging on any open gate, doorknob, or any dangling rope, that without even thinking I naturally grabbed that horse's extended flopping ding-a-ling as high and tight as I could, and pulling my sopping little dripping legs out of the water I gave myself a push and started swinging. It was great, like swinging from the sky.

The horse began moving, gently walking forward out into the watery field with me attached to his penis happily swinging along to the motion like a baby monkey from a jungle vine!

After seeing me joyfully dangling and swinging away, attached to a walking stallion's penis out in a field, it was my mother's turn to be horrified. In a flash she unlatched the field gate, and leaving it down and open, like a horse herself, walk-ran with as much control as she could muster, sloshing across the irrigated field, knowing better than to run or yell so as not to frighten the horse and risk getting me killed, trampled beneath his fleeing triple zero hooves.

But the horse jumped out and ran anyway and I lost my grip, dropping *kerplosh* into the drink while the horse's hind legs rolled over and past me in a considerate flash without even touching me, but leaving me very wet and alone in the water, furiously weeping for having lost my toy.

Smokey, who was really barking now, succeeded in herding that stallion right out of the field, past the gate my mother had left open, and after returning proud, panting and smiling to where my mother was busy scooping me up out of the water into her crying and laughing arms, marched alongside us as she hauled me off back to the house for a bath, fresh clothes and an instruction course on the danger of grabbing just any old unpredictable horse's wee-wee without thinking it out first, and made me promise I would give her fair warning the next time it occurred to me to go swinging from a horse's penis.

That was my very first horse ride, and it was a good one too. I can still remember how sad I felt when it came to an end. Now you know: my crazy horse-riding life didn't start on top of a horse but underneath as an inspired ding-a-ling swinging fool!

I never did get to say goodbye to my loyal sidekick Smokey, for as to be expected he disappeared shortly after. Everyone tried to convince me that he'd just "run away" like so many dogs and cats were said to do, but I knew he'd run to me for safety in the first place and had no reason to leave.

For a long time I sighed and grit my teeth, sure that it had been those bad cowboy owners of the white horse, who were mad cause it took them three days to find and gather up their runaway prize stallion and had probably shot Smokey in revenge. But years later I came to my senses, realizing they would've actually been thankful to Smokey and us all for getting that giant beast away from killing himself on green alfalfa. So of course, it had been my own father who took Smokey away, no doubt at the insistence of my mother, terrified at all the danger and ruckus with snakes, skunks, and wild horse-penis-riding the dog and I together had wrought in less than three weeks. I know my father wouldn't have killed my little dog and hopefully Smokey ended up in some other worthy adventurous existence no matter what happened.

Dogs, horses and people all come and go but the beauty we make keeps everything alive around us so life can keep coming. I hope God and Nature were fed at least a little by the beauty and humor of such uncontrived full-living as carried to fruition by the inspired courageous love of a 28 lb. little kid for his 9 lb. dog, skunks, snakes, a swinging horse penis, hot chocolate, cake and mouth-clamping jelly.

Chapter 1

Like a Goose Shot from the Sky

We'd blown ourselves over ten-foot holes; hopped, skipped, jumped around, over and through eroded upper cuts of canyon tributaries; flown over live, running coyotes; slogged, pushed and slid down the unstable, sandy sides of vertical cliffs; we'd put our heads down, increased our speed, and with our wings folded up like swallows, cannoned ourselves clean through culverts in front of flash floods in time to avoid our demise in a thrashing wall of water.

But Amarillento and I had never before been shot down from the sky or ever stumbled together out of view to land square beneath the earth... until one afternoon we did.

Thirty-three years after my first wee-wee ride, twenty years away from the Reservation, and five years after returning from my Tzutujil life, with twenty-eight other good Barbs in my corrals, Blue and Amarillento were still the horses I went to every time. If I had been a samurai and those two horses swords, they would've been my favorite *katanas*, my greatest swords: one heavy and intrepid for getting through, the other light and brilliant for flying and flashing; both for hitting every mark in a way beautiful each in their own distinct fashion.

Like a rock guitarist with a thousand fancy guitars, Amarillento was the old Stratocaster for every high, long, luscious lead, and Blue the 12-string Martin who when played right was an entire symphony sewing the mountains to the sea; and that afternoon, my blood stirred, powerfully coursing up the last rise at Las Golondrinas with a thousand people watching, I intended to end the day by boldly exiting the outdoor museum of old New Mexico Spanish and Native life arts with a dashing ascent onto the ridge upon whose flat summit the parking area and exhibit hall were perched. My reins loose, both arms recklessly raised in the air, the bravado of urging my Yellow Boy on without any steerage made the crowds cheer, and in my grandiosity I committed the greatest "meat-headed play of all time," completely forgetting about the old 18th-century irrigation *acequia* thoroughly hidden by the overgrown Sacaton and Willows that ran along the entire escarpment. Without a care in the world, like two idiots we galloped at top speed, disappearing straight into that tangle to drop like a shot goose into the antique ditch. The tall grasses grew so evenly, covering the entire east face of the rise up which we had charged that the gigantic *acequia madre* (the mother canal), some five-feet-deep and eight-feet-wide, was completely hidden from view for a quarter-mile in either direction.

Of course, there were breaks in the cane and little bridges where all the visitors and exhibitors could cross into the lower fields down by the most appealing springs and rivulets, whose unexpected presence in the high desert caused this volcanic canyon oasis to have been populated and farmed by layer upon layer of cultures for several thousand years.

Singing my song of flying and swinging my sword of haughty hope on the head of Chance's absolute reign, I brashly drove my little horse, all silvered up in his old Spanish and Native hand-hammered bridle and saddle and breast collar, crashing straight into the grass-covered hill at such a speed and angle that to the observers in the valley below it looked exactly like we'd somehow ridden magically right into the hillside, disappearing utterly from view, without reemerging anywhere.

No one knew what had really happened; no one had seen the reality.

I didn't even know myself until I regained consciousness, for both Amarillento and myself had been knocked completely cold. When I came to, Amarillento was already back on his feet, still a bit stunned and a little wavy. He stood behind a man who held his reins in one hand and with the other, cradled my neck and head up off the floor of the ditch where I still lay, having fallen in and crashed there while moving at speed.

This old cowboy kind of guy sat me up, gave me several swigs of water, and then grabbed my face and stared at my eyes for a good while, checking for a concussion while he filled me in.

He'd seen the whole mess because he'd been down inside the *acequia*, between two walls of six-foot-high grasses and five feet beneath those at the dirt bottom, running up and down its dry length looking for his girlfriend's stray dog when Amarillento and I came unexpectedly crashing right over him, tumbling square into the canal.

In some bigger way than most he understood everything about me and about Mari and hadn't run for emergency help. After explaining to me what had happened and making sure neither man nor beast were seriously broken anywhere, when my buzzing head was ready to hold a thought this good man told me what I will now tell you:

"Son, don't be too hard on yourself for stupidly washing out like that. That was a really impressive wreck. The crowd below is still milling around waiting for you to appear out of the ground! Nobody knows what happened. They think you pulled some kind of magic stunt up here. My advice is, if you can handle it, when you're ready, get back on this beautiful little rascal of yours and ride hard out over there (pointing to a low spot where the banks had caved in a bit) and pretend like you intended the whole thing. Like you didn't crash, like you went into the hill and came out again. We all need that magic. People long for living evidence that there's more to life in this world than the scared little gray lives they waste watching life on the tube. There is real magic. Plus you owe God for saving both of your necks.

"Now, remember kid," laughing as he pulled me to my feet, "There's only two kinds of riders:

the ones that fall off

and

the ones who are gonna fall off!"

I nodded and tried to smile.

He continued: "The main thing is to live life and ride in such a way that everything you do is beautiful because God lives on the beauty we make. Even when you fall make it good, make it worth having made the mistake, make everything you do beautiful, even your failures. And I'll tell you what kid, that was the most beautiful crash I've ever seen! It was stupendous. You two fell right out of the sky!"

I was still too dazed to ask the man his name, who he was, or where he came from, but when I could finally get back in the saddle we rode out of that ditch just like he said we should, and the world was cheering. I've always tried to live up to what that man said.

He must've been a spirit.

Amarillento recovered quicker than I did.

I was sore for a month.

Chapter 2

Blue Sets Me Straight

Not long after the barn fire*, and with no courteous warning, we were forced to leave the home where we had been living so well. The creekside land up in the beautiful mountains did not belong to us. We'd been caretaking this wonderful little place at the base of the mountain wilderness for almost ten years. It had been our only home during our exile from Guatemala. The rich absentee owner mechanically sold the area to the faceless agency of the National Park Service, which had economically pressured the owner to sell the land pending its condemnation in order to establish a "Civil War" monument.

*See the last chapter of *The Wild Rose, Volume II of Stories of My Horses*.

This agency subsequently designated my family and our horses as squatters, our cabins and fancy teepees as non-historical trash, and all of a sudden we were illegally occupying condemned government land! Though initially they told us we had a month to relocate, once the papers were signed that "month" was instantly disregarded and with great satisfaction they began to robotically dismantle and burn every plank of our demolished cabin and barns; hauling off our appliances with no compensation. After removing every rail of our corrals, they bulldozed our campsite until no trace of our ever having existed remained. It was like reverse archaeology; where layer by layer all traces of *what had been there* were erased to make room for what the powers in charge said *should* be there! We joined the many Natives in history whose presence—like us with no money, lawyers or advocates—had been swept out of the story, the land and the sequence of history to make way for official shrines to white American military history. Out of sight, out of mind.

Unprepared, we were lost. Our family integrity ruptured. Held together only by the already strained thread of hope that someday we might return to Atitlán, we had painfully navigated that daily hope, barely surviving the spiritually erosive effects of the treacherous murky canal of modern American culture for ten years. Only the relative freedom and unpeopled, mystic, indigenous nature of New Mexico's wilder land, into which we had become so thoroughly a part, had kept us relatively whole.

A unique but tenuous single-family culture had formed in that decade. But the amazing thing we had become was wholly dependent on our presence in the land, and when we lost that we came apart. Dismantled just like our rough-sawn cabin and hard-earned barns, plank by plank, piece by piece, as a people we smashed up like a beautiful, frail boat of indigenous identity on the trashy, unfeeling concrete banks of modernity's money-mired cultural mind. The floating chunks of our broken hearts were swept straight downriver by the impossibly strong current of the globalized one-size-fits-all pop-culture-mind of the 1990s, in which direction was pulled what remained of our struggle to survive as "Natives" inside an unsympathetic modern world, into the dreadful immensity of consumer culture.

In the mountains we had been proud human beings, but we had to leave the mountains, and when we did we were just another jumble of anonymous nobodies in an urbanized world.

Though paddling for air and surviving that initial confusing free fall into modernity's crowded bucket, as individuals, each of us were altered and no one agreed with my over-principled insistence on trying to keep our original-culture-mind alive. It all ended with each of us thrown away from one another, scrambling scared and desperate to vastly different shores. We would never really find each other again. Wounded, befuddled, angry and no longer trusting one another, the family scattered, each of us heading our own separate ways.

While I had always assumed that all our horses had been a part of the family, now there was no longer a family. To those who'd been the family, the horses became just unrealistic possessions. Everybody wanted money, not animals—and now having no land with which to feed and keep them, I was tragically forced to sell the horses and divide the money. The herd of Barb mares I'd spent so many years, so much inspiration, strategy and joy outwitting the settler mind to gather them together, all had to go. Even old Juniper went. The heartbreak of portioning out the pitiful cash such quickly peddled horses brought, marked the official entry of that era into the exclusive realm of memories.

All the horses were gone, the land was gone, the family was gone, those days were gone.

But after a year, when some of the dust settled and the heartbreak small enough to safely tote, Old Blue was still standing there, still looking back at me. Who else would advise me and ride the hard inclines to pray on top of mountains and haul me out of my sorrows? And if Blue remained, Amarillento had to be there too, and he was—what other heroic horse could track autumn Woolly Bear Caterpillars to their hibernating places, ride the wind or race the world and always win?

Though all the mares I'd planned for him to breed were now gone, young Punk was still there with me too.

Because he could breed and make more of his kind, he was for me a spirited, zany, horse-shaped trunk of hope for the future. Into this one crazy stallion I folded and carefully stacked all my hopes for Horses to once again reappear. The big herd was all gone, and in order to economically survive I would now have to get social, leave the mountains and begin traveling, start doctoring people on the road, teaching and doing what I'd become known for. But still in my crazy little kid heart I kept a flame of hope lit, holding fast to the idea that if things ever went right and I miraculously found real love, a new life might jump up and become a reality again. Then maybe I could reopen Punk like a magic chest and from him unfold the hidden genetic majesty of all the other horses I'd lost, all those great old-time horses who were just standing hidden, waiting to reappear from his genes from a time of history long obstructed. If I were fortunate enough to discover a couple of real Mesta mares again—like those old Ute horses Punk himself had descended from—themselves hidden in some forgotten canyon or desert backyard of people who still loved these horses, then maybe, I dared to hope, maybe we could begin to bring back a line of Barbs just like Old Blue, Amarillento, Zajlani, Cicatriz and Punk himself.

I could dream a big herd again. I could see them clearly in the landscape of my heart's body, but to the world they wisely kept themselves out of sight, running solely inside the world of Punk's genes.

With only these two good geldings, my stallion, my saddles, my gear, my guitar, my profession and my old truck left to my name, I cleared off the officially designated boundaries of the Park Service's Civil War monument. But I knew those New Mexico canyons, highlands, shrines, springs and trails in a way that stayed living in my body. So I went away, but the land came with me. While the empire had won for now, like a displaced solitary nomad of old, I left the mountains weeping and hit the road back into the land of people; I still had a tribe, just no people of my own. From the first my horses took it all a lot better than I did, but slowly I came to see it their way.

Always practical, Blue wouldn't let me ride him until he'd infused me with his saner attitude: "It's too easy, Martín, to allow your bitterness to make you feel important just because you've been trampled and dissed by the same unfeeling institution as the old-time Natives. Do you think you can just sit immobilized in a comfortable toxic pool of self-pity, getting your identity by endlessly legitimizing your victim status? Look, I don't want to be the horse of anyone who isn't willing to keep expertly struggling by means of spiritual integrity to make beauty and fight for what that person loves! Sure, you and I lost a lot, but we've won more than we lost just by the fact that we are still here. If our kind are moving toward love and life when we get knocked back, we never really lose. So let's get ourselves moving again toward life, man."

So we did, and when we did he let me ride again. The horses and I kept our heads high and proud and moved as needed from here to there, and there to where, wherever there was room for me and my three hard-riding friends. Kept alive by the knowledge that we hadn't been conquered and we were still part of something bigger than modernity's white noise existence, we moved toward finding our "Herd" again somewhere, someday.

Meanwhile Punk and I concentrated on growing back our burnt-off eyebrows and manes, and prayed for someone to love.

Chapter 3

Growing Back Our Manes

For months after living through that barn fire, no matter how well we washed or anything we tried, both Punk and I stank like stale burnt hair. Worse still, we both looked like a couple of rumply pit-cooked vegetables.

My own head of hair, which up till then I'd always kept hanging in long Viking curls down my back, had been singed off down to my blistered hide and for a while I looked like a baked chayote crossed on an exploded fiber optics cable. When it all did grow out, my hair never attained its original length again, stopping at my shoulders. Punk, on the other hand, did better. His mane and tail had both burnt to stubble but when they returned they actually increased beyond their original length, growing so exuberantly that both his tail and mane would eventually surpass in length what had burnt off by five times. And his mane hair utterly morphed in character as well, changing from a stiff bristly broom into tiers of luxurious, black, sausage curls that reached to the ground. It took four years for his mane and tail to drag magnificently along the earth and this corresponded exactly with the time it took for me to break him into a wonderful riding stallion. A fierce one, but a good one.

It was as if some forgotten ancestral mind of ancient human-horse culture was steering our lives, because the time it took for me to grow myself into a better man corresponded to the time it took to grow back my hair, and in a parallel way, Punk's development into a rideable warrior equaled the four years it took to grow out his mane and tail to their adult form.

Throughout the world, particularly in Spain, North Africa, Scandinavia and continuing among all the various layers of Eurasian pastoral steppe nomads for more than 3,000 years, male horses in different stages of training always had their manes cut into different types of complex designs whose distinct shapes presented readable messages signifying different stages of learning had been achieved. Anyone seeing horses thus marked running in a crowded herd would know at a glance what stage of "educational development" or initiation an individual horse had completed (or not). Various stages of training a horse for a particular capacity were also marked by certain "haircuts," something still carried out a bit today in the

California Vaquero, *bozal*-type training. But its ancestry goes way, way back.

This haircutting tradition extended to the horse's people as well. Most ancestral nomadic horse-living peoples signaled their own human life changes and rites of passage by haircutting ceremonies that paralleled the stages their horses were going through.

All horse-riding steppe nomads made elaborate haircutting, nail-cutting and naming ceremonies for their little boys and girls at the exact same age as their prospective riding horses' first mane cutting and hoof trimming, which meant these horses were taken in from the range herds for the first time. Even today various divisions of Mongolian horse-raising pastoral nomads still make big festivals for their small children's first springtime haircut. Relatives and well-wishing visitors dressed to the teeth in their tribal best pour in from everywhere to wish a long healthy life for the child, and then after blessing the honored child each visitor carefully trims tiny bits of the child's hair, which is then stored in a small specially made little pouch. After the blessers give the children gifts (often very fancy lifetime gifts), the relative formally naming the little ones shoots an arrow up through the smoke hole for good luck and blesses all the stowed little hair cuttings and nail parings, which stay with the child for his or her lifetime. A feast ensues, accompanied with the very ancient custom of communal drinking of fermented horse milk by all men and women, who then sing the traditional music of these horse people, which stirs the soul of any sane listener.

Steppe nomads everywhere of every station have always been buried with these little sacks of blessed hair cuttings. Indeed in modern excavations throughout Eurasia of even the richest two- and three-thousand-year-old burial mounds of horse cultures one always finds little bags of hair and nail parings that had accompanied the interred throughout their horseback lives.

These peoples lived parallel lives with their horses: during the time their riding-geldings' manes and tails were growing back, the horses were being trained. Once the manes had grown out, these geldings were now "ready" to become part of the family and took their place as indispensable, rideable herding horses. Likewise as a child's hair grew out, traditionally boys and girls were initiated into the vast ins and outs of the work of adult herding life and a milk-based existence. Anciently, boys were further tonsured as adolescents in a way that left a central queue of hair to grow down their back like a horse tail, which when it reached a certain length was often braided or folded in a way that signified their graduation into useful young adulthood. Women on the other hand, just like their mares' manes and tails, never cut their hair again except in the case of extreme bereavement.

When someone passed away both men and women cut a piece of their own long central braid to put in the grave. This was a big meaningful gift and delivered great energy to the dead person's spirit journey into their next world stages. While some of the dead person's horses were killed and buried with the owner, the riding horses of the survivors had their tail hair cut back just like their owners' queues, the hair braided, and this braid placed inside the burial mound alongside the people's own hair braid offering.

For horse cultures hair growth was all about time, for once the hair of the survivors—men and women and horses—had grown out again, it was known that the dead person's soul had passed into the next stage of life-giving existence.

In some world traditions the method used for cutting hair on both horses and people was accomplished by the expert use of a flame instead of knives or shears. Even horse hoof trimming was done in many places with a red-hot steel hoof-trimming tool that cauterized and sealed the hoof.

Other peoples, both settled and nomadic, simply trimmed off a portion of the horse's mane and cropped the tail altogether to signify branding, gelding, and that they had begun his training; by the time the mane and tail were grown out everyone knew the horse could be fairly confidently chosen to ride, while if the mane and tail were still short, this meant no one should yet try riding the animal except the one person by whom that horse was still being suppled and educated to the rigors of being ridden.

So here we were, both Punk and I, seemingly arbitrarily singed to the scalp, but it was life's expertise with circumstance that had worked on us to cause a contemporary ceremonial "mane cutting," both of us trying to turn ourselves into fuller males, growing our manes out year by year to show the world we were trying as hard as we could in our own ways to develop into deeper, nobler beings a little more useful to the world.

By the time Punk's mane and tail hit the ground and my hair and eyebrows had resumed a reasonable presence, we fit into each other's spiritual and mental form well enough to where I lodged inseparably into Punk's back and he fit under me in such great deliciousness that together in great confidence we could move as a single creature through the world. Though he had logically developed into an even fiercer stallion and was still definitely a law unto himself, he would nonetheless listen to me and defer to my desires. And on my end, I always tried to be even and honest with him, and brave enough to be able to be as kind and useful a man as possible. For bravery is not about getting your way, but the strength of character to ride out whatever comes your way.

* * *

When Punk's hair had originally burnt off, the hairs of his I missed the most were his wild face whiskers!

So many mammals, birds and fish have impressive and even peculiar face whiskers. The young of most furry animals have beautiful whiskers over their eyes and around their muzzles, but most people pay them little mind because generally whiskers are very clear and monofilament-looking, and therefore, as seen against the rest of an animals' markings they can seem rather insignificant or even invisible. But they should not be glossed over, for these filaments are extremely important and a spiritually powerful part of every real horse. To cut them off, except for the treatment of an illness, is brutal evidence of certain people's callous disregard for an animal's natural way of being.

These whiskers are hard to clearly see.

To see a horse's whiskers properly you must see her or him in silhouette against a good New Mexico sunset. You can't always choreograph such a thing, but if it happens you will be amazed at the intense variety of whiskers bristling out of the face of a single animal that you never even noticed were there. The variety of styles, colors and shapes on one horse as compared to the face of the next horse of the same "breed" are as idiosyncratic as human fingerprints.

And like fingers these little hairs can feel the mood of the world. The elegant face whiskers of horses are important to their existence, for their whiskers strain the world's vibes for direction and deliciousness like the antennae of Butterflies, Moths, Katydids or a singing Cricket! Foals have such fine, sensitive little face hairs that they feel the shift in things happening 100 yards away. Their whiskers are already adult length at birth, but start in the womb all curled up. Like a butterfly's wing in the cocoon, their whiskers unfold a couple of days after the birth to form a very fuzzy muzzle indeed. These long filaments as they are at birth are what you must slowly work with to gain friendship with a new horse. The whiskers over their eyes and around the muzzle are very, very sensitive.

I always look at how a horse's whiskers go before I listen to his or her whinny. If as an adult their whiskers remain undeveloped and uninteresting, so will their whinny be and so is the horse.

Good horses have impressively shaped and well-placed whiskers.

Most horses have eye and muzzle whiskers in the general shape and translucency of a trout rib bone. The horrible custom of constantly trimming away a horse's whiskers as practiced by show people and a lot of horse trainers to "tidy" their horses and "desensitize" them has left a lot of adult horses with short, gnarly stubs of non-returning whiskers, like the stumps of a mountain slope clear-cut for lumber. This often makes for a jaded, uninteresting horse.

Horses in nature, like all animals, periodically molt their whiskers one at a time to regrow filaments even more extravagant and evolved than the originals. These new shapes are intended to more excellently navigate the changed conditions in which the horses now find themselves. They adapt. Whiskers are in every way "feelers," as old-timers call them.

Pay attention and respect the sensitivity that whiskers give your horses and they'll show you more about themselves than any other part of them ever could.

Punk's whiskers were like light-conducting fishbone threads at their tips, but where they emerged from the skin of his muzzle and lips they pushed into view as tiny corkscrews! Like ballpoint pen springs pulled out and extended, Punk's snout, chin and eyebrows were covered with clear three-inch bouncy springs; they were definitely communication oriented, for anyone looking at the sun through any horse whiskers will see that, like polar bear belly hair, they transport a spectrum of light down the filament and into the horse through the skin just like fiber optics!

Punk's "spring" whiskers were even wilder still, for they sent spiral spectrums down and out around his soft spotty mouth. When they were burned off, I mourned their loss. I waited and prayed they'd bounce back, and by the following year they had all literally "sprung" back to life out of his bossy squealing face.

Both Punk and I had our eyelashes burnt away in that horrid fire, but like a pruned Willow thicket Punk's came back thicker than before, while mine never grew past the shortness they'd been singed to, and I've had short eyelashes ever since.

On the other hand, Punk's actual eyes had been severely glazed in the heat of that wicked fire. After a few years his eyesight would begin to show signs of moon blindness in both the brightest sun of summer and in the brilliant snow of winter, but this never stopped him from discerning one mare from the next, one person from the next, or one enemy from the next.

At the time, Punk's pink coat had been singed down to his tough coal-black skin, which showed a good amount of superficial blistering. I'd been well taught by the same Pueblo herb healer who had shown me how to mercy-kill a horse and pull cars out of the mud with horses. This old-time magic and very good plant medicine, once applied to Punk's hide, by the time of his next shedding caused a full crop of seasonally-staggered colors to return even more glorious than the past. Like birds, Mesta horses often grow their "plumage" into adult coat colors that are much different than those of their youth, and depending on breeding-season hormones, seasonal temperatures, what kind of graze they find, and the water, coat colors in Mesta horses can also shift dramatically.

People who keep their horses' winter coats from growing out to keep them "sleek" and don't allow them to naturally grow seasonal hair and shed at least twice a year are doing their animals a great disservice.

In the rough and tough of a natural wild existence, mammals and birds, and all plants for sure, need to annually renew their worn coats and sometimes do so more than twice a year. Not only are horses naturally set up to replace and revitalize their old worn out hair, but like birds do their feathers, trees do their leaves, bark and roots, the substances that make the colors in the individual hairs of a horse's coat are "cognates" with other internal hormones in the horse's body: hair growing and shedding calls into action the metabolic changeover needed by mares and stallions to become fertile as they go in and out of annual baby making, baby carrying and baby birthing, i.e., in and out of "season".

Hair shedding and regrowing of hair is also an integral part of a prehistoric symbiosis upon which all sorts of other creatures living in traditional horse herds' territories depend. Even the lives of Birds and Insects, Lizards and Mammals are triggered hormonally into action by the corresponding coat changes in Horses, Deer, wild Bovines, Antelope and others.

Thus the body of a whole herd of horses in shedding mode is part of the whole body of the steppe, forest and wild lands, where the molting stages of a horse's hair give signals to smaller animals who depend on these signs in order to begin to line their nests and burrows with horses' spring shedding of winter-heavy fur. Even the hormones and pheromones in the manure and urine of horses generated during the "molt" time also call into action the springtime activity of insects whose life stages feed the birds during the brooding of their eggs—eggs cushioned in horsehair nests.

But even so the horses also need to grow and shed hair just for their own sake. If a horse doesn't grow hair for winter there is something amiss and is judged to be ill by "down-to-earth" horse nomads and Natives worldwide. Not only can he not keep himself warm in the winter's cold, but without the winter months' long old shaggy hair presence to be shed off in spring, the vast inner changes in a horse's body necessary to make new spring hair of a totally differing composition are not there to stir into life the necessary spring hormones and enzymes that cause a horse's digestion to gradually reopen from a tight winter mode, so they can survive the rising presence of chlorophyll and sugars in the "greener graze" of the imminent warmer weathers without foundering or suffering weather-change colic.

Because of all the gorgeous coat colors possible in horses it's difficult to resist just breeding horses for certain colors, but like birds, "real" horses should also be able to change their colors from season to season throughout the year. I've never heard of any modern horse "breed" registry selecting stallions and mares for their ability to seasonally grow hair for winter, shed out, change color, shed again, change color again, shed out and then regrow their winter hair in a tonality and type of body-heating, light-holding, refractive hair filament different from their summer coat. But that's exactly how natural horses actually function. The modern horse world thinks this is all nonsense and just some primal romanticism, but it's true. And I'll tell you, those people have not only lost the core of their horse's reality, but are themselves pretty atrophied.

It's show and performance horses who have lost the most, for whole castes of show horse owners and their backstage trainers think it's just fine to house their horses in warmed quarters to ensure that their horse's coats don't grow out so they remain "sleek" during the winter months, then neurotically blanket their Arabians when they go outside to graze. But their horses' coats don't actually get sleek, they just stay short, dull and worthless because they never renew themselves; the old hair remains unshed and unrenewed. Then worse still, in order to make their dull horses *look* shiny, these appearance-addicted fools spray them down with all sorts of commercial concoctions as if they were polishing a car. When normal coat-shedding is impaired, delayed, or never happens—after a couple of generations such horses can't digest properly—they sicken, then develop thin skins and become flighty and shallow-souled, with a very compromised fertility. (Just like their owners!)

Horses become the high-strung manipulated product of civilized fakery because of such synthetic standards of appearance that have nothing to do with what horses really are. Enforced by horse shows and contests, horses are damaged in the same way certain beauty contests damage the mental well-being and physical health of human women.

● ● ●

Natural humans, Native people worldwide, have since forever easily read the nuances of seasonal change in the Natural World's animal calendar of seasons by the big clumps of winter wool and hair shedding off and renewing itself on the spring hides of Deer, Buffalo, Musk Ox, Moose, Elk, Gazelles, Antelopes, Wolves, Foxes, Wildcats, Bears, Ibex, Wild Sheep and Goats of every sort. This is still recognized by pastoral nomads who can "read" the news of the season's changes in their horses' coats. And of course, these horses live outside close to the natural earth.

For people who live in a natural way, these sheddings and regrowths of animal fur are far more useful in determining natural changes of time than astronomical observance because animals' natural bodies directly and very sensitively anticipate seasonal changes in conjunction with the annual shifts of the bigger multi-year cycles of plants and weather. Their bodies have an inbuilt spiritual intelligence that can read when the season will actually *shift* instead of when it is astronomically "supposed" to happen. While certain domesticated animals, if they live out of doors, have retained some of this ability as well, all wild animals shed and regrow hair accurately in response to what their beings know is going to happen meteorologically, and it is these animals who have kept time for us humans all along. To this day, certain Native peoples commence their ceremonials in a calendar determined by watching the hair growth of wild animals, not because they don't have the capability of calculating time mathematically, but because the animals are the direct representation of living time in conjunction with what actually happens in the stars and the electromagnetics of the solar system and beyond. Science and mathematics can be wonderful, but they do not determine what happens; they only record and measure what the natural world already knows and makes happen.

Once slave-powered, farm-sustained, city-centered civilizations took hold, they distanced themselves from the pulse of the wild land and Her water, mountains and deserts, and from that time on they conspired to organize the universe from the vista of their civilizations. Crowds cloistered in city buildings, reading seasons by sun, stars and timepieces, were constantly surprised and disappointed when reality didn't match calculated probabilities. Only recently is astro-earth-dynamic-weather as predicted by computer, interpret multiple data in such a way as to come close to what natural humans originally knew more easily, adequately and elegantly by reading it all in the behavior of the way ants make their mounds and by watching hair growth in the coats of animals. People knew how to read the natural world before they lost their place in the original world to the limitations of urbanized civilization, which thinks it should be able to manipulate the Land and Weather at will but has only succeeded in raising Nature's ire, to their own detriment.

Unlike most plants (but not all), wild animals don't all change their coats simply according to the stimuli of temperature and the changed sunlight angle of the seasons, but for more subtle reasons much akin to how certain birds read the bigger cycles in the flow of magnetic, plasmic, solar and stellar layers. For our nomadic ancestors, horses were always our calendars and clocks; the stars lived in their fur.

Though he hadn't made any babies yet, Punk's body was a meticulous calendar. His four-season coat-shedding and -renewing alone meant his breeding patterns and mindfulness of the seasons in which foals could be born would be a powerful trait worth keeping alive in his descendants; a good thing to recognize.

But I knew of no one at that time who even thought about such things. I only did so because I'd been given such awareness by my old friend who taught me how to doctor and euthanize horses in my youth.

♦ ♦ ♦

After the next ten years had crashed, creaked and rumbled by, and my horses and I had been able to finally stay put long enough to taste a full year of seasons in one place, both Blue and Punk became the favorites of a grateful string of handsome nest-building birds who would queue up on both horses' dorsal stripes and wait their turn to pull out their share of the thick winter hair molting off those shaggy horses' backs, then fly off like puffs of fuzz to incorporate the horse fluff into their nests to cushion and insulate their early springtime eggs.

The longer four- to six-inch winter belly hair went for nest foundation material, along with sticks and pebbles, into whose coarse sieve-like basket the horses' shorter, denser back hair, like blocks of sod, were put in as insulating pillows and shock absorbing cushions for eggs inside the mud nests of Swallows, the open cup nests of Flycatchers, Canyon Wrens, Thrushes and Bluebirds. One could definitely distinguish which horse's hair had been used to build which nest throughout the open desert land and bosques that now surrounded us. One set of Magpies specialized by carefully grooming Blue's tail and increasing their already enormous nests every year, extracting the red tail hair and lacing it expertly between large clunky twigs; then, after lining the nest with his white belly hair and the top with Punk's sod-like, pink back hair, the Magpies' eggs would sit in a fur-cushioned castle of sticks and horsetail hair.

For a full mile around, nests of all kinds of birds had our horses' molt hairs incorporated into their construction. And, of course, these were the same birds who so gracefully groomed my horses in the summer, jumping up from their backs to eat the flies.

On the other hand, Amarillento, the little yellow buckskin, was not so popular with nest builders because he would allow only certain birds to sit on him one at a time, especially tiny birds like little Hummingbirds who didn't much use his hair because they preferred spider webs, old leaves and lichen, and only sat there as a spiritual togetherness thing.

But Punk and Blue, like tribal kings, thought all birds were their servants and loved the birds to groom them of all their itchy spring-shedding hair. When Punk got very old he eventually became the permanent summer roost for three Ravens who basically lived on his dorsal stripe and groomed him everyday all season long, especially while Punk was eating. Ravens are all cheap opportunists, gossips and spreaders of lies. But Punk was never taken in. He liked their highly intelligent conversation, overlooking their cowardice and unreliability as friends in order to keep their cool iridescent colors on his back. Punk was always very hip and stylish and loved how the string of Ravens looked against his seasonal coat-color changes!

Even very early on Punk loved all the birds because he knew they made him look good. After all, naturally raised stallions are really into looking *good*. But for Punk the birds of the world were his jewels, a kind of barbarian splendor, a warrior's jewelry. He'd huff and strut around, striking, stamping, sheath-squeaking, snorting and squealing arrogantly, keeping his mares in line, wearing a string of Flycatchers, a Tanager, several Red-winged Blackbirds, and a Mourning Dove perched in a row down his back as he thrust about. The birds enjoyed the ride and Punk felt powerful and well dressed.

Sometimes with a bird perched on his poll right between his ears and another at the base of his tail, Punk swaggered around looking mighty mythological. Of course, when you get down to it he really was. Like a primal native hero, Punk wore an armor of live birds who crowded, cried and stayed on him as he moved toward a mare or viciously charged down on an enemy male horse for a challenge. He had no use for fake Protestant PC humility, he knew he was special, fabulously handsome and unafraid, and he made sure everybody knew about it.

I felt very special as well; after all, how many horse-people can proudly boast they have a stallion that dressed as an indigenous hero in an ever-shifting array of brightly colored birds?

• • •

Most people keep stallions to breed mares in order to capture or continue traits in a bloodline, or to "improve" certain traits in their descendants in order to get a "faster" race horse, a more "savvy" roping horse, a "higher jumping" eventing horse, a more "painted" paint horse, a more "breed conforming" show horse, a bigger, more "powerful" draft horse, on and on ad nauseam. But all that is only about money; it's just business both big and small and very mechanical. The health and "horsality" problems so widespread today come from the fact that most of the horses regular people end up owning and riding are not bred to ride and own but are by-products of big business: they are equine culls from those big, frenzied, multi-owner competitive horse-breeding operations.

Were there no horse people left who bowed only to the natural magic of horses' original place in our human souls?

Were there no real horse-living people hiding somewhere on this beautiful spinning earth? People like there used to be, who loved Nature's will and still bowed to that will as it manifested in the motive of a highly regarded spiritual animal's inborn magic to make more of themselves?

Well MY reasoning for keeping Punk as a stallion had nothing to do with commerce or even color, or anything else the rest of civilization cared about. I simply thought to keep alive the presence of horses as magical as Blue, or Amarillento, or Punk himself: recent avatars of the horses I grew up with, so as the animal-seeds of an original type of greater substance and indigenous integrity they might continue to thrive relatively unhindered beneath the obscurity of modernity's overwhelming details and mental tyranny in order to be there when the world wanted and loved them again.

Though Punk could easily "pass" the common-sense checklist of what modern people claimed made a horse a really good horse for breeding, what my heart wanted was to keep alive the most precious core of living horse mystery that a whole self-rationalizing imperial history had neglected, and for which certainly nobody was breeding, because of course there was no money advantage in doing so.

But just looking at Punk, he was a whirlwind of excellent parts put together in exactly the way wilder natural horse people would have always wanted their horses to be. Even before horses were shuffled aside at the beginning of the 20th century to make room for fossil-fuel machine transport, Punk's old-time breed was not the gigantic horse that the early industrial ages and European world-colonial emplacement employed to power their mega farming wagons to carry grain to mills and then to the railhead. Punk's type of horse was not the horse of industry, of the settled aristocrat or the turnip grower but the horses of worldwide Indigenous tribal freedom. When slow-plodding, grid-oriented settler culture and industry kidnapped the land, Punk's ancestors were discarded and disregarded as "Indian" horses; too wild, too smart and too small to subjugate into colonial industrial civilization. And then when steam- and fossil-fuel-driven trains, tractors, automobiles, factories, and trucks took over from civilization's horses, these little Barb horses left over from the Imperial settling of the tribes, were further slaughtered to feed the poor conscripted soldiers of the world's industrialized wars all senselessly dying for fossil fuel and territory to fund their machine-dependent empires.

Because of all this, just the presence of Punk, Blue, and Amarillento was a political movement. Punk was the epitome of all the attitude, capacity and parts you needed to be a wild and unfettered human. When civilization worked at eradicating such humans in Persia, Russia, Europe, Africa, and especially the Americas, the first thing they had to erase were the free living people's horses, and by that method the people were reduced. The same pattern existed in China and Eurasia in wars 2,000 years previous.

The dimensions of that Horse-freedom lived in Punk's body: starting from his feet upward (as you always must because a horse's feet are the foundation of all his motion, and without good feet everything else that's good above them will crumble and fall—literally), Punk's hoof wall was three-quarters of an inch thick all the way around, never becoming brittle but resilient and hard as fire-hardened mountain mahogany. This is at least three times the thickness of any of "civilization's" horses.

His frogs took up most of his sole; his fetlocks were graceful, well planted, and sturdy with no feathering; his leg joints strong, large and straight; his cannon bones were like cannons, his forearms like a steel mace, long and flexible to the shoulder such that he could scribe a circle at a gallop while still stretching out like a tiger. His hocks were ball joints, his stifle an unkillable rubber roast that never came out of the groove, his hinders well sloped but powerfully arranged with tendons the size of ship hawsers. His tail could've clamped a calf's head if he wanted it; his neck was too massive for the Euro-Americans, but he was an old Mesta and while all of them have real necks, the stallions have even more neck, which is why they don't need wide draft horse chests but have beautifully deep ones instead, as Punk most certainly had. He could pull better than any other horse his size. Over the years a lot of skinny-necked-horse people thought all my Barbs were foundered for the size of their necks. Punk's face and forehead were handsome and as flat as a Bulgarian anvil, neither dished nor Roman-nosed, from which the dense twirl of the hair of his white blaze under his bangs shed out and renewed itself every day of the year, so you could always get a tuft of hair from his forelock whorl to burn in the nostrils of his babies to bring them out of a fright or to tame a bronc. (That's old Native medicine and Punk was a walking medicine chest.)

His teeth were grand like fossil shells in the matrix of his gums.

His eyes, though compromised in bright sunlight due to the fire, were very large and beautiful and set so wide in his head that no modern bridle fit. They were big and black and never looked away but always straight into your soul. Though hurt in the barn fire Punk's eyes were full of far-seeing and emotion.

His nostrils were elegantly curved, tough and just the right size, and spoke when he did, which was loud and often. His wind never roared. His throat-latch was capable of swelling up like a Frigate bird's neck when he ran, keeping him well supplied with oxygen. In his well-sprung lung-holding ribs, his heart had an athlete's strange atypical heartbeat, and his shoulders were both sloped in such a way to make his shuffle through sand dunes as smooth as a sleigh pulled by the moon.

With incongruous cute tufts sprouting out and plugging up his horn-shaped ears, he was still very capable of hearing even the slightest belly grumble of anything on the range sneaking up, which in order to confront he could jump a six-foot fence or a ravine fourteen-feet-across, and would do so without the slightest reluctance.

Nothing scared that crazy stallion when you rode him. His immediate response to anything that would cause a normal equine to balk was to stop and look whomever or whatever it was square in the face if he could, then either kill it on the spot, or if he rationally assessed it as harmless or beneath his dignity to react, he'd simply walk past. If it warranted a strategy he'd think it out and come back at whatever it was again till it jumped, then he would move on but he never ran away, never retreated, never reared or gave in.

Punk did have a firm routine you had to accept if you were to ride him. Most people would have tried to squelch this routine out of him but I always respected the fact that Punk had to buck every day whether he wanted to or not, just to keep in practice and to retain his self-respect. It was his way of making sure everybody knew he'd not been conquered. He never once felt the need to buck you off, it was just that his nature and general health demanded of him that he should at least once a day squeal, leap, kick out and go all-out bucking until the delicious storm was thoroughly grunted out of his gut and the sharp splinters of his daily edge were sanded off.

For Punk bucking was a kind of nutritional supplement; it kept his blood moving properly. He never did buck with me in the saddle, but I could always tell when he hadn't done his daily bucking and needed to buck. So every time I saddled him, for which he stood very steady, and before putting on his silver bridle, I'd stand back and say "Okay 'Father of the Herd' let's see how many bucks you got in there today," and right on cue he'd arch his back, take three choppy steps forward away from me, and commence bucking higher and harder than any rodeo stock you ever saw.

After a few minutes when he stopped bucking, he'd just stand there breathing deep and thinking, then when he was normal again, at my cue he'd come calmly walking back to where I'd been standing, watching his magnificent saddle-on bucking display, at which point I'd bridle him and climb on board. We could ride all day without one spook, balking or any episode of bucking. Unless of course we ran up on someone riding a mare in heat, in which case I'll spare you the details—after all, he wasn't just a soulless old tennis shoe with a horse suit, he was a natural born stallion who knew he'd been born to keep the entire world organized to his plan whether they liked it or not. But he didn't buck just to do it.

Sometimes in the mornings you could tell he was brooding about something and pouting too much to really buck. When after only two or three pitiful crow hops he'd lay off, I could tell something was eating him. So I'd ask:

"Older Brother of the Herd, are those really the only bucks you got left in there?"

He'd stare at me like a ticked off teenager with his big pool eyes full of unleashed tears and war. I'd chase him around a couple of times with my quirt; he'd buck hard till he was sweating like a rain storm, then stop and turn his head sideways as if listening to himself. "You got more in there I can tell, come on let's do it," and away he'd rip, kicking out all fours and flying like a horse trying to jump the Sun. I'd force him to buck until I could tell he'd finally bucked the grudge out of his system. Then together we'd go for a good fast gallop to conquer the world with the beauty of how we looked doing it, raising a streak of desert dust like a zipper opening up the land. It was only right to let him saddle-buck.

On rare occasions, mostly in the mud when running alone confined in a corral, getting up speed to buck he'd lose his leads, slip and roll head over heels. Like any horse worth the grass he's squeezed out of, Punk had his pride and it was best to look away when this happened, pretending you hadn't seen it, otherwise he'd mope all day long for the disgrace. One had to love such a proud horse.

So Punk more than passed muster on how I judged horses, and whether or not he would have easily passed the checklist of what modern horse breeders require in order to rationalize reserving a male horse as a money-making breeding stallion, I can't tell you, but while all of these details were grand enough and definitely necessary they were not in and of themselves what caused my great admiration for Punk.

Though I know Nature's spiritual plasmic motion is not concerned with human intentions, inventions or insistences, the fact is, miracles and magic do happen; pretty much every natural thing that does happen is already a miracle and magical. If you see life correctly, magic is all that happens. So in that way of going about life, I knew that the magic in a horse or a person could only develop in a foal or a child if the parents of such foals and children truly loved one another. While I was judged a naïve fool and a romantic in most modern people's eyes, Punk certainly felt the same way I did. For mysteriously and very uncharacteristically for a stallion, Punk for years refused the company of all mares until the real love of his life, the life partner created for him by the Holy in Nature, showed up. So many mares had snuck in, come by, or been afforded him, but until the "Mother of the Herd" showed up and she said okay to him, he would never breed. I loved Punk for this. We were both hopeless romantics, heroically charging against the flattened stupidity of modern life with its money dependency and its mediocrity. Together we were both honorably waiting for love to appear and life to begin again, for our manes had grown back.

We were patiently waiting.

Chapter 4

Badgers in Love

Real horses don't just breed horses, stallions out in the world don't just breed mares, mares don't just breed stallions: together they are cells in the body of the land's existence, for the entire world lives in their bellies and they inside the land—so much so that the whole world is procreating when real horses begin their lovemaking.

All Natives know wild Elks don't breed just to make more Elk. Bull Elks don't just fight for cow Elks. Cow Elks don't just casually choose a bull and make babies. No, when wild male and female Elk breed the entire rolling landscape, the rivers and the forest are in their bodies; the whole world lives inside them and they inside the land. All the wild mountains and grasslands are breeding when wild Elk breed.

Wild bull Whales in the Great Mother Oceans don't just jump and twist, dance and dive to impress lady Whales in order to secure the future of the species. No way. When Whales breed the entire waterscape of the wide Ocean is making love. The current with its Krill, the whole Sea lives inside herds of whales and they inside the vast Sea; so the Sea Herself is breeding ecstatically when wild Whales breed, all life bolstered by their echoes from the deep.

And like a Whale, an Elk or a Badger, Punk himself was as wild as he could be, and in the truest old native sense he was always waiting to begin his lovemaking in order to do his part to keep the whole world alive. When Punk put his ecstatic fierce seed into the womb of an agate-hoofed mare she would be the entire world to him and he the entire world to her, both of them making natural foals by bringing their part of the natural earth back alive in their lovemaking.

Some of the funny old New Mexican ranchers in our area, God bless them, secretly admired what they thought were my "four" old-style stallions running with the geldings on the bosque bottom we owned down by the Green-Stain River.

These were Spanish-speaking men and women of Comanche, Jicarilla, Diné, German, Spanish-American, French and more ancestries, who lived at our New Mexican edge of the world's strange drift into cyber wasteland. The urbanized global computer emptiness was crashing in on them, but these ranchers still lived in a magical landscape: a New Mexico mind-and-soul-scape. Thus while out gathering up their range cows they would get occasional glimpses of crazy Punk, whom they matter of factly interpreted to be four different animals because, like the land, Punk had seasonal colors that made him *seem* like four different animals. Most of these old timers very clearly recognized that the horses I was raising were of the same type of animals their own grandfathers had been riding. But because white "cowboy" culture told them those horses were "passé trash," there were none of these Barbs left.

But every so often I'd find that one or two of my compadres from our canyon had craftily introduced some gigantic Thoroughbred mare or a couple of eligible Quarter Horse fillies or an Arabian or once a Paso Fino mare in heat onto our land through a suspiciously "down" fence in hopes of catching an accidental-on-purpose range breeding from "one" of my fierce little Barb stallions, all four of whom were Punk!

It was always a fond source of whispered village gossip how their time-tested methods of stealing breedings seemed to backfire with Punk. Punk simply refused to mount their mares, going so far as to even drive all these fine ladies out of his "territory" and back through the cut fence they'd come in on! These horses were not horses as far as he was concerned. Plus he was not *in love* with them. He hadn't courted them!

All the other stallions of other breeds I'd ever seen without any qualms would mount and breed a truck's tailpipe in a second if it smelled remotely like a mare in heat, and a flesh and blood mare in heat of any size, type or age they'd never turn away. But Punk like the land itself was governed by an older ethos. There were even experts who told me Punk would never breed, never make babies, that there was something amiss with him. Such frog farts.

Don't get me wrong, like any stallion worth his grass, Punk would viciously attack any gelding within a mile of him accusing, convicting and sentencing all male horses in one motion as a threat to some imagined herd of "mares" he didn't have yet. Either trying to disable or kill the perceived competition, he always succeeded in at least driving the competition off.

No, Punk was truly a romantic horse and would not make babies with any old mare just cause she backed up to the fence in readiness.

Though he'd been in my corrals for 16 years, and was already 19 years old and at an age when a lot of "civilized" breeders begin to retire their stallions Punk hadn't even yet begun to breed. He was still a bachelor and still holding out for just the right girl! He wanted to be in love with the lady with whom he made his babies!

Everything that happens in Nature is ritual, and while the ritual of keeping your ancestral line alive is an ecstatic interruption in the routine of Nature's everyday life, it is a routine part of Nature's bigger cyclic vision. Inside all of that there are animals who definitely find partners with whom they become ecstatic lifelong lovers.

In the bigger motion of Nature you have to be awake to see and hear all the subtlety, terror and ruckus of a natural romance to begin to understand how all the fluting and bellowing of male Elk and the fierce clank and clack of the fencing with their antlers is part of that romance. Contrary to what is commonly taught, this drama has less than nothing to do with "sorting out the fittest" for reproduction. But still this ritual must be done, as it is an obligation, an instinctual contract with Holy Nature's gift of life. The Elk ladies need the pheromonal immersion of the male's elegant jousting, they need the sound of antlers clanking and clacking, the grunts and moans, the power of this impressive martial ballet, the tournament of expert twists and turns of the males, in order to shed their winter coats and pull their ovum down the river valleys of their tubes. They need this messy noise and atypical life for one week out of the year so the land inside them could open up and become receptive to the placement and growing of new Elks. But... they only rarely breed the victors!

Science's mechanically-minded fiction insists that Elk males fight for eligible females, who stand by waiting for the "victor" to mount them. Baloney. The girls choose who they want to breed no matter who wins, which in my personal experience is only rarely the best swordsman at the ritual grounds! The breeding dance of the Elk is to artistically and ritually continue the species by putting the entire world under the spell of the luscious waterfall of erotic life-making. When it comes to the Holy in Nature it's best to humbly watch and keep your senses awake before tightly designating any human-generated pseudo-rationalist assumption as "scientific" truth. Just because things seem to appear how you've been taught doesn't mean that's how they really are.

More than once I've seen a pile of sexy young recently-come-of-age Elk girls sitting together with a pile of sexy crusty old dog-eared matron Elks on a little ceremonial mound where annually they traditionally watch the jousting of the young bulls with older bulls. Seated in an open grassy swale whose short enclosing ridges are fenced with thick conifers, the young cows chewing their cud look like sarcastic human teenage girls chewing gum, viewing the proceedings from the corner of their eyes. With a feigned disinterest they watch the hard struggles of all the eligible one-thousand-pound jealous males fighting, dancing and singing their beautiful forest-echoing bugles, the bulls running out from the tree line, down the open slopes into the parkland, gaining momentum from opposite sides until heads down they spring up as they meet, locking heads while rearing, then sometimes getting into a sumo push-and-pull antler-locking match like dueling bulldozers.

Meanwhile, every once in a while, but continually during this ceremony, one of these Elk girls will rise and leave her gum-chewing post to run off into the loving arms of a really funky-looking, mangy old bull with a dented half a rack hiding in the woods! With no intention of fighting anymore in these dangerous energy-expensive ritual games, it is He who ends up breeding all the females, one by one, who then return to the mound to continue watching. Though brought into season by all the traditional sex-inspiring ritual, the lady Elks are usually already impregnated on the sidelines by the time they pair up with the "winners" for the winter, who may appear to have bred their female partners, but it's not the winners' calves who drop into the mossy forest ground months later!

Maybe as individuals these animals are not romantic, but the entire herd as a single organism inside the organism of the Wild as a whole is a romantic lover of life and gives more life to the whole as a result.

In my youth on Pueblo lands there were a number of Badgers whose big ancient dens were dug in under the wild horse-running hills and arroyos I grew up in. Badgers live mostly hidden in the dens of other animals. After expertly digging out the original resident Ground Squirrels or Prairie Dogs, whom they voraciously and gratefully devour, they just move in.

Rough characters—imagine somebody eating your neighbor and then moving into his house!

The famous world-reading olfactory precision of Badgers' tough pushy little snouts and their close-seeing eyes signal their long claws and iron-snapping jaws about where and whom to snag there in the dark underground. After carefully ingesting whosoever had presented themselves from the hole, the sound of Badger gnashing, slurping, crunching and humming always scared off the remainder of the eatable underground citizens, into whose abandoned labyrinth of holes our Badger would dig and dine, remodeling and amplifying the rooms in the west and south sides of hills until it all fit his bulk and into whose comfy grass-lined confines he or she would take up residency and fall sound asleep. It's hard to see any of this 'cause no Badger likes to be watched.

I've always found that it's pretty rare for life and love to unfold when one is noisily seeking it, but more often it elegantly happens in rare unexpected conjunctions when one is simply sitting and watching quietly, expecting no more than the beauty of the world.

As a teenager, one day in exactly such a way, miles from any other human, while squatting alone out on a gentle slope of an agate-cobbled hill, holding my father's little rabbit rifle vertical between my legs, my knees up by my ears, I saw a mythology come alive.

I wasn't actively "hunting," but had the gun with me, as I always did so any Native who might see me on the wild hills wouldn't think I was guilty of just "hiking" but doing something useful like hunting to feed someone. If I came across a Rabbit or Prairie Dog I'd probably take a shot.

Breathing shallow so my ears could sort out the sounds in the magnificent breadth of the wild desert valley spreading out below, I sat as still as a boulder, scanning the yellow-flowered desert stretch for any Jackrabbits or Cottontails that might present themselves in the splendor of that cool morning; one early summer day and in that condition I began to hear, long before I could see, the rarely witnessed morning approach of a Badger heading off to his daily job excavating rodents and reptiles for his breakfast.

Like Porcupines, Badgers are famous singers and they always sing on their way to work. Most people, if they are ever fortunate enough to hear one sing, might mistake their song as some abstract muttering as they saunter about snuffling, and then… stopping all of a sudden and cocking their funny sideways ears to listen, scraping out a few test pits, and mostly abandoning them, still singing as they move on.

Of course if you say that a Badger actually just mutters and complains to himself and is not really singing at all, then you've missed the concert, for though it's true that Badgers constantly complain, they always do so very musically. They sing as they shuffle along about the unfairness of the world in which they, the honorable, hardworking Badgers work, searching and digging hard for a living while everybody else in the world does nothing at all equivalent and still eats. The songs Badgers sing as they move through the day are definitely complaints and you can hear their whiney blues coming a long way off if they don't know you're sitting there, because Badgers don't like to sing if they know people are listening. At least I never met one that did. That's because this animal knows most humans today can't really hear the mastery of the Badger's music inside the bigger music of the land, where, backed up by all the birds as he rambles through the orchestra, he's Caruso in the world's opera. Since people think he's only "muttering" and are too dull to hear his sound as music, Badger refuses to sing for the dull.

Sitting motionless, shallow breathed and waiting, I could hear the Badger singing his beautiful complaint coming up the draw to my right some fifty feet off and below. His song faded, then got closer and soon enough, right there within clear view a good-sized Badger, low to the ground, side hair quivering, head bopping back and forth, came moving along in that very concerted, forward, workman-like fashion all Badgers have. In a high-pitched gravely mutter he whined and sang all the way, this time not only to himself but to two Coyotes who strolled casually right along with him, one on either side, their opportunistic red foreheads nodding in condescending agreement to his every word. Like chums on their way to work, unflustered all three sauntered right past me on their way to somewhere, either paying absolutely no heed to my presence whatsoever or mysteriously not seeing that I was sitting right there not ten feet away. I held my breath and my mind.

Once past me and all the way up the arroyo, they disappeared over the small ridge, onto the flat and out of my view. I crouched down and moved up carefully to get a peek of where they might be heading. Hearing what I took to be the accustomed sounds of Coyotes yipping after a flushed Rabbit, by the time I'd got on top and could see, I had to duck and push down the laugh inside. For one Coyote had run up ahead to the mouth of a big hole on a Prairie Dog mound where he started yipping and digging, which caused the Badger to rush up to the same hole and disappear, digging inside to get what the Coyote seemed to be after.

Meanwhile the second Coyote had already rapidly spiraled out around running in increasingly bigger circles behind where the Badger had disappeared, until he found the "other" hole, the escape tunnel, and was crouched down there, quivering with wide-eyed intensity hidden beneath the little dirt mound of the hillside hole.

Badger was now down deep into the mound digging and digging; every once in a while, frantically clicking and grumbling, he would back out of the hole like a mine drill, pushing a big wave of moist underground earth into the light. Rising up onto his hind legs he'd take a look around, then after not seeing any "food" running around, Badger would dive back into the hole again like a coalmining machine, digging and digging some more, hoping to eventually come upon the animals he could smell in there to eat.

Both Coyotes, on the other hand, with their positions between the escape holes with hardly any effort caught Prairie Dogs one after the next, flushed from their dens by the Badger's ardent tunneling! Prairie Dog after Prairie Dog, the Coyotes very quickly snatched 'em and dispatched 'em, cracking their necks and crunching them down almost whole like seals gulping fish!

Meanwhile the poor hard-working, ground-digging, snuffling, growling, workman-like blues-singing Badger was driving Prairie Dogs right into those shameless lazy Coyotes' stomachs without ever getting one for himself.

I couldn't believe what I was seeing. It was just what the old stories told: Badger, after marrying Coyote's sister, hunted with his lazy Coyote brothers-in-law who everyday ate up all the animals that poor gullible Badger chased out of the holes, coming home so gorged while the honest Badger only ate what the Coyotes couldn't finish.

And there right before my eyes, snuffling and grumbling, Badger every now and again would back out and scurry to the top of the Prairie Dog mound to see if any terrified animals were running out to get away.

But the glutted Coyotes, belching and lethargic now, always claimed they hadn't seen a thing sending the honest, disgusted Badger to huff himself back into the hole, where complaining in a high-pitched whine all the way about the hard work it took to live, continued his futile digging causing those rascal Coyotes to feast again at his expense.

Coyotes and Badgers are very different beings, one made for running, conniving, ambushing and stealing, eating rotten meat or fruit, while the other digs and works hard. But they both have salt-and-pepper coats, which Natives know comes from the ancient intermarrying of both their tribes. Though Coyotes are famous everywhere for their self-aggrandizing nighttime singing, and their shy brothers-in-law the Badgers sing quietly in the day, Badgers nonetheless are way stronger and could kill a Coyote in a second. And of course everybody knows that Badgers are better lovers, which is why long ago Coyote girl fell in love with Badger's quiet breeding song to begin with.

Badger, they say, used to have a really big set of eyes with far-seeing vision. Coyote they say had really funky shortsighted eyes that he got stuck trying to see out of after he bet his beautiful eyes while gambling with Cedar Waxwing. After stealing some eyes from Tarantula (who used to have ten but now only has eight), Coyote badgered Badger to play at stick dice (Badger had never gambled) in a game where they both bet their eyeballs. Badger lost bad of course when Coyote cheated. Coyote even ended up with Badger's once-upon-a-time luxurious tail! For this reason the once big-eyed Badgers with long furry tails ended up with little close-seeing, underground spider eyes and short bear-like tails, and Coyotes are the way they are today.

They say after all of that betrayal and abuse, Badger has remained forever paranoid, touchy and dangerously reactive. And because of his nearsighted underground-seeing eyes, until Badger gets a good sniff of you (his amazing nose really works well) he just assumes that everyone's out to "take" him for a ride; so Badgers always bite first and ask questions later. Viciously gnashing their tusks, hissing and fighting everything on the spot, Badgers are so powerful that they are capable of nipping a broom handle in half like a breadstick.

And while all of this is very true, there are three or four days a year when the normally vitriolic steel-necked Badger becomes a calm drooling lover who stops singing complaint songs and starts crooning sweet bird-like troubadour tunes! This you have to hear and see to fully believe.

For years, I'd heard old people tell me this about Badgers, but I didn't know it for real until one time after Punk had already grown out his burnt-off mane and tail, and all the tresses of my own hair and eyebrows had grown back again, when I would see for myself how two animals of such snarling, spitting, reactionary, cursing, vicious, suspicious, nearsighted, combative everyday manner could become the sweetest, trusting, slavering, honey-eyed cooing sweethearts of the deep-earth sort in a way no one would have ever surmised.

Punk was now well broken to the saddle, but for safety we rode together only in the big wild unpeopled stretches of the arid highlands where we weren't likely to come upon any riders or wild horses, for he was still a stallion if you know what I mean.

Punk and I were out for an amble in the once wide-open lands west of Santa Fe, some eight years after the crazy fire, and there on the top berm of a big Badger hole drilled into a small knoll of polished agate-y alluvium sat two Badgers side by side, unmoving, gazing out together toward the afternoon sun like a couple of stoned California hippies.

Sliding quietly off my saddled perch I let Punk out, dragging the reins to graze at whim the Sacaton shoots, and crawled on my belly up for a closer look at these two Badgers. As I didn't really know what I was witnessing, I was tense and cautious about coming so close, for all the Badgers I'd ever met were fast, frenetic, quarrelsome and solitary, and never just sat around enjoying life together; in every case always primed to spin around and explode.

Lying on the hillside I waited and listened. When the breeze stilled I could hear both of the fierce animals humming in the cutest little way, each taking turns at first, then singing together. They never looked at one another but with their powerful front legs locked vertically and their hind ends squat, they sat identically cantilevered, staring up and out at the beautiful world. For an hour I waited and listened to them both humming high-pitched a cappella love songs and actually drooling from their trembling jaws in the breeze, taking in the world.

A Fly landed on the white strip of the forehead of one of them, and immediately a Yellow Warbler nailed the Fly but stayed sitting on the same Badger's head! The Badger couldn't have cared less but just continued humming and drooling!

These were not the Badgers I'd ever known, Badgers who like lightning would have devoured such a relaxed bird in an edgy second! But today the whole world and this warbler knew these Badgers were in love and it was safe to be in their presence.

This turned out to be my first glimpse of two Badgers in love and how Badgers in love wouldn't hurt even a Fly much less a Flycatcher!

There are a lot of honeymoons among natural beings in the wild, but people mostly miss seeing them because one has to be very immersed and constantly awake to the cycles of plants (by whom all animal's lives are mandated; whose cycles are in turn managed by the Moon) and the dance of the electromagnetic astro-plasma of the Sun and both the temporary and orbiting motions of the Universe to even get close enough in timing to know when and where and how to look for natural "honeymooners". There have been fine original humans throughout time for whom, like Snakes, Ants, Birds or Butterflies, the subtlety of Nature's next movement can be seen just as clearly as knowing where to dig for a clam, but for most people today, blink and they'll miss the tranquil version of a set of Badgers in love, or the wild underground orgy of Snakes making babies, or the lovemaking of Bears in the bush. Science seems to declare as fact that there is no love, longing, grief or beauty as a motivation in Nature; this they say is all just romanticized nonsense, some poetic imagined flamboyance of human behavior. This implies that love and romance are the sole domain of "humans." However, from where I sit on my Horse, both love and beauty seem to be pretty much the domain only of Nature, natural peoples and the Universe, while the emotionally-eroded humans inhabiting a lot of this modern age come in with a pretty bad showing. Instead of feeling the deliciousness of being alive as the main meal, to them love and beauty are sparse condiments on modernity's thoroughly over-cooked, bland stew of sarcasm and shallowness.

Elks have their ritual of love and it thunders on the surface of this wild ground. Badgers have their love inside the ground. Two Eagles in love have their dramatic courting ritual by free-falling from the heart of the sky at hurricane speeds, where with talons locked they drop and spin together, each learning to trust the other to gracefully break apart a second before both would die, whacked to pulp on the Holy Earth. Is this not a powerful courting tradition among Eagles to establish trust before joining in the well-attested lifetime monogamous marriage custom of all Eagles?

Every living being in the world has their courting, their love, their wild ecstatic togetherness that is always out of the ordinary from their everyday lifeways. Normally impossible to see, shy underground Badgers will continue their open air, ecstatic, friendly staring for three days and three nights. Then, every now and again, the lady Badger's eyes will all of a sudden grow strangely big (their eyes are very small so this is startling), at which point she turns her head away from their combined staring and grooving on the world to scamper like a dust mop, as only Badgers can, down into the remodeled, much widened Prairie Dog hole behind their "thrones," her sweetheart grinning and waddling out of sight right behind her.

The sounds of their private mating come bubbling and reeling up from one of the echoing chambers deep inside the lovers' den: squeals and shrieks, then growls and yips reverberate out into the wide desert world as if the Earth herself has satiated Her desire somewhere deep inside by the mating of the Badgers.

Then a ripple of silence.

A Mockingbird sings, then a Meadowlark, then the Forever Wind.

After a while, surging up out of the ground like a little wave, one Badger pushes moist sand to the surface behind him, emerging shoveling backwards out of the hole with all four paws and their huge claws. When his head finally hits the air he spins around a couple of times to shake off the sparkling mica dust from his salt-and-pepper bristles, then retakes his place on the top ledge of the hole as he waits for that second burst of sand out of which his lover, her head and body quivering, will pull back on up and plop down beside her fierce and furry sweetheart, where they both calmly take in the world. Once again staring and crouching for hours, they drool and drink up each other's company as only Badgers in love can do! The one strange thing about it all is they never actually look at one another but together stare out at the world, in love with being in love *in* the world.

Like the dedicated hardworking beasts they are, their sweethearts' honeymoon is a factory worker's vacation: three days a year is all the world will ever get of amiable mild-tempered Badgers, for on the morning of the fourth both wake up, shake their ornery heads in disgust, and hungover from the ecstasy of the annual love-trance, their breeding accomplished, the honeymoon is officially finished. Now instead of looking out at the beautiful world of tinkling birds and wild open land with all its possible cool creatures to dig out and eat together, they both turn around and finally take a good look at each other, and it is a loathsome, revolting sight to both! Insulted and horrified at what each now sees in the other, they both let loose a terrible guttural whining which increments to a fierce growling, spitting and hissing, and right out of marriage they both aggressively leap and spin, each one heading right toward the other's throat. Rolling around in the flying fur and dust for a tense half minute, they gnash and claw away until the lady succeeds in getting the upper hand and sends her former love—the sweetheart of their luscious three-day honeymoon dream—off to find his own goddamn house!

Back to grumbling and singing his complaint about the unfair world as usual, away he rolls with a Badger headache, all pissed off and bobbing his front end back and forth like a hoodlum, mopping up the world with his long quivering rib hairs until his song disappears back into the matrix of the sounds of the wide-open land.

You can still hear the angry lady Badger's muffled kvetching rolling off endless chittering threats deep inside the new mansion she earned in the divorce settlement, until eventually, of course, all is quiet except the Forever Wind and the tinkling of birds.

But the world-at-large has been fed by the ritual of the Badgers' marriage.

And life goes on.

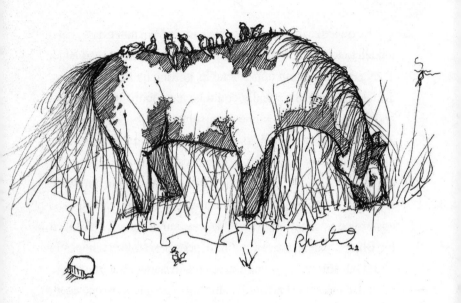

Chapter 5

Punk Builds a House

For the praises they sang of him, Blue prized all the little birds that sat sunning themselves perched up and down his spine. And like a hornless, dreamy-eyed, cloud-spotted unicorn, Blue would always be enchanted by truly beautiful women and loved having the fur covering the hard bone of his rhino-like head caressed by any of the same whose own noble natures recognized his, but he would under no circumstances ever allow any human being besides myself to climb up on his powerful back and ride him. No man. No woman. No child. No matter how amazing or beautiful they might have been. I was the only one who could seem to ride him.

Knowledgeable horse people, riders I'd known for years, tended to fear him. Male riders in particular bad-mouthed Blue. They considered him unpredictable, unfriendly and dangerous. To tell the truth Blue really could be a stubborn rusty old nail and would certainly become a fearsome one-of-a-kind monster if anyone but me tried to ride him. What caused many to dislike him was his policy of aloofness when anyone fearing the massive warhorse he was trivialized him to make him seem less. Blue's utmost contempt was for people who masked their cowardice as superiority, and this was democratically balanced by Blue's huge respect for timid people who were honestly afraid but still brave enough to approach him with admiration.

All these same knowledgeable horse people were outraged, horrified and aghast when they saw that wild Old Blue boy let the love of my life, that long-curly-haired princess of such fine lines, to climb up onto his powerful warhorse back and ride him calmly like a queen in an Arthurian romance!

Mind you, I had a straightforward talk beforehand with Blue about how I would cook his meat if anything happened to her.

But it wasn't really necessary because to everyone's chagrin, Blue loved my little Hannita and became so embarrassingly cooperative and inflated to be ridden by such an exquisitely beautiful and decent-hearted girl that for once in his life he went riding right along pretty much quirkless, his fierce and opinionated nature so transparently charmed by how luscious the two of them looked moving through the New Mexico dust and up the trail together, that Blue's lifelong dream of having only such beauty on his magical back reconfigured his tough warrior persona into something resembling that of a gigantic loyal old family watchdog, whereby he practically became my new wife's personal bodyguard. Like myself he was utterly beguiled by Hanna and nobody was to mess with her. If I was Blue's man, she became his lady! Most people couldn't see it but that's how it was. A decade had passed since leaving the mountains and both Amarillento and Blue were now in their mid-twenties. The love of my life had finally come.

Though when we met she knew very little about the life I loved to live, and learned to love it better than I, she ironically knew more than me about how to live the life I'd been forced to follow in big cities, with all its rules and banks, scheduling, airports, taxes and IRS, and proceeded to fix up my exorbitant phone bills, double bookings, financial blunders and general incapacities with modern life on the road in such an expert way that we could finally stay home together a little more and follow the lives on the wild open land we both loved being in together.

While that little girl was a fine chef and could handle big really sharp knives, real hot ovens and hotter stove burners, she interestingly knew nothing about making fire outside or about Coyotes, Hawks or Eagles, Swallows or Beavers, or growing chile or eating it as a main course, and had most certainly never been on a horse, much less my crazy broncs. But Hanna learned how to saddle, how to bail when things got too rough, how to ride the crumbly cliffs and stay afloat in a storm, and was brilliant and brave and took to moving on horseback like the warmth of the Sun in a summer's dawn moves across the purple hills. Soon enough we coursed together through the arroyos of my homeland like a couple of wild Antelope, inseparable, in love and courageously facing an unsympathetic human world, making tea and lunch on our fires under the mountain mahogany on overhanging cliffside ledges.

None of this of course was lost on Punk.

For when he saw my new life, how my new bride rode out on Blue with me on Amarillento, he could tell better than I that *his* bride should not be long in coming too. Now that love had found us, and life and home and land had begun to gather again, Punk knew for sure that I'd go hunting for some mares for him and start up a herd again, a decade and a half after that barn fire.

Because Punk knew the love of *his* life was on her way, like a wild stallion he began to prepare a home for her. That's how I knew he knew. It was all uncanny and seemed a little precipitated, but Punk knew what we didn't.

Natural stallions *do* build homes, wild-horse-style homes. Overdomesticated male horses know nothing about any of this. For though Punk as yet "had" no mares whatsoever and was living in a 65' wide, 6' high circular corral of welded steel pipe, one morning after Hanna and I had moved in together for the first time, Punk all of a sudden went about creating those characteristic stallion piles of his daily droppings in the corners of his tiny realm. In wild open land, a herd's "house" can be about 50 miles square, some seven miles by seven miles, and is invariably marked in each "corner" by a three-foot-high pyramidal stack of horse droppings from the resident stallion. Unlike herd mares who poop wherever they stand, herd stallions never allow themselves to poop where their digestion commands but hold it and use their feces to add to their piles, which in the wild can be five to ten miles distant from each other. These piles are the corners of the herd's house and form olfactory boundary markers from which all horses outside his herd's "house" or territory can inhale a myriad of messages, just as if they were reading a long sign. The main message written there is a warning that this talking pile of poop is the threshold of such-and-so stallion's territory, and if any other male horse should be audacious enough to cross into that territory he will be automatically assumed to be on a raid to steal mares. The presence of an outside male horse was a threat and would rouse the ire of the resident stallion, who as the protector of his realm and harem of mares, like a local feudal aristocrat, would come unapologetically charging against any such careless trespasser. If the intruder be a stallion young or old who did not instantly turn and flee out of this territory, each contestant would circle round and round sniffing the other to get the details of his foe, until a vicious combat ensued which not uncommonly resulted in the death of one or the other, or in both being so maimed as to die later, leaving the herd to disperse to other stallion's herds.

But my Punk was not ruling a fifty-square-mile range. He had no real competitors, and at this point his herd of mares was physically invisible. At least I couldn't see them in his 4,900-square-foot territory!

Even so, after two months, four three-foot-high stallion mounds had emerged in each corner of his "inner" territory, firmly in place like the pillars of his mansion.

I'm sure *he* could see his mares, his herd, his open land inside the timeless inner landscape of his fierce Barb soul, where all the spirit forms of his babies to come were no doubt already dropped and up and running alongside their mamas under the stars in that wide, free world so prophetically written in the lining of his cranium. And Father Punk's house was ready and furnished; all he was missing was his first sweetheart.

But where were the mares? In the past I'd always been a good horse finder and now ten years later I still assumed I could scare up one mare, or someone would know where they could be found, but having focused my efforts in other directions for a decade, when I turned to look again the breed had totally vaporized, only more completely than before.

Computers and cell phones had come into vogue during those years and seemed to utterly rule the minds of all civilization. Horse people were not the least of those instantly glued to the addiction of their megabytes. In my search for Southwestern Indian Mesta mares, I would become acquainted with more than a dozen men and women ranchers, some wealthy beyond telling, but each of them cursed to spend their entire existence locked in their computer rooms, glued to multiple screens; getting ulcers over the rise and fall of market indexes, the price of wire, steel culverts and fence posts; manipulating tax shelters; buying and selling; giving orders to fence riders on ATVs by computer and computer phone; getting even paler skin and thinner souls, bigger bellies, physically ill and mentally impatient, no longer able to spend any time outside in the beautiful wide-open land they claimed to love. To me this was a very unappealing leaching of the beauty of what it meant to be living; a strange and stupid modus operandi for raising animals, accepted by some as a human advancement.

And with that convenient opinion held very tightly in my one hand, in all honesty, after finding no "good" mares of my style, my other hand was embarrassingly forced to peruse the "horses for sale lists" and horse registry sites on a computer as well. For in my search for a girlfriend for Punk, gone were the days of letter writing, feedstore posters, newspaper ads, homemade roadside billboards and word of mouth. All the mouths were glued to cell phones.

No one understood why I was being so particular about mares, but the horses that corresponded to Punk's history, those horses I was looking for, in a short dozen years once again ceased to be a presence and were washed out of people's minds. It seemed nobody remembered what such horses even were, much less something to find. It was bizarre.

But these horses had magical indigenous spirits watching over them and these spirits were wild subtle beings for whom miracles were their daily fare, and so by following one thing I found the other.

I'd never given up hope of someday reclaiming those first silver saddles and headstalls I'd made, purloined now 14 years previous. It wasn't that I was actively searching for them, but in my exhaustive hunt for the right lady horses I kept at least one eye cocked in case something might spark a clue as to where they might have ended up. It was silly of course, as my good bride reminded me, for the "bad medicine" of the thieves' heartless action would remain with what they stole and who stole it. Why would I want any contact with such hateful beings to retrieve things tainted as such? True for certain, and wise. Plus, she said, you can make new ones, which was very true, and I did, and they were good too.

But I was descended from clannish Irish people and Natives, and I was a New Mexican as well, so still I hoped.

Thumbing through one of the piles of books people sent to me as a teacher, in one "authoritative" coffee table book, I came across a photo of an old-style silver-mounted headstall touted as the definitive "artistic and cultural link" between Native American silversmithing and fancy central Mexican saddlemaking silversmiths. The photo credit read that this "artifact" was in the private museum of some wealthy collector outside Dallas, Texas. But comically, this "old" 18th-century silver headstall was one I myself had hammered out from Mexican pesos less than 14 years previous, the one that had gone missing along with the beloved first saddles I'd ever made. Obviously sold to collectors as an old relic, it was hopeless to think those publishing the book or the "museum" owner could be held in collusion with the theft, for no doubt they were as much a victim of the "thieves" as I was and were led to believe what they so desperately wanted to be true. But we checked on it all anyway.

At the distant edge of the trail of our search, we casually came across a site on the computer where a very talented African-American Texas cowboy was selling his hand-braided rawhide horse equipment: *riatas*, *bozales*, reins, saddles and bridles. He lived in the same town where the museum housing the silver "relic" of my creation was located as well.

To demonstrate his "old-time" Luis Ortega type gear, this man had photographed several "old-time" horses suited up with all the tack he had created. To my great surprise, the horses wearing his beautiful handiwork looked for all the world like horses descended from one side of both Punk and Blue's ancestors!

Once I got him on a landline telephone, we struck up a conversation in which it turned out I was correct that these horses of his were the last ones left of those taken out of Valencia County by helicopter when the owners of old "Long Mane's" herd had passed on.

They were all beautiful little Barbs but they were geldings—no mares, and none for sale. But on the computer screen in an advertisement, this lover of the Old-Time West, its gear and these original horses, had a photo in which he himself was seated on a powerful black-pointed buckskin gelding sporting his handmade saddle, bozal, and rawhide reins; and there behind that horse off a ways stood a very tiny, fuzzy silhouette of a horse I could just barely make out. It's funny though how much you can sometimes discern from just a stance or an attitude.

Standing at least 100 ft. behind this mounted artist, I could tell the horse was a Barb mare. It was difficult to be certain but I felt sure.

"That horse," I said to Hanna, excited and crazed, rudely poking my finger onto her laptop screen, "there she is, that's the one!"

"That's what one? What horse?" she asked. "What are we looking at, you mean the horse he's riding?"

"No, that's a gelding. Nooo, the horse behind him," I blurted.

"What horse? I don't see another horse in there."

"Sure, look hard, can you make the picture bigger?" And Hanna did but it was all a blur, but I could still tell… she was the one!

"She looks to be a solid red Barb mare," I told Daryl when I finally got him on the phone again.

Shuffling through his site he came to the picture in question. "You can see that tiny dot there is a horse?" he laughed. "You can tell she's red and she's a Barb and she's a mare?"

"Yes of course."

"You must be a lion or an eagle. The image is only 2 mm tall. How can you tell?"

"Is she from Valencia? Is she about 4 years old?"

"Well, that's exactly how old she is and yes she is from Valencia, and as a matter of fact that's the name we registered her under."

We rolled in and around the subject then after I commissioned him to make me one of his cool rawhide ropes, we got back to talking about this little red mare.

"Won't you sell us your little red mare, Daryl?"

"What do you want her for?"

"Is she broke?"

"She's a joy to ride for green broke," he said very authoritatively, which is cowboy horse jargon for I got a saddle on her once, otherwise not broke.

"Great, how's her health?"

"Never foundered." Which is horse trader talk for she had some other health complications.

"Good. Have you tried to breed her?"

"No, we didn't catch her off the open for that purpose." Which is a horse trader smokescreen for we did get her for breeding but she can't seem to carry a foal full term, i.e., the health problem.

"How is she around people?"

"She's a little standoffish at first, but once she gets to know you she's great." Meaning she's pushy, probably bites, doesn't kick but tries to rush the gate, and is a general hard-to-catch pain in the rear.

"How about with other horses?"

"Valencia is always first, she's your lead mare." The truth for once, meaning she beats all the other horses up.

We talked and talked some more and finally he sold her to me for $1,000 to be shipped at my expense to Colorado Springs in six weeks, to where I would drive, pick her up and trailer her home into Punk's waiting arms.

Her presence was so strong that from a tiny 2 mm silhouette you could just smell the past, see the old form and feel her *Aleika* six hundred miles away!

Chapter 6

Bears in the Barn, Kite-String Corrals

In Northern New Mexico, Rain is everything. If the Rain Gods are captured by the south mountain demons, and our world gets dry—and that means really *dry*—New Mexicans get paranoid and irascible as a normal everyday running mood.

For Rain is love. And if Rain should rain and the highlands turn to all mud and a riot of wildflowers, then New Mexicans run around irrational, crazy and relaxed, becoming cooperative and friendly overnight. They love everyone to a fault. It's been our downfall from the beginning because depressed unhappy people from wet places, who are chronically never happy and just don't really know what truly dry means, have always come to exploit New Mexico during Rain times, conquering us with just the blow of a feather, for we in our rain giddiness can't wait to give everything they desire, and of course they have always shamelessly taken it until New Mexicans are left with nothing but their love of Rain and New Mexico.

In New Mexico water runs our souls, for every natural-born human here is just a water course: a flinty, edgy, dry-bouldered arroyo waiting for July's flash floods like Christians wait for Christ.

Well, I was making money now. Moderately famous everywhere except New Mexico (thank God) and like the real New Mexican I was, I knew cash like water would evaporate in this glorious, rocky dry land unless that money was turned into a place for Rain to gather, so I put all our humble funds into buying land, magical land.

I knew land didn't really *belong* to people; in Native thinking land *pertained* to people. But I also knew that "white man" capitalist society had kidnapped all the land and only respected your intended occupation of land if you paid them to get it back.

Like the horses who were once only in the lands and hands that pertained to Natives and local peoples when there was originally plenty of land, beautiful New Mexican Rain-appreciating land, old time Horses I'd been consigned to buying back one by one from white people to put them back in their original land and lifestyle, in a more small and moderate way I began to buy magical land as well, to give a place where those magical horses could bathe again in the rare rainstorms of their ancient indigenous homes, running strong in the canyons of our Native hearts. I would ransom both the Horses and their Land to get them both back from their kidnappers.

In New Mexico there are still places you cannot find on a GPS and roads that have no map names because our hearts have spiritually willed them off the maps. There are places with old names every local knows, but if you look them up and try to go there you might end up as much as 280 miles away in a peculiar location not even in the state! Modern people hate this. They want to be in control. As neo-colonials they want every inch captured, measured, categorized and known. New Mexicans, on the other hand, are easily recognized by their joy over the fact they can't be found or understood, comforted by the fact that they live in a land that continues to be magically protected by something older than 21st century humans and their invasive contraptions, a land that can't be seen even by those who actually do find the locale they seek because the spell of the land hides the land from those with no magic. So people always come looking for us but only find themselves staring at more of what they think they know—namely, the world they bring with them—while New Mexico's real face remains hidden to them, thriving beyond their sensors right in front of their eyes staring at the coordinates on their phone.

If we should succeed in getting Punk married and should his mares' bellies be blessed to swell with foals, I felt his babies should have their original Native magical land and magical water on which to tumble from their mothers' wombs, from where slipping down as from the womb of the sky onto the womb of the world's sparkling grass-home of earth, drinking snowmelt water from the wild mountains they could be truly part of the land again.

Far east of us past the mountains, almost still in the mountains, in a hidden nook of timber, where in a snowmelt mountain creek under a straight up stonewall-bend of a cave-lined canyon lay a seep pool of beaver-dammed water that had never dried up in living history, a spot whose mythological presence had been quietly famous in tribal people's lives the same way that fog is famous to the sea.

This land was not big, at least not to the unmagical imperial mind. It was definitely beautiful—not just beautiful but the biggest kind of beautiful, and mystically important to all local culture's unwritten history and to the Holies in particular who inhabited the Eagle-nesting crest one thousand feet above the Beavers' springs.

Though more than one hundred and eleven miles from where we parked our life and love, and the same distance from where Punk's poop pillars lined the mansion of his dream, it was this very place I'd first seen and loved as an eighteen year old, knowing it instantly as the deepest of all places. And for the first time in written history it was mysteriously for sale. And I even had the resources to buy it. And so I did.

It was there that all my horses from then on out would be born.

A Nut Seed Sedge, Tule Rush and Willowed stream ran through the land's Canyon entirety. Full of small nervous Trout and white-jawed, gold-eyed Water Snakes, and into which noisy, chatter-beaked Kingfishers like Pterodactyls dropped, the creek was ruled by a dynasty of unique enduring Beavers.

For centuries these Beavers' dams on three springs along the creek made it so the pools never dried up, even during the occasional happenstance of extreme drought that not rarely dried to dust the entire thirty miles of exquisite meandering creek of snowmelt waters, as well as every other stream in the area, the Rito was held by small bluffs of mica-infused orange earth whose small flat expanse that ran the whole canyon was filled with Crocus in March, Lavender Flag in May, *Estafiate* everyday; then all summer long: Bluestem, Pink Penstemon, red-flowered short Barrel Cactus, *Afilerio*, Cota by the fieldful, Grama, *Yerba Negrita*, pink Oregano, white Oregano, odorless Sage, Poleo, Sedge in places, small gold-eyed Frogs, Horned Lizards, Voles, Silver Foxes, Coyotes, Least Weasels, stands of Wild Carrots, Wild Plums, Chokecherries, Gooseberry bushes and Golden Currants, wild Bluebells, Columbines, Mariposa Lilies, Bluebirds who nested in the bank cliffs, and Swallows of every species. Eagles—Golden and Bald—Vultures and Peregrines all nested in the their sandstone apartments in the caves riddling the vertical eight-story columns of agate-embedded sandstone, which like a claufoutis whose matrix sheared every pebble strewn there for twenty square miles, looking as if every cobble had been sawn in half by a diamond blade.

Everything was different here. Singular. Nothing matched any books on the subjects of geology, birds, mammals, plants or climates, bugs or lizards.

Even the Beaver royalty who presided over the stream-course-dominated-canyon built domes of sticks very elegantly and to code, but never in the water like the guidebook says, rather only on dry land. Three feet tall and eight feet wide, these were the Beavers' daytime summer bungalows, whereas they actually lived throughout the year in caverns along the streamside bluffs with underwater entrances, whose twenty thirty-foot-shafts to the bluff tops they only used for skylights and breathing holes.

Beavers love singing, and when these Beavers came swimming to hear your prayer all the other beasts of that magical zone would begin to show themselves as well. The

97

Lions though only rarely seen were often heard, their rumbling screams echoing between the maze of caves and cliffed pillars, raising the hair on every being's head.

Bears are always holy and they ranged everywhere. Though hardly allowing themselves to be seen you could always smell them. Like the Eagles, Vultures, and Red-tails who all raised their babies in natural holes higher up in the rock towers, the Bears lived and raised their children in the endless stone maze of caves and vertical walls beneath, their echoes seeping right through the depths of the rock, making their presence a constant, but detected mostly by that unmistakable bear aroma and the occasional hoot or grumble.

Generally red, these "Black" Bears were famously feared by the few people of the area because of their fondness for atypical nighttime wandering in family groups, including males (science says they don't), to find and kill heifer cows with calves, communally eating only the udders and leaving the calves orphans, who they rarely touched.

Gigantic wild red Goats had been left four centuries before by Spanish colonial buffalo hunters who bivouacked here in the shelter of our canyon, where they sallied forth daily to compete with Pueblo Natives, Comanches, Jicarillas, Kiowas, and Cheyennes over on the flipside of our stone walls, which formed the very westernmost barrier fencing of the original Ocean of Bison of America's central corridor stretching out onto the grassy rolling plains. These red Goats were fully wild and rarely let themselves be seen, but when they did, they did so only running: running from one side of the canyon to the other, splashing through the stream, disappearing clattering up the steepest cliffside.

The Bucks were formidable and fearless with huge curved horns not unlike a Mongolian Ibex, and they stank like seven dead devils in a compost heap.

The Lions ate the slow ones, so the Goats were always moving. It was startling to see them cross your path and they did so in a lighting flash, there and then gone, the Buck thirty seconds behind and always red.

Wild Geese, Curlews, Snipe and Wild Turkey loved to raise their young here, strangely laying their eggs nestless on top of huge box-like chunks of sandstone twelve-foot tall, twelve-foot square, surrounded by the huge old Ponderosas and Douglas Fir that covered the rock maze of the cliffs.

The Turkeys of course had planted all these trees for millennia with their constant cultivating of the pine needle build up in their dedicated scratching search for Beetles and the seeds to fill their bulgy crops and iridescent souls.

The place was full of life known and unknown, sacred, and nothing ever for sure or by any rule.

One day an animal showed herself that was said by biologists to not actually exist, but a beast of tales and Native imagination.

I'm not the only one who saw one, so you know I wasn't dreaming, but all of us who did see them saw them separately in places within ten miles of that land of timber, grass, snowmelt, Beavers, deep canyon walls, no people, no electric lines and no name on the maps.

I couldn't praise the Holy in Nature enough when I found out this particular chunk of watered canyon was up for sale, though no one could hardly buy it because nobody bad could seem to ever find it and the chicanery to find the seller was all old-time New Mexico to the T, but in the end Hanna and I became the ones whose name was read upon the deed.

A place for sanity to rule, plants of medicine to thrive, baby horses to drop and romp, had itself dropped like a foal into our life.

◆ ◆ ◆

During that era when Hanna and I were working on the details of how to bring Punk's new bride and another mare to New Mexico the next spring to start up the Herd once again, late one November night returning sleepy from a day in the inner bigness of our enchanted land off to the east of where we lived, when I went to feed Blue, Punk and Amarillento their evening hay, none of the three would come near me and all refused to eat.

They were milling on the east fence line, wide-eyed in the flashlight, keeping as far as they could get from the barn, stuck on the fence like loose leaves blown by a wind blast onto a screen.

This was pretty odd because my horses always ate, even in the middle of a battle, and tonight... well it was late, maybe they were just punishing me for my tardy service. We were tired and the horses were fed and if they wanted it they'd eat. We needed to sleep and so we did. No doubt it would all explain itself in the clean light of dawn.

And indeed it did, for when I arose to feed, after entering the hayshed to cut a bale to toss three breakfast piles of grass to my rascally equine companions, while reaching for the bale most exposed, I noticed that unmistakable animally smell of the presence of a Bear.

So... that was it. There had been a Bear or two wandering about, maybe getting a little something in the barn before heading off to their winter quarters. Well that made perfect sense. But the only thing that didn't was the fact that Blue was not generally afraid of Bears and today he was the most standoffish.

Just as I was turning on my heels, intending to go look out around the sandy banks and arroyo course for tracks of who was smelling so clearly like a Bear, my hand brushed a bristly, warm, furry Bear's butt just barely sticking out from the very center of the stack of baled hay in the shed! There he was.

A Bear was sound asleep in a very snug and insulated cavity of our hay bale stack, his breath full and pulsing, stinky and comfortable, snoring at just about eye level a foot off my head and shoulders.

That's how I learned that Old Blue (he was twenty-six now), who was not excited by the presence of live moving bears, was terrified of a snoring Bear! Punk, who had all the rules of what his kind of Horse was supposed to do written in his soul, was brave about the Bear but pretty sure Horses were not supposed to be housed with Bears. Amarillento didn't pretend: he was terrified, snorting and pacing, getting ready to jump his confines, too nervous to eat.

After a while we all got accustomed to the inoffensive smelly presence of a snoring Bear with his exposed butt. It was kind of comforting in a way 'cause to people like me he was Holy, so I let him sleep peacefully, actually buying more hay to feed the horses in order to leave him his nice little insulated hay-lined hole undisturbed. One early morning in late February, when the Sandhill Cranes start wandering back North again, the drowsy Red Bear wriggled back out of his hole, bumbled off into the red Tamarisks, and after wandering down the arroyo to the Ojo Caliente river, where he got a good drink, he splashed through the water and headed up onto the cliffs opposite, into coming Spring.

◆ ◆ ◆

Even though I hadn't formally informed him that a young lady horse of his own ancestral horse band was on her way, Punk's bigger herd-mind already knew his bride was coming. Snorting and snuffling about like a bug-eyed fiend, Punk renewed his corner piles, pooping up a storm. After sniffing a corner pyramid, he'd stand and stare, his eyes taking in the great distance, then screaming he'd strike the earth, raising a puff of dust; making the rounds, he assessed the shape of his markers and anywhere he deemed them slightly uneven, he'd turn around and with the greatest precision drop a load of "road apples" exactly where they were needed. He never missed his mark. He could even drop one here and two there with perfect sphincter control!

Punk definitely knew She was coming, for every day he grew wilder and more frenetic, getting to the point where one day, when we weren't looking, he decided to jump his corral and go walkabout, hunting for the beautiful gift-girl he knew must be there hidden from him somewhere.

A dear friend of ours, who at that time was working as my secretary and our house and ranch sitter when we were away on the road, Marilyn Bacon, lived in a house down and off a ways on our little ranch. Now first and foremost, Marilyn was a magical person, a kind of rare cross between Jackie Chan and the Fairy Godmother you'd always wished you'd had. She'd raised three children, made documentary films on the lives and high-speed moves of almost supernatural martial artists, on peace gatherings in India, and filmed dog sled races in -50°F in Yukon and Alaska.

Every child and dog on earth loved Marilyn and every-where she went dogs, kids and wild animals—unsolicited—would follow her around like the Pied Piper. She was meant to be a teacher, a peacemaker, and probably not cut out to be an administrative secretary, and though she sent more deadbeats packing than she brought ships to anchor in our bay, for Hanna and myself she was always the most loyal friend. Blue, Punk and Amarillento loved her too and Marilyn loved them, for she had no fear whatsoever of any of their pranks or power; real horses fear cowardice.

That morning when Punk got so excited, Marilyn calmly called us on the phone. This was strange because she lived only one hundred yards away, and when we had to parley we generally just walked over to the other person's house and talked.

"Martín, is it normal for your horses to bash through plate glass windows, jump into your living room and stand there snorting?"

"Not really, Marilyn, why do you ask?"

"Well, Punk is here in the house, tromping all over, sniffing under all my sofas, and he's eradicated all my front windows getting in."

Running out the door, grabbing my rope off the veranda wall, I sprinted the one hundred yards to Marilyn's and sure enough, her bank of seven-foot-tall plate glass sliding doors and windows were demolished, lying about in a glittering pile of thick razory shards, and Punk in a riled up mood was wandering around her living room pounding the hollow wooden floor with his front hooves, grunting, his neck all arched up.

"I don't think he meant any harm Martín," she said, "he just wanted to come in and I guess... he did!"

By the grace of the spirits neither Punk nor Marilyn had so much as a scratch on them.

Speaking gently I asked, "Punk, what happened? What are you doing in here anyway?" After slipping my rope loop over his big old stallion's neck with the swirly pink spiral cowlicks on the sides (we call these speed buttons!), making an Indian halter I led him out of Marilyn's house, through the kitchen door, still arched up and squealing his macho head off.

He fought me and didn't want to go where I was leading him 'cause he had a reason to be where he was, but what that reason might've been still remained a mystery. Though not for long: as I wrestled him, trying to head us back to his corral, we had to pass the north wall of Marilyn's house, where another bank of large glass windows still stood intact. Like a tank turret Punk spun around to stare into the glass, and with his eyes bugged out he reared and emitted an ear-splitting, wild grinding honk, pounded down on the earth, and made a powerful dash to fight the window.

Managing to cover his eyes with my big scarf, I got him turned around and gradually (really gradually) was finally able to shuffle His Lordship back into his six-foot-tall corral and feed him. He was such a dangerous life-loving nut, but now we knew why he'd thought to smash into Marilyn's front room like a cannonball.

While out looking for "his mare," the girl he knew was soon to arrive (which was true!), Punk had come across another stallion just as handsome and powerful as himself right there in his "territory"! And this beautiful threat to his sovereignty was none other than his own full-length reflection in Marilyn's plate glass sliding door! Punk's own mirror image looked to him like a legitimate threat, a rival standing inside Marilyn's house behind the glass. No doubt it was this evil creature who must have stolen Punk's girlfriend, so when Punk rose up on his hinds, rearing to fight, the ruffian in the glass unwilling to back down did the same inflammatory thing, rearing up, swinging his angry front hooves to meet Punk head on. Outraged and in a fury, Punk attacked this non-retreating interloper just as his mirror image attacked him, and when his hooves hit the other stallion square in the glass, the force of his powerful full-body strike shattered all the windows on that side of the house. Unaffected and not in the least bit deterred, Punk the eternal warrior rushed right into the house to "kill" his audacious opponent, whose presence had strangely vaporized. So Punk went looking for the coward under all the furniture! Punk naturally felt this image of himself was a threat to his "mare herd" (mares he didn't yet have).

So much for horses not seeing two-dimensional images.

The main difference between Punk and Blue was that Blue knew the handsome guy he saw reflected in a plate glass window was none other than his own dazzling self, while Punk didn't recognize himself and only saw a worthy equal enemy. But Punk was so natural and wild, a one of a kind jewel and a fearless noble presence.

Luckily no one was hurt, and though I was down a few thousand dollars, life kept rattling on down its funny old New Mexico path.

● ◆ ●

Weeks later, while jumping from town to town in Britain on an exhausting whistle-stop book tour coordinated by a publisher, one night after returning from a 2 a.m. interview on an all-night radio station located three stories up and across from Harrods in London, just as little Hannita and I after three sleepless nights were finally dozing off in our room in an old-time hotel across from the Liberty calico store (from whence came a lot of the cloth Native Americans received in those terrible colonial times), the phone rang.

It was Marilyn, frantic and weeping, calling from our house in New Mexico where we'd left her to house sit and feed and watch over the horses.

"Martín, they all ran away."

"Who ran away?"

"The horses, they're gone."

"Horses? What horses? Our horses?"

"Yes, Blue and Amarillento and Punk, they've all run away."

"Away?"

"I went out to feed them and they're all gone."

"What do you mean? They can't be gone, where are they going to go? They have to be around the land somewhere, did you check? How did they get out?"

"Well, they didn't really run away, it was all those other horses!"

"What other horses?"

"The ones the cowboys were riding when the cows came through!"

"The cows came through? What cows, what cowboys?" We didn't have cattle yet. "Whose cows?"

"They had guns, Martín, they were yelling—whistling and swearing and throwing their live cigarette butts everywhere."

"Guns, what guns? Cigarettes!?"

"When the cows came Punk got crazy, I mean really crazy, Martín, he jumped out and then the cattle just flattened Blue and Amarillento's corral and now everybody's gone off with the cowboys!"

"What cowboys, what cattle, whose horses? Marilyn, where's our horses now?" Then the line went dead.

All silence.

"Marilyn, hello, are you there?"

"Marilyn!!! Hello!!!" Silence.

Then she was back:

"Uh oh, here come the cowboys again, they're yelling and whistling and look, they've built a couple of fires on the other side of your house. I gotta go I'll call you later…"

"Wait! Marilyn, wait. What are you talking about? Fires? What fires? Who—what cowboys?"

Just a dial tone. Now she was gone!

We were about seven thousand miles away and couldn't do a thing; we were jet-lagged; after being dragged around to 20 different cities, lecturing and signing books in bookstores all over England, we were back in London and hadn't slept. We were fairly used-up to say the least. It was now past 5 a.m. and I was scheduled to be on "Good Morning London" TV at the BBC building in an hour.

We are here, I thought, and she's over there. My horses are close to me no matter how far I wander, so I knew somehow that their spirits had to flow and would come around again. No doubt they've gone hunting for us like they had sometimes in the past when I'd been gone too long. But cowboys? Technically I was a cowboy in my neighborhood. Cigarettes? Fire? We didn't permit any fires or smoking around the hay sheds. Guns? Horses?

Figuring we had to do what we'd come to do with what we'd taken on wherever it was we'd ended up, and couldn't do anything about the horses so far away so... one thing at a time. First wash up, drink black tea, eat, forget sleep (we could sleep later), drink more tea, wake up, put one foot in front of the next—and let's go walk to the big BBC building rising up down the way. But all while we walked, rode the bombproof elevators, met agents, etc., it kept rolling around in my head: "What cowboys, with guns, fires, herds of cows, cigarettes, yelling, whistling, runaway horses?"

Just as the very nice British talk show host, a lady in a red suit, asked me my first question on the morning show, I realized what must've happened. It finally all came together. It was spring branding time, of course! Local guys, per local custom, no doubt cut my fences to get all their combined herds to the Maestas' land next to ours, where on the side opposite several families could share each other's roping and branding expertise, making their combined branding and castrating a normal communal event. No doubt they'd come on their horses in their normal rambunctious fashion, yelling in Spanish and whistling to move the mama cows and calves, building fires next door to heat up the branding irons and cook on their *discos*. Probably my animals got wound up when all the herds thundered through, and ran off with them to join the general milieu of excited animals, smoke and people. Punk was no doubt attacking all the geldings! Marilyn knew us well but she was from the coasts, and had never seen the normal tumult of annual calf branding, especially Northern

New Mexico style, and this time coming so suddenly out of nowhere. Marilyn, always a willing believer in the wondrous and wild, probably thought we were being attacked by some old west hooligans like in the movies.

After fulfilling my promise to do this one crazy spot on a TV morning talk show, there were then two BBC radio interviews, between which we had to sit out (standing actually) a full BBC Tower security lockdown due to an alleged IRA bomb scare, in which Hanna and I were methodically shuffled by guards into separate zones and I found myself standing with two others in a tiny bombproof steel-tube shelter, pulled unceremoniously into the arms of a gigantic half-dressed lady (a Norwegian weather announcer) and a naked Swedish anchor woman, who because of my long hair backstage figured I was a woman and whose breasts kept bouncing my face into the bosoms of the other lady as we were forced to stand there, embracing in the narrow steel tube, until the all-clear signal rang its ear-splitting pulse and the red steel sliding doors snapped back open.

Luckily they kept calling me ma'am all the way through. But then the doors opened and all hell broke loose when they realized I was a man. I'd never known big city women wore high heels before they dressed. They were very nice about it all though—after they stopped yelling and we all started laughing.

Pretty worn out by the time Hanna and I had dragged our very dogged selves back to our Victorian hotel, the concierge handed me a note; I could hardly focus to read it, but it was a note from Marilyn:

"Blue, Amarillento and Punk are all back! The cowboys helped me catch them. I fixed all the corrals. Don't worry, everything's fine. Have a good time. Blessings, Marilyn!"

• • •

Ten days later, after driving home at 2:30 a.m. from the airport two and a half hours away, when the delicious morning dawned and I finally realized I was waking up in our own bed, the loud Red-winged Blackbirds, Meadowlarks, Goldfinches, Tanagers and Towhees of spring pulled me outside to greet and feed my Father the Sun just rising, always a grand daily event in New Mexico. Then right away I went over to say hello and feed my wayward horses.

I was still only half-awake when I got to the corrals, but a sight which defied all nature and science met my momentarily unbelieving eyes. It held me bedazzled with amazement for its frailty, anxious for its improbability, and bent over in a full-body laugh I couldn't control when I realized what I was seeing.

When Marilyn told me over the phone that all our corrals had been knocked down when the cattle had been herded through, I'd envisaged one side of the corrals to have been tossed about, with a hole knocked through big enough for them to push their way out. I had not realized that the entire length of jackleg corrals had been utterly demolished and the steel panels of the farther sides flattened.

The truth was that there were no corrals left at all, except a very basic outline made up of a few wobbly upright posts starkly marking where the corrals had been before they were smashed into piles of sundered firewood.

BUT...

Right there in the middle of this bizarre ring of debris stood three beautiful, unscathed Spanish/Indian Barb Mesta Cow Ponies: a yellow buckskin gelding, a red Medicine Hat paint gelding and a strawberry roan stallion with a long curly mane and tail, all in a row looking at me grinning while I unsuccessfully tried to control my laughter.

Marilyn said not to worry, that she'd patched up the corrals.

But this was Marilyn. And her idea of having fixed up the corrals was pretty whimsical. Like the web a giant spider stoned on acid would have concocted to snare some intergalactic animal, a single thread of pink cotton warp-string draped five feet above the ground ran around and between each of the remaining upright posts; onto this Marilyn had tied pieces of rags, old shoes, satin ribbons, kite strings, twigs of free swinging driftwood, a couple of bead necklaces and several old socks, all of which hung down from the sagging, flimsy top string, each gently swirling in the desert breeze! Though it looked faintly like a gigantic little kid's mermaid necklace or one of those driftwood mobiles 1960s hippies used to make, the biggest miracle and surprise was the fact that behind this very abstract curtain of spread-out, colorful, waving debris, my three horses had been very obediently keeping themselves for over a week without ever once attempting to escape! This "corral" was so humorous and nutty I couldn't stop laughing for days. But in truth the horses did stay in; for it was a magical structure: not unlike drawing a line in the beach sand with a twig in front of a Tsunami and assuming it would not cross it!

One could walk right under the cross-thread into the "corral" without hardly bending down. There was literally nothing containing these wild-headed ponies of mine or anything keeping them from leaving except Marilyn's straightforward little kid faith that simply assumed all that wonderful swinging rubbish could be a fence, and the power of her clean-souled will that ordered the horses to stay inside, a command which the horses out of their love for Marilyn, and not wanting to disappoint her, all mysteriously agreed to obey. They agreed to regard that bizarre, frail collage as a legitimate corral, and while they spent each day taking turns bumping the suspended stuff with their chins and foreheads to see it all spin around, it never occurred to any of them to escape to greener grass! They would never have done the same for me.

It was an unexpected incredulous delight and we laughed in joy over something so tangibly enchanted, but we never laughed in derision because I'd known since we returned that I would now be required to erect a for-real horse corral to hold the little rascal horses, and real quick, for it was only Marilyn's magical character that had kept these ponies in there. Anyone could tell those *picaro* horses of ours had been only waiting like little kids to show me the novelty of that crazy corral, but once I'd seen it and once I was back in charge again, the spell would be broken and away they'd fly if there were no physical corrals to hold them! It would all be back to business as usual.

It took me a week to achieve that, and when I had it all fairly tight I didn't have the heart to remove the crazy horse-containing, driftwood magic-mobile, emergency thread-line corral. It remained fluttering for several years after, adorning the heavy-duty structures we put up behind it until gradually it began to drop scrap by scrap back down to the Mother Earth as the intense New Mexico sunlight ate this thing, and all the pieces had finally merged back into the sandy belly of this high desert earth, buried by the Forever Wind as all things here eventually were. A little of Marilyn's magic still lives on in the very ground that once surrounded those three broncs, for even now, years later, after we've had dozens of corrals, whenever leading other horses past or over where that original kite-string corral used to stand, invariably every horse will stop and snort and stare right into the ground there. It always takes a lot of convincing to get them to cross Marilyn's magical invisible line into the pen. The good in real earth magic is never destroyed by human insistence or time.

There is usually a magical person hidden in any crowd, a magical horse or two in any herd, and in every stretch of land there is magic somewhere if you've got the eyes to see it.

Chapter 7

Valencia

Valencia was Punk's bride-to-be.

A solid, well-put-together, little red Mesta mare whose chest-thundering whinny was so unexpected, so low-pitched and deliciously musical that, along with her long, wild, disobedient dreadlocked mane, her crooked smile, languid stare, self-assured stance, unerring footwork and clean beautiful legs, Valencia had more than one cowboy sighing, wishing she were his, everyone of them unbeknownst to the other comparing her to Tina Turner. They were both smooth, they were both rough; they were both the same glowing color.

Where I grew up we all loved Tina Turner 'cause to us she was an Indian and all the Natives claimed her for their own.

From our banded cliffs, timeless fields of Blue Corn and Pueblo Indian existence of unending communal ritual trying to sing the world back to life, all the Native youth of my generation watched America from that remote cultural perch, what seemed like, in those days, a safe enough distance, how that smooth red-ochre-colored siren sang her way in and out of the jaws of that soul-devouring monster of white-dominated big-city betrayal, with its empty promises of respect through so-called stardom.

Where we lived every person was known to everyone else. For better or worse everyone had their day in the gossip headlines. We quietly marveled at what we recognized as the horrors of Tina Turner's struggle for air and honest dignity in such an anonymous, crowded, heartless, synthetic urban sea of endless buildings and nameless people.

Those few of our own who'd ever been enticed into those same waters had always drowned and disappeared completely. Those rare individuals who did miraculously reemerge returned to the reservation with minds so shattered, bodies so addicted, and lifestyles so unrecognizably Native that they were considered war casualties: people we used to know, now Missing in Action with only half their souls, wandering the village as babbling ghosts.

Because of this, to the Indians of our neighborhood Tina Turner was a miracle, for when that soul-sucking insatiable scene had done its worst and was through pounding, sucking and chewing up what they thought was Tina Turner, Tina Turner was not only still standing but even better than before: still tall, still herself and still on her toes.

You see, it wasn't just the whispering heartbroken roar of anything she sang, or the brilliance of anything she had to say or how she did what she did, but that her very substance remained undefeated right in the pocket of the oppressor's suit coat. That fact alone engendered hope in a lot of young people caught between cultures, especially young Native women.

Though Valencia's wild, range-matted tangle of very stylish, cocklebur-stiffened, standup mane-dos, her voice, beauty and color made the comparison an easy association for more shallow pop-infested minds, to others of a deeper heart and life experience the comparison still held.

For both Ms. Turner and the little red mare radiated some other unmeasurable thing: some force field of erotic magic whose invisible organic flood defied all science with the crazy effect it had on other live beings.

Real Horses pride themselves on not being definitely definable. Modern people pride themselves on being able to categorize and control everything, by stuffing everything they don't really comprehend into boxes with shapes they do understand, the shape of which they then declare to be the shape of what the box contains! But horses always jump out.

Horses are made of wind and ancient dictates that run in cycles, for sure, but which are just as easily and consistently renavigated to accommodate what the bigger mind of the Herd as part of Nature's motives decides, often, if not always, foiling the best computer system's attempts to "nail down" a defining pattern.

When you get down to it, no matter how finely you cut it with horses, if a rule is determined to exist for certain cycles and functions in their lives and physiognomy, there are just as many instances of horses consistently circumventing that same rule as there are those that adhere.

Old-time Horse-culture people worldwide are mostly considered to be historically interesting but not scientific — prone to believing a lot of "folk" beliefs about horses (and everything else) that science spends a lot of time refuting.

For instance, the old people where I grew up knew all about the fertility cycles of Horses, Cattle, Deer, Dogs, Sheep, Goats, etc., on which science claims to have an exclusive grip, but they also knew that in none of these cycles would a baby be conceived until the "heat cycle" corresponded to certain Moon cycles, and that all animals had plants they needed to be eating when certain stars were in the sky for "fertility" to happen, and that if a foal, for instance, *was* conceived outside of these conditions then that foal's life would be regulated by that irregularity and become either anomalously magical or a rough individual.

All the old-time people and myself included were also very certain from experience that mares could become fertile at will, especially whenever they met "somebody" they really wanted to have a baby with! If a cool young stallion showed up out of nowhere, started fighting and strutting and spreading his sound and pheromones everywhere, all the unpregnant mares inspired by this newcomer could go instantly into heat all at once, no matter where they stood in their reproductive cycle!

Science says this is nonsense. It may be nonsense but that's how it works.

Veterinary science says very authoritatively that all mares come into season, into their adult fertility cycles, in a rhythmic way every twenty-one days all year long. Simple science says mares are therefore fertile for three to five days every twenty or so days toward the end of each cycle, during which they will "accept" a stallion mounting them.

Simple science also says during the next few days the male horse's semen remains alive and vital and can cause the mare's egg to fertilize and signal the womb to build a home (placenta) inside of which a foal can develop to be born out into the world eleven months later.

Maybe this is all fine and true for horses made by science, but it doesn't account for the huge pile of authoritative papers, presented PhD studies and clinics dedicated to explaining the general failure of mares to do what any of these books say.

The beautiful Natively-landraced little Spanish Mesta Horses of my youth who grace my present-day corrals, aren't actually refuting science, instead they enrich the awareness that horses are not mechanical devices like the cars, trucks, planes or trains who usurped horses' rightful throne in the lives of all civilizations and whose original natural way of being does not give predictability much clout.

Animals should not be required to be machines any more than people should.

Nothing female in the Universe wants to be figured out, categorized and forced to fit a predetermined pattern of action or form. Mares are dedicated followers of this religion.

Valencia was one of the original magical mares descended from magical mares (whose traits jump every other generation just like they do with people) and she not only made every stiff rule go floppy, every human assumption into a doubt, and turned hopeless situations into ecstatic miracles, she caused a lot of havoc without lifting a hoof, was fair to the smallest detail, and just as romantic as Punk, her husband-to-be.

I'd already purchased Her Ladyship from her owner in Texas, paid for her, and was waiting to go retrieve her in Colorado to where she'd been shipped with another yearling Mesta filly I'd found in Wisconsin, when it was whispered down through the talkative horse-people grapevine that Valencia had been determined by veterinary examination to be lacking some of the apparatus necessary to conceive a foal. They said she'd been sold to me because her owner had been unsuccessfully trying to breed Valencia and had finally consulted some vets who determined it was impossible.

But I already owned her, and since I was such a romantic and Punk was even worse, we both knew Valencia had to be a romantic as well. Valencia was the only mare I'd found who still really had that original Indian-Spanish bearing I'd grown up riding into life.

Only seven years old and from the same old wild land as Punk's grandfather, Valencia was probably just waiting for the "real thing"; the real love of her life to show up, and in the meantime she'd just willed herself not to conceive until he came along.

Chapter 8

Yakatche

This close up the Spanish Peaks gave the impression of a row of mythic giants hatching straight up out of the plain like forest mushrooms breaking into the clouds of rain that would come rolling south to our land. With the beguiling voice I was in love with ringing loud right in my ear—"Look! There's still snow up there above the timber line!"—Hanna craned her elegant neck to look past me at the wheel to get a view from beneath the truck cab's window.

"It's so beautiful up here and the breeze so cool in June."

Neither of us spoke, drinking in a Meadowlark's sparkling riff and the wide majesty of the unpeopled land.

"I'm glad you took us off the highway overland onto this wild, unmarked bumpy trail, but sweetheart, do we have to take it this fast? Am I missing something? Are we in a hurry for some reason?"

"Look over there," pointing with my lips New Mexico style, "there's a bunch of Antelopes swirling under that horde of Swallows. So many babies. It's an Antelope daycare, but look at them run. So young, so fast, so amazing, so graceful— even the Swallows are racing them!"

"Can we please slow down? I'm a chiropractor's daughter, do we really need to ruin our tailbones, knockout our fillings, mess up our necks? And what about the mares in the back? At this pace that trailer's going to be thrashed to bits."

After a couple of seconds she grabbed my arm, "Please, I need to get out and collect my nerves. This is too rattly and too fast for me. What are we running from anyway?"

Sure I'd fail at what for so many years I'd been holding my breath to accomplish, clenching my teeth I headed us square into the well-rehearsed trajectory of my imagined mission, unthinkingly turning what could be great joy and not a little victory into a tense, plodding job.

"I was running all these ancient wagon routes to avoid the preponderance of Colorado livestock inspectors who swarm along this border, and to detour around the weigh station at Ft. Garland with all those sheriffs and state cops.

"I learned these routes long ago from old timers growing up on the Rez. This time of day we can pretty easily cross into New Mexico with our horses by this heading without being detected, and once we're on the New Mexico side nobody's gonna stop us and we can take it easy all the way home."

Just then the entire rig began to tremble and rock as the bright red mare bellowed from the back of the trailer, her echoing scream announcing her return to the Motherland. Once more, her body shaking like an earthquake, she screamed. "Did you hear that? Isn't that something, that little mare locked into the trailer knows we just crossed over the line into New Mexico at that painted boulder right there."

Slowing our thrashing bump down to a thundering rumble, then down to a mumbling bumble and finally to a stop, I settled the rig onto a levelish grass-surrounded open space, from where the high mountain plateau would have run off forever on the authority of its sagebrush flatness if it had not been stayed by the knees of the San Antonio Mountain fifty miles to the west.

Hanna had already popped out, eyes closed, leaning up against the trailer bed catching her breath. When she was breathing again and her color returned, I said:

"Let's make tea, little Hannita, we're in friendly home-tribe territory now."

"Good idea," she said and reached into the truck bed for the cups and storm kettle while I unloaded the water and my fire kit.

The little red mare, Punk's prospective bride, kept up a thunderous pounding with her front hooves on the back gates of the trailer.

"Looks like she wants some tea as well."

After I lit a tiny teepee of local twigs beneath the kettle and the initial rude rankness of the burning sage bark had settled into the fragrant curative redolence of Juniper sticks, I went to let both mares out of the trailer to graze the Grama Grass of Home.

Once out, the red mare wouldn't eat but just stared south as if in a trance, breathing in the delicious clear air of the wide-open unfenced land of home, then whinnying a heart-rending blast of hope.

"Look little Hannita!" I whispered to my bride, "She's remembering. She's thinking. I think Punk can feel her coming too. They're both talking to each other in their souls. Look!" And she screamed again, the whole land reverberating with her body-quaking whinny. Staring straight south-southwest to where we lived 90 miles off, Punk was no doubt pacing and staring and bellowing just like Valencia but back toward us.

The tea was welcome and reviving, with goat milk and the honey of home.

When it was time, after a nap to the crunching of the grazing fillies, we reloaded the mares, stowed the tea kit, latched the sliding crossbars of the trailer doors, climbed back in the cab, and after "slowly" driving five bumpy overland miles back to the main road, we headed down the big smooth highway toward home at a saner speed.

"Why?" she asked.

"Why what?" I asked back.

"Why did you want to avoid the livestock inspectors?"

"What do you mean?" It seemed like a silly question. "'Cause that's what you do. Nobody wants one of those angry, underpaid, uniformed, racist paranoids peering into their affairs. If they feel like it they'll always find something to fine you for, pull you off the road, and quarantine or confiscate your animals; they can make your life miserable. Everybody avoids them."

"But aren't we totally up-and-up-legal to the eleventh degree? The truck is new, everything works, we have all our documents, the horses all have health papers, Coggins tests and traveling logs; there's nothing we overlooked, so even if we got stopped, don't we just show 'em our papers and they let us go on our way?"

Though stunned not only by the realization I was married to someone who believed the world worked that way, but also by the fact that she was right or at least should have been, I hadn't quite gotten cuddly with the notion that lately I was totally legal and socially kosher for the first time in my entire existence! We both understood the world from two different experiences. Since our marriage she had all my taxes in order, all my phone bills paid. (They even paid us money back after she talked to them!) I owed nobody any money anywhere.

I'd never had modern choices before: "Martín, would you like a brand new, one hundred percent functional red 250 truck, or a white 250 truck under warranty, which the dealer will repair if it fails?" Who ever heard of such a thing?

In my upbringing you had lots of choices. But all our choices were between one bad situation or another hard situation. There were never any choices that involved having anything you wanted, just between whatever was there to have and what you could get.

Either you got a very used truck where most everything kind of worked but one cylinder was getting ready to blow, the rod already knocking; or a truck for even less with no mirrors, where nothing really worked at all but you could manage, tie the door shut, tie the carburetor on with bailing wire, start it up by priming the gas, and since it had no truly functioning clutch you just jammed it into third between pumps; or another truck in perfect running condition with only one dent, but which had been stolen in Arizona, with no paperwork, and if you bought it and got caught it was prison, and so on. It was never a choice of what you wanted, only choices of what you were willing to put up with and learn to like, or just wait for better days.

Traditionally in New Mexico, no one could afford to be legal, to pay for health records on cattle, much less horses; no one could afford to fix a faulty turn signal or keep up car insurance. So if you were going to thrive, you got good at dodging any authority that said it was illegal to be that poor. Just like never leaving home without your blanket, your pocketknife, matches and water, or watching for rattlesnakes and blizzards—avoiding authorities was all part of a person's survival education, and we lived on. In New Mexico, some of the authorities themselves came from the same upbringing, knew what it was like and were more lenient. But never in Colorado, everybody knew that. Yet still, in principal little Hannita was right and I had to laugh at myself.

My laughing got so loud, I startled my wife. Banging on the steering wheel in the glee of realization of my new liberated status, I vied with the ruckus Valencia was making, who had never stopped pounding the trailer and whinnying at the top of her ecstatic lungs ever since the border.

"I hope you will forgive me. I'm pretty new at being a legitimate citizen," I said. "It was old habit that took us on that beautiful bumpy ride. Besides, in Colorado it's illegal to make a fire on the side of the road to cook your lunch and have tea.

"I much prefer having tea with a beautiful girl like you, with our horses grazing beneath the great "Picketwire" Mountains, with Antelopes and Swallows, than choking on the bad cologne of some underpaid pistol-packing brand inspector who'd be so jealous of our beauty that he'd fine us just for being born. So I hope you will forgive me my outlaw upbringing and Native culinary sense."

I'm fairly sure she did.

At least she smiled.

• • •

From that wild red herd of Barbs in the wide-open canyon country this side of Magdalena, in the shadows of Ladrón Peak west of Valencia, NM, the little red Mare had been originally hauled as a baby to Texas, then shipped with the registry's name of Valencia to Colorado Springs, from where we retrieved her in 2006.

Though born in the bush sometime in 1999 on a day no human could say, she was captured as a young foal alongside of her mother who was killed in the helicopter roundup, brought in with several others and subsequently named Valencia. The minute I set eyes on her my heart renamed her to rematriate her back into the Motherland of New Mexico's Spanish/Native cultural landscape.

Valencia was the official name her kidnappers gave her. It was the kidnapper's name for a designer horse designed to "continue" the wild Native Barb breed in a designer horse setting in the wealthy Dallas suburbs among designer "Westerners."

But now as an adult Barb mare back in her old neighborhood, from this moment on, as she was ardently banging another million dents into my 18-foot trailer to match those put there by her direct cousin Old Blue eighteen years previous while returning back from Iowa, she would no longer be known by her captive name Valencia, but by her freedom name, Yakatche.

From the first weird moment I first set eyes on both little mares staring back at us with those tagged hangman-noose-shaped shipping-company nylon neck ropes in the rodeo stock holding pens right in the "bad side" of suburban Colorado Springs, I put my saliva and breath into their beings, and as per Native custom I gave both mares real names, thereby spiritually winching them out of the anonymous stifling context of "whiteman" existence, back into New Mexico's roomier free-air matrix.

I hadn't studied or rehearsed or researched these names, I simply waited till I could see each of them in person, and Yakatche was Yakatche instantly because Yakatche is a Keres word for the greasy seams of bright-colored red ochre earth that startled the soul for their unexpected brilliance, running high up along the Eagle-nesting tufa cliffs radiating out of the Pajarito Plateau where all the Native priesthoods gave offerings, whose beautiful substance was with great difficulty scraped to gather a little for their rituals to spiritually protect their officials. Yakatche was the color of vibrant life.

And Yakatche the horse was "Yakatche"-colored to the nth degree and she liked her name.

The other mare was a wild color too, not unlike purple native corn ground to meal, so I named her the name Kotona. From both Yakatche and Kotona all of Punk's living representatives to this day descend.

* * *

The closer to home we drove, the longer the episodes of trailer shaking grew and the deeper Yakatche's incessant screaming became.

The whole rig rocked back and forth with it. More than once this shaking caused me to pull over, go back to look in the trailer to make sure everything was all right, where all I got was an air-ripping horse bugling right in my face. She was excited. She knew she was coming home. She screamed the entire blessed way, and that's how it was Ladies and Gentlemen, with all her offspring too ever since. They were all screaming trailer-rockers.

But then, without my really noticing, about a mile from the turn into our little ranchito in *Acequia* Gavilan, all the whinnying and commotion went dead quiet.

As we rolled smoothly right into the narrow entrance to our place, there to our left stood Punk's welded steel pipe six-foot-tall stallion pen inside a couple of acres of wild Sacaton, behind a very old unconvincing barbwire boundary fence we'd inherited with the land.

Punk was soaked with sweat head to foot, having obviously paced for hours before we ever arrived. Serious pacing in a trance. He knew Yakatche was coming.

When we came to a halt, Hanna dropped out of the truck to open the main gateway and let me pull the truck and trailer with two mares from Texas and Wisconsin into our beloved land.

The only animal sound was the tread and sheath-squeaking of Punk's endless pacing along his north fence.

Hanna got back in the truck.

We pulled up to the next gate...

and then,

an echoing

Ka Booooomm rang from the back.

The trailer sank to its wheel wells as a horse's weight dropped onto the floor of the trailer, accompanied by a horrible, deep, heart-wrenching raw bellow as if something had shot and dropped the horses in the back. The racket was so sad and stultifying.

Instantly turning off the truck I leapt out and running to the back saw that Yakatche had been thrown, cast utterly to the floor of the trailer, her neck bent up unnaturally against the opposing trailer wall; her eyes quivering and terrified were rolled back, her sides heaving and shivering, the little mare grunting in pain.

But worst of all,

in a way I couldn't even quite grasp, from under the trailer's closed back gate, up against which Yakatche was crumpled and jammed inside, a hind leg protruded outside the trailer, trembling in spasm from the unbelievable cleaver-like binding weight of the closed gate on her leg.

There was not even half-an-inch clearance at the bottom of that steel door, and for a foot five or six inches wide to have forced its way under such a heavy panel would have completely crushed the bone of the leg upon which it was horribly clamped.

The pressure of the gate on the leg was so tight and intense I couldn't begin to budge the fasteners and crossbars with all my mortal efforts to open the door.

The mare kept trying to move but was wholly pinned. I was sure it was all over for her. There's no way to save a horse with that bone crushed as it must've been.

So close we'd come. Right to our doorway, within forty feet of old Punk.

I was weeping like a baby as stumbling I ran frantically to the closest hay shed for a sledge hammer with which to bust the welded latches and free the suffering horse, sure I was going to have to shoot her soon after with such a crushed cannon bone.

I whanged and whanged on the latch, and the bar slowly started to inch up with each whack, the mare grunting with every blow. It was exhausting. I was spent in every sense when the bar finally lifted.

When all of a sudden—

Kashlam

Pop

Boom and *whinny*

—the back door flew open like in a dynamite blast, and because I had been standing right in front of the door resting on the sledge handle, I was tossed through the air several feet, but not so dazzled as to miss the fact that out of that trailer sailed a very not-lame

Yakatche, who in a single very able bound popped to the ground, took an instant right, stood on her hind legs, and like a ballerina in a very credible *levade* leapt over and cleared the first barbwire fence. Then in less time than it takes to tell, she landed from that first leap, instantly bounced square up onto the top rung of Punk's fortress corral and shimmied her red-ochre-colored-butt right into Punk's mansion, hitting the ground running with Punk and his erection in close stallion pursuit, both screaming like Banshees.

After mule-kicking Punk a couple times just to save face, Yakatche lifted her tail, backed up to Punk, peed the bold acrid milky piss of a mare in heat, lifted her tail again and let Punk mount her and breed, then they ran around again and repeated the whole for a couple of minutes, and then it was over. They both settled down and went off to the corner to eat peacefully like the old married couple they would be forever on, Punk dutifully obeying Yakatche's every bossy command.

It had all been a big ruse. I couldn't believe it. What a monstrously giddy, manipulative joker.

Yakatche was even more original and cunning than Blue!

In less than three minutes she'd arranged to be let out where she wanted, when she wanted, with the stallion she wanted, and was now pregnant with what would become the first of the new herd!

And what was more, that very moment every eligible female animal on our range and our neighbor's went simultaneously into heat: every cow, goat, cat, dog and yes, person, bred all the respective bulls, bucks, dogs, cats and menfolk, and all gave birth during the following year.

Yakatche had come.

Chapter 9

Eight-Legged Horses, Square Pumpkins, Chile Feathers and the Color Genes of Stones

Hardly any mares ever give birth to twins. Those rare mother horses that carry full-term twin foals often perish trying to birth both little horses, all three usually dying in the process. And in those few pregnancies blessed with full-term twin foals whose birth doesn't kill their mother during delivery, usually only one of the foals survives. For this reason, among horse-living tribes worldwide, the event of the healthy delivery of twin foals and a live, standing, milky mama is a thing of immense joy, wonder and ceremonial celebration. To sing of the beauty and rare presence of Twin Foals is a well established metaphor for the beauty of a lover in many popular Horse Nomad ballads, even to this day. Twin horses and twin children are regarded with great supernatural portent.

Though I've known a couple of families in whose horse herds the majestic generosity of Nature's life force has manifested as mares birthing healthy twin foals, none of my own mares has ever dropped visible twins on our flowering sandbars.

I say visible twins because one of the greatest realities about all the horses in the world is that they each start out in the womb as one in a set of twins.

Yes, every horse ever born into this world has a live twin with whom he or she has shared the first month or so of life in their mother's womb. As she traverses the earth in search of short grass to eat, salty earth to lick and delicious wild water to drink the mother horse cultivates these two tiny horses living in her belly everywhere she nomadizes with the band.

When a stallion's seed fertilizes a mare's ovum, two fetal horses are started. One of these is a Hero, the other the beneficiary of the Hero's action. Two proto-equine cell clusters develop. One decides to bounce about inside the mare's womb-space. Everywhere this original horse cell cluster touches the womb walls, patches of placenta begin to form until an entire placental sack and corpus luteum have developed, inside of which the other twin roots him- or herself with what shall become the impressive umbilical cord that feeds this one growing horse-child through his belly from the mother mare's belly.

At this point in the pregnancy, the first placenta-making fetal twin horse—the Hero—stops developing, stops moving and sits still for a little while, alive with a tiny spine and a tiny placenta of his very own inside the matrix of the Holy Female's substance, where this hero filly or colt eventually dies, voluntarily relinquishing his womb-space and future life so that the little horse we see poking her head above the slosh and birthing sack upon the ground ten months hence can join the matrix of this air-breathing reality with the rest of the world's living creatures.

Every standing horse you see is only the visible half of two originals: a single twin whose sibling lives unseen to normal eyes but remains vital and powerful, spiritually ruling the deeper dimension of his visible sibling.

Remembering this helps a lot when treating with horses. As everyone knows, even living twins are not the same in character, but balanced opposites. If you keep in mind that the horse upon whom you would charge out into life is only one half of what sits beneath you, that another horse runs invisibly right there inside your horse with an equal power but opposite character, then you will realize why what sometimes seems to be inconsistent behavior, mischievousness, side-jumping and crazy antics one day and not the next is because no horse is one horse but always two. And they are! In the telling of so many of the old mythologic stories of Nordics, Mongols, ancient Vedic Brahmins, Persians and sub-Saharan Africans, magic divine horses are almost always described as having eight legs. Live twin horses are actually four horses: two visible and two invisible.

Because this invisible twin is a visible horse's spirit-self, tribal-oriented horse people have always known that to tame, treat, heal or raise a healthy horse, one must address and spiritually care for their horse's invisible twin.

This invisible twin is not only the Hero that gave up his future of running, jumping, playing and becoming a living horse in this world so that his sibling could do exactly that, it is inside this unseen hero where the *orenda* of the visible horse is occulted. By caring for both twins, a sound, lucky, strong, whole, tangible, magical Horse can become a living reality.

After dropping her foal onto the grassy earth, with any luck, the mama horse will not be long in "birthing" the afterbirth—the placental sack and supporting cables and spent baby-making gear—into this world as well. People of my tribal background and lifeways consider this "shedding of the placenta" as the "birth of the twin foal".

If you are diligent and search very carefully through the initial slop of the shed placenta (which when fresh on the ground looks a lot like a big, complex, beached jellyfish) you might be fortunate to run across a very tiny, bean-shaped, second placenta with a tiny little being inside, no longer living but with a minute spine. This is the body of the newborn horse's brave hero sibling who gave up his life to let the other thrive. Every horse has one of these undeveloped twins as a sibling in the womb. This is a very mystical thing and an amazing feeling to actually hold in one's hand the "other" Hero-half of a living foal's being.

This tiny placental package and her passenger must be dried and dressed and kept in a sacred circumstance where it is ritually fed. It is here that the health and power of your living foal is housed.

The secret name of your horse also lives in this little placenta. Natives have whole groups of these placental twin horses kept in fancy bundles called the Herd. These bundles are also bundles of names carefully kept and ritually fed and ceremonialized by the herd's owner in his or her abode. These bundles and the feeding rituals are passed on from grandchild to grandchild, each of whom over centuries continued to add the spirit-twins of their own horses to the bundles. Most of the new additions are direct descendants of those already in place!

Every Horse is a twin. We who would live with horses and fly over the earth on their backs must care for our horse's Hero-half. This is a deep thing everybody once knew, for these twins can talk to us in dreams.

The existence of an unseen twin for every foal was magical and secret knowledge of people with horse medicine and herds. Bundles filled with fetishes of placenta-twins were ritually feasted at periodic intervals—these were special events where the soul of the herd was fed and people with no horses but desirous of having them went to petition the "Mother of Horses" (as these bundles are often known) to grant them horses. People could borrow such bundles to heal a sick horse, the collective power of all the past horses in one of these precious bundles easily rebooting the vitality of a weakened horse.

Though as a young man I'd always kept this all to myself, there were other details of equal depth and amazement pertaining to these same older knowings, many of which my younger self had already put together on my own before I was generously taught their place in the sacred context of Indigenous Horse medicine.

One of these principles had to do with how certain solid-colored mares, mares the color of died-back winter grass or purple stone or red clay cliffs, with coal dust points, would after conceiving a foal gradually begin to add patterns and the color of her coming baby onto her own coat color and pattern!

If the baby to be born were a stud colt, then the coloration of the baby's papa would begin to mysteriously creep into the mother's original coat color, sometimes leaving a buckskin mama with large smoky patches of amethyst boulder hues on her flanks and belly as well as white "eyeglasses", or a solid red mare would develop a general snowball-roaned color! The mare would adopt the color of her baby boy.

Month by month, hair by hair, the mama's color would change and intensify as the little horse inside her grew bigger and bigger and more horse-like. Eleven months later when her new baby dropped onto the wild earth, both mother and child would often match the colors of the stallion.

Then, by the next shedding the mother's original color and pattern would reemerge while the foal continued to develop his or her own colors, to the point where oft-times a dark red mama could be seen suckling a long-legged, handsome, bratty, bright snowball foal with a dark head the color of purple stone, each horse as distinct from one another as the skin and meat of an apple.

On the other hand, if a mare were a solidish color and pregnant with a girl, the mother's own original color would deepen and she started taking on the look as if she'd just been swimming in a pond, her original color enriched in a way that would match her newborn filly. When this happened the new "wet" version of the mother's color would last the rest of her life without reverting to her original tones. Birth is powerful.

These changes are everywhere, if you're willing to stay put long enough to notice. Many human women experience very similar changes while making children.

Another subtle majesty of horses was that the palette of available coat colors for the foals born into a specific band of horses living in an area for several generations was governed more by the colors, textures and changes of the very ground where the horses ran, and the seasons of land there, than science would dictate with its genetic rules. The "genetic" colors of real horses are handed down alright, but they descend from the herd's original ancestral adjustment to the color and nature of the land of which they were a component. Like Horned Lizards living in an ant pile, whose colors match the constituency of both the ants and the ant gravel, the land Herself that the horses lived on gave them their color patterns. Horses living for generations on any wild land were not like most invading human cultures—horses were not a superficial conquering colonial addition—wild grazing horses were themselves happily conquered by the land that fed them and they in turn became a part of the land.

A whole reservoir of horse colors waited inside a herd and no colors busted into view unless these colors agreed to be something that added to the whole of the land and the changing color and patterns of the rocks and vegetation throughout the seasons.

Because of this, even though mares took on the colors of their baby's father and the baby's father's color came originally from his mother's father, *all* those colors themselves came originally from that horse herd's ancestral adjustment to the colors in the land from long ago.

Of course, when no constant outside stallions or mares from other districts and bands found their way into the herds, bringing their own land-given color patterns, eventually all colors would go entropically back into the tribal suitcase to be stored away 'til later. Every horse born for even a century after would end up as a red horse. A herd of red horses with black skin were always just a sack of hidden colors waiting like fireworks to come thundering out when just the right newcomer showed up to light the fuse!

Deep down, the Twin Horse inside all horses is an artist, a painter who lives so as to be part of the land they love to run in. When horses lose their land they start hating their lives. Then they all turn into "bay" horses. Among the southwestern Mesta Barbs there were no real legal bays and no paints with bay and white markings, but every other pastel—purple, blue roans, reds, yellow, grulla, very few blacks, sabinas of every ilk—was there. No official "English" colors: no flea-bit grays, no chestnut bays, liver bays, etc.

The color of every horse running in a real half-wild Mesta herd that descended from distinct naturally-decided dynasties of stallions could be understood as a "note" in a visual symphony of colors that changed its composition to match the tones of the land as the land changed its tune throughout the year.

If Horses lose their land and get stuck in barns, their breed begins to lose its colors and the foals born there become "barn" colored. They lose their score in the original symphony and start mimicking the monotone spiritual landscape they are forced to live in.

Reflecting not only the vividly distinct look and character of the land between summer's piles of thundercloud-inspired green fuzz in the low spots and the purple-flowering red cliffs and sun-glazed stones in the high places and winter's blanket clouds, ice and very dark, wet patches of ground between snow-topped chunks of amethyst boulders, dried yellow clumpgrass and dormant needle nests of gray-green cacti, many Barbs shedded into spring colors to match the violent dry winds of tree-pollen-yellowed-haze and light that grind boulders into pink sand, and the postwinter rumply, swollen slopes of loose earth at the bases of a million red flat-topped bluffs.

Some horses specialized in autumn, their hides reflecting the fierce blue skies of fall in a steel-blue grulla-roan phase, others turning gold to match the Chamisas while others took on a purple roan to bolster the confidence of the purple starflowers running like seas for miles, their hearts full of yellow dust marking all the dark horse's knees as they shuffled through the galaxy to find grain-laden prewinter grasses.

For the most part, each of our Native horses as individuals had no single, fixed breed color. But like the ground they were born to, whose grasses fed them and upon whose bosom they ran, lived and died, their coat colors did adhere to certain inherited fixed color "phases." These were usually four annual changes of color, yet some had as many as seven and were famous for it. Because of this, single horses were often mistaken for several different horses throughout the year by those who didn't stay put long enough to see the seasons change on the horse's back as they mysteriously morphed the colors of their seasonal outfits to match the natural annual shift in the surroundings.

What needs to be said and heard, I feel, is that somewhere along the line of settled civilization's overdomestication of people's minds and senses, that just like their exploiters, owners and keepers, the horses that had powered these same civilizations until machines took their place, now no longer living in a landscape of natural substance, saw their inborn color phases that had once matched the land in her seasons atrophy at the same rate as their exploiter's ability to live with, see and feel these changes.

Horses raised in single static farm and city environments stuck in stalls, square monocropped green pastures and mani-cured paddocks took on the monotones of their surroundings. In the same way that the people creating civilization's one-size-fits-all thinking-production-and-acquisition-oriented-mono*tone* culture also lost their sense-capacity to recognize the color phases of true horses as a trait of real horses. On that day they began designating the limited solid colors of their cubicled equine power sources as legitimate evidence of their breed purity.

As a result, today, there are entire breeds of modern equines whose individual colors no longer change pitch or hue, remaining the same in spring as in fall. These horses are the results of centuries of careful culling to create equines whose color corresponds culturally and genetically to mostly Christian and Muslim religiously originated color biases that are now strangely required for entry into the registries of so-called "pure" horse breeds!

Civilization's people, unconscious of the oppressive religious origins of their need to strain people and horses into color races, freezing both into single categories of status according to color, appearance ignorantly enforces social prejudice and business culture wealth castes among both their people and horses. This abhorrent phenomenon has been weirdly paralleled for horse coat colors where certain "breeds" can only have certain colors and all others are considered to be "impure" mutts. They even recruit genetic science hoping it will support this nonsense but science doesn't back this up.

Science should always open minds, not restrict them. Technology is useful only insofar as it can serve to make humans a more welcome guest at Nature's already impeccably beautiful and ever-changing feast, instead of using partial science to ruin Nature's gift.

I, on the other hand, as a kid assumed that all the obvious seasonal changes of the colors in the Mesta horses, whose hooves rumbled by us every morning, was simply the result of the changeover in diet these horses experienced coming off five months of dry winter's grasses, cottonwood bark and leaves, into summer's flowers, herbs and renewed wild grasses. I figured that our horses' coat colors were no different than the feathers of the tropical parrots New Mexico's Native Pueblo people have for centuries kept as sacred pets (brought anciently from far away lands to the south).

Some Natives had big Macaws and yellow Parrots living with their families (some had eagles too!). These birds were and still are considered blood relatives and Divine visitors. The families who cared for these bird relatives sunned them on their flat roofs by day and sheltered them in their houses by night. These birds supplied the village with the prized tail feathers needed to carry out a profusion of communal life-sustaining rituals. We all knew that the color of the parrots' feathers could be intensified or even coordinated to make particular colors, depending on what those beautiful ornery birds were fed.

If fed quantities of dry chile seeds, bright red and yellow feathers would sprout. Black sunflower seeds caused more blue and green feathers; piñon nuts made every color appear. Some parrot people had their secret recipes, but it was all in the water, salt and diet. So I very logically assumed our Mesta horses were no different. While that probably contributed to their coat colors in some small way, the massive annual change of color of all the roans, buckskins and grullas lived right inside the horses. Just as the horses lived inside their particular terrain, the nature and season-color-changes of that terrain lived inside the horses.

Just as our half-wild Mesta-raised Spanish-Indian horses were made of the plants they ate, plants whose own natures came from the nutrients in the feldspathic dust, decaying boulders, and beetle poop they absorbed, these horses' bodies became the land Herself by eating the plants' intake of the land. The Mesta Horses were hoofed, wind-blown agate boulders and Grama Grasses in all their seasonal phases running around as mammals; wind crossed on polished stone, suckling their breezy babies with the milk of decayed stars (meteoric dust).

When Horses and people truly "belong" to a place and are indigenous to the land, they take on the colors, textures, changing expressions and physical appearance of that place. Genetic function doesn't fight any of this, but actually works to make it happen.

But it works in all directions.

Like pumpkins grown in a box come out as pumpkin cubes instead of a beautiful, natural, round-ribbed pumpkin shape, people and animals grown in cities come out shaped like a city, behaving like a city.

You can easily see this, where knowing nothing different and having been convinced they're on some air-ride of progress to a glorious future, people and their pets with lives embedded in the limiting shapes of a life in concrete, surrounded by manicured trees and drywall cubicles for homes, who with bent-over heads focus only on their iPhone-inlaid-palms— begin to function and actually look like very specialized larval stages of synthetic insects with little bug-like antennae, earbuds and iCaps, who live like the soft parts of some bug lodged in the exoskeleton of their automobiles in which they scoot about in aimless city-commanded directions, emitting cyber squeals, beeps, alarms and tweets. Baby: you become whatever you're immersed in!

The good thing though, is, if it's only you, and you're one of these square-box-brained city-grown pumpkins, your seeds might still know how to grow a "real" pumpkin if liberated to sprout in the right open place and space. In this case you might be able to retrieve a real person out from a city-bug person.

The bad thing is when several generations have landraced and morphed into overspecialized neotenic techno-larvae who think that cubicle-grown square-pumpkin-head techno-life is normal and real, then their seeds will only grow techno-adapted morphs which are never truly viable outside their limited techno-dependent phone-charger environment.

By this point it's no longer a matter of just getting out of the city or away from your computer or dumping the iPhone, because you've already unconsciously morphed into something that will ruin Nature if you go into the Land without somehow first reindigifying your tangible soul. I say reindigifying can be done, but ironically *not* by the part of you that wants it, but by finding the lost viable spiritual seed of Real Life riding in your soul beyond the personal insistences of what you've become, which are morphed city-bug square-pumpkin thoughts.

Even artificially rooted in cubicle Hell, if you can "re-member" what it is like to be immersed in the natural shapes of real Dawns and Mountains, in the songs of migrating Birds,

Wind and an endless land filled with all types of life and the face of the Holy in Nature, without neurotic modern-culture supremacist people, then maybe a real pumpkin can be grown on a square pumpkin's vine. Maybe. It's worth a try.

The horses that coursed the wild open cobbled hills of their Home were themselves the containers from which to grow the heart of the wind. Their movements, like the Hero-womb-twin of all foals, carried a place for the world to give birth to another year. That sandy land once the bottom of a sea millions of years past was the placental welcome upon which the horses, like a windy hope of continued real form outside the slavery of the pumpkin box, could drop their free-born foals from the amniotic sea in their bellies onto the sandy bottom of that disappeared ocean, to grow into the wild nomadic beauty they were meant to be.

The colors of our horses were not the required restrictions of designated race, but the shifting seasonal colors of Nature's liberty of expression.

Chapter 10

Hunters, Rustlers, Horse Burgers and a Dream

Kotona and Yakatche had been carrying Punk's foals since the past June. I was nervous to casually set them loose on the magical Beaver-land, first because I had been trying to revive these particular New Mexico Mestas for over twenty years and I unrealistically had all my hopes riding on the outcome of Punk's children, knowing full well you can't revive an entire culture of horses just by getting a few foals.

But I was nervous because I knew a lot could happen to two lone pregnant mares on the wide open, and in the wild they'd normally belong to a larger band of their own, but we didn't have a herd... yet.

The world being what it was made it such that I couldn't just put old Punk out there on the wild magical land, for he'd attack anybody else's horses that might materialize in the area, so even if I put his pregnant wives in the magical canyon to live on wild grass, drink snow melt and give birth in the open as I had always thought was best, Punk couldn't be there with them to protect them from all the dangers.

What dangers you say?

Everything! I worried about everything. Tense because these mares might actually birth horses that would be the beginning of something precious that was a long time coming, still I knew they were horses and to be the original horses they had to be able to negotiate the reality of real unmanicured living. But I worried. The first worry of course being the Lions.

A number of Mountain Lions roamed that territory, a few big males and a resident mother with young. They could very easily kill and eat a young foal, especially if they had their young kits to help them. The remains of several Elk calves, all lion-killed, lying about on our land attested to this fact, each Elk about the size of a young horse.

Then there was the reality that a mare might get into a tough labor and need outside help, but if we were living one hundred and ten miles away... well, you understand.

Then there were the occasional difficult humans. I was worried about hunters because a lot of Deer and Elk grazed on our wild land, and with those Elk-sized mares in amongst the Elk, who knows what could have happened. Inebriated or nervous, inexperienced rifle hunters are often blamed for killing a horse, mistaking one for an Elk. In my neighborhood more often than not, angry hunters from the city, frustrated with not having seen any Elk or Deer to fire their expensive new guns at, itching to shoot something, will get tired of shooting road signs and drop a wild grazing horse to get their need to conquer out of their system. They rarely ever get caught, but if questioned later by the authorities they can always claim that they mistook the horse for an Elk, and only get charged with trespassing or shooting from a vehicle, receiving a heavy fine, not the seven years in prison the real crime carries.

Then there were professional livestock thieves. Some modern people probably think that "rustling" is the romantic subject of corny pulp fiction, bad western movies or at least something that took place long ago that no longer happens. But in the American West, brand inspectors spend half their work time chasing down the whereabouts of large numbers of "reavers" who run as part of every well-organized illegal meat business.

All cows are required to be marked by branding in the West, whereas branding horses is by choice. I hadn't started branding my horses so they were unmarked. If lost or stolen there was no easy way for anyone to know whose animals they were.

Professionals in the business of supplying illegally gotten meat to restaurant chains, supermarkets and hamburger joints never wanted to be caught with a trailer full of live animals, especially if they were branded, for then of course they could be easily convicted of cattle theft, which could carry half a decade in state or federal prison, not to mention all sorts of other penalties. If they captured unbranded animals, thieves could easily brand them with their own mark, but then moving them was difficult because until a brand has "healed" it's always suspect.

So, since once it's cooked meat is meat and the majority of horse owners didn't brand their horses, if found grazing in groups, horses were the preferred easy prey for "cattle" rustlers to run into a portable funnel chute, onto a stock trailer and haul off to butcher.

Excepting the case of elite "commando"-type livestock thieves—industrious criminals who could afford all sorts of gizmos and transport, who meticulously planned crimes and stole fancy horses or expensive prize Bulls to sell live to prearranged wealthy buyers usually in Mexico or some other far away location—most rustlers were meat purveyors and they preferred horsemeat because horses were unmarked.

No matter what animal they gathered up, each group of rustlers had their particular style, but they all had speed of action as part of that style. The best scenario for them was to quickly herd cows and/or horses to an out-of-the-way location, kill them all, gut and skin them, load all the meat under tarps into a stock trailer, or better still into a large travel trailer gutted of all appliances for the purpose, then, leaving all the heads, hides, legs and innards behind, drive up to two hundred miles in the cool of night to their receiver's cold storage unit, usually a refrigerated trailer of a semitruck, where butchers hung the sides of "beef" to cool.

This meat was purchased by a lot of stores and restaurants at a price less than a quarter the cost of their normal legal sources.

There was one little New Mexican hamburger joint in Santa Fe where I loved the green chile cheeseburgers with homemade buns, etc. I knew the meat was colt meat, everybody knew. That place lasted a long time until they tried to expand into a chain and their competitors in Texas blew the whistle on them. In this case the meat wasn't stolen but served illegally as beef. A lot of the "beef" served in truck stops, steak joints, etc., was horse.

Anyway, I didn't want Yakatche and her coming foal, or Kotona and her coming foal, Punk's only mares at the time and his first children, to risk being served up as burgers, nor did I want to feed the Lions with the mares (though I do love the Lions), and I didn't want any hunters mistaking my little horses for red or blue roan Elk. So I decided to put Old Blue out to guard these beautiful mares.

It was a sacrifice because I rode that old gelding up and into all those incredible mesas of eleventh-century Pueblo grid gardens and shrine-layered, cobbled desert magnificence every day I was in the state.

But no one could steal Blue out on the range unless the rustler was a beautiful girl. I took the chance that most bad rustlers were ugly boys.

No Lion would eat my horses because Blue could crack an adversary's skull in an instant and Cougars could usually sense this and never even try. And though Blue was a very fancy-looking Paint and would be attractive for someone to illegally obtain, he would evade all capture, taking his "mares" with him, pretending like Ojo Sarco from before that he was actually a stallion.

Plus, because he was so brightly marked, with bright blue eyes and white and sorrel paint clouds all over, Blue could also never be claimed to have been mistaken for an Elk by a frustrated hunter.

That's how it was: Blue, big-bellied Yakatche and bigger-bellied Kotona—a herd of three—became the very elegant equine inhabitants of that magic Beaver-owned land, grazing wild Grama, Bluestem, Dropseed, Indian Rice Grass, Nutseed Sedge and drinking snowmelt from the Mica-sparkling stream.

Blue took his job seriously, one hundred and ten miles away, watching over his niece's safety, but I really missed him.

Punk was in a telepathic trance, somehow right there in the magic canyon, occasionally struggling and yelling out orders at things we couldn't see.

It became a custom for us to visit the mares and Blue in that wild, hard-to-find canyon every ten days or so to see how things were going.

Still warm during the day, winter was closing in, and at the altitude there at the mountain's edge the temperature had begun to drop at night and freeze the grasses, turning the scrub oak leaf red, though the streamside willows still had their leaves, albeit all a deep yellow now. The smell of fall and the Beavers was strong throughout the rush of that rito's run.

Some nights a dream would come, causing me to think I should look in on the girls. I'd leave alone, arriving midmorning from our ranchito west of the Rio Grande, east of the Chama River, smack on the Greenstain River of the Tusas/Ojo Caliente drainage.

On one of those rather summer-feeling presunrise mornings, after a dream with Blue talking, I drove my truck to the Beaver-land, entering from a different side than usual, coming in on the unnamed road from another unmapped road, just to see the valley at sunup from the north for the change.

At the distance of even a mile I could see Blue's markings and the two darker Indian Pony moms, snug against the north fence.

As I rolled in closer the land of ours utterly disappeared, magically swallowed into the sheer cliff bend, not to reappear until I was less than two hundred yards away. I was startled to see a muddy truck parked down in the neighbor's rolling land, the truck's snout square up against my north side fence, the whole mostly hidden out of view.

Out of some strange old Reservation instinct I decided to drive in past the dropped wire-strand gate, onto Mando's land, and after turning off my engine I rolled my truck silently behind the other vehicle and stopped.

I slid out of the cab very quietly and without shutting the door, to avoid any noise, I peered into the bed of the other "foreign" truck as I tiptoed by. I noticed a "come-along" used in fencing, a bolt cutter and a lot of hand tools. Everybody within five miles was known to one another, New Mexico-style, for better or worse: what they drove, where they kept their animals and what animals they kept.

But this truck was unknown to me.

Walking downhill to the creek on my neighbor's side I let myself into the stream and, sloshing quietly, crossed into our land through our north fence, whose wires had been deliberately cut and rolled back across the stream. Silently padding midstream around a big overhanging Cottonwood, to my great delight I came upon Old Blue with both mares also in the water, striding straight toward me in the creek.

Then to my relative terror, downstream on the west bank a big middle-aged man appeared, who I saw before he saw me through the Cottonwood leaves. Throwing small rocks toward something farther downstream, he was yelling and hooting.

Like a Deer I froze stock-still in the river shadow caused by that big Cottonwood tree.

Blue was already rubbing his neck up against me when this fellow got close. He hadn't seen me yet and was swearing when the two mares ran away from him up the side of the cliff. I helped him curse a little harder still in Spanish, at which sound he turned and saw me in the creek. Though his eyes were wide and his face gone white, not losing a beat, he feigned normality and croaked out:

"Oh, hello sir, say, do you know who owns these horses? Sir, I was trying to keep them from getting through that fence while I get these cows off this land."

I switched my stare from this fellow to the smell of cows there in the creek, where quite unexpectedly thirty or so of what I took to be my neighbor's mixed black and red mama cows, a bald-faced little bull and a bunch of half-grown calves, all on my side in and out of the river, trotted right toward me.

It took me a second to add it all up at first, and though I actually didn't want those cows grazing out my sacred mare birthing-land, I went ahead making motions to help this guy drive the cows through the fence; but when I turned to look his way again he was gone. A revved-up truck engine moved off onto the unnamed canyon dirt road to the north, the sound disappearing at a pretty heavy clip, the echoes holding on for a while.

Blue, Yakatche, and Kotona were now wisely out of anybody's reach, way up into the cliffs, safely inside and below the capstone boundary of our magic land. While I really wanted to drive Mando's cows off the land to save the grass and wild plants, I couldn't at first deduce how they got in our place to begin with if it wasn't through the same cut fence, crossing the stream through which I myself had entered. By sheer instinct I pulled and jury-rigged the wire crossing the stream to provide a makeshift barrier until I could come with tools and more material to properly heal the cut fence. This left all the cattle fenced inside our land.

Hurrying back to my F-250 I drove on our beloved unnamed dirt road south to a big 19th-century adobe "shotgun" house shaded in a grove of wonderful Cottonwood trees, an Apple orchard and Weeping Willows, right on the same creek my horses drank from but a couple of miles downstream.

The crumbling adobe ruins of a former paddlewheel mill sat on the opposite side of the unnamed road, which ran clear between the very functional old house and the dead mill, forming the courtyard of Mando's home.

I would have waited in the truck of course, but I had my good knee-high boots on and decided to risk the inevitable ankle-biting of Mando's three cattle dogs.

"Yeah, I didn't know that man, but he was about forty-five, wearing a straw hat, taller than you or me, had a moustache, and he took off north in a dark blue Ram up the canyon."

"What did he say his name was?"

"I was standing in the creek and he was on the hillside as we spoke, but he got going before I could get close enough to really hear what he was saying."

"Did you see his plates?"

"They were all mudded up, but his passenger door was bashed in and the mirrors all gone. Do you know this guy? I'd never seen him before." Mando, who had opened his house's fence gate when I'd started talking, leapt up into the driver's seat of his truck cab, was already speeding back up the unnamed road I'd just come in on, signaling to me with his arms to follow him.

And I did.

To my surprise, all the cows had already drifted half a mile south of my place and onto the land of one of Mando's cousins. Here we stopped our trucks, hopped the fence, and I watched as my companion counted his cows and found five of his neighbor's in with his, and though two of his own calves were missing, one heifer calf and a little steer, we found them later, right on the unnamed road another mile north.

Much relieved, Mando and I rolled back to my land. He had me go look at the fence crossing the snow melt creek to the south, and just as he'd suspected the fence had been deliberately lowered into the creek to allow all the livestock in the valley to be driven up the creek into my land and then out through the cut fence on the creek to the north, to what real purpose I couldn't immediately grasp. As far as I could figure, if some cattle thief was preparing to load all these animals into a large gooseneck stock trailer it would've been in plain view of anyone traveling the unnamed dirt road, not to mention it would've taken a while and several people to accomplish, making it almost impossible to pull off such a theft without getting caught.

But Mando pointed up the canyon just three hundred yards past where Blue, Yakatche and Kotona, like specks of color, stood mountain-sheep-like out on one of the steep cliffside overhangs.

"Do you see where your horses are up there very wisely trying to hide? Look hard and you can barely see a rough gash that goes up in the rocks of the side of that steep *questa* at an angle, then reverses zigzagging back down and up again, disappearing between two walls of straight-up sandstone. That's where this guy was going to send your horses and my cows: up that cliff. Once they get in those rocks you wouldn't be able to see anything of those animals or that man on foot.

"It would take an hour to get them all up there to the very top and over, but from there on it's a kind of rolling forest and it all lowers into a string of connected wild ponds that never dry up. There is no way to get up there except with a "guacamole" horse or on foot.

"But once all the animals are in the old pens by those ponds, they'll butcher them all and pack the meat down to trucks in Ojo Feliz at this guy's dead auntie's old abandoned adobe house. Then off to the restaurants. Didn't you ever wonder why so many Eagles and Vultures nest right up around that cliff? That's because all the guts and skins are left there by these rustlers.

"You did us both a good favor showing up to check your horses when you did, you not only saved my cows but probably saved your horses too."

I looked in my binoculars and there was painted Blue, red Yakatche and blue-corn-colored Kotona still grinning and waving down at me from their safe perch way up in the straight rocks beneath the capstone of the vertical canyon walls still technically on our land.

The Canyon Wren was singing, his echo sewing the amazing past to what would happen, knowing like me how miniscule we humans really were in such grandeur, as I rolled proud and still worried back to our house one hundred and ten miles off to the east.

I left offerings at all high mountain headwaters alongside my route and prayed that the Mothers of Horses, the Holies who watched over my precious Indian Ponies and the possibility of a herd appearing in their new foals, would continue protecting them and sending me warning dreams upon which I could act, dreams in which it was always Blue who spoke. He was magical and would always be the spokesman for the Holy.

Chapter 11

In a Swale of Wild Carrot Blossoms

Every couple of weeks, even over the treacherous icy mountain passes, we'd make the trip to check on those three horses. They did well on the winter grass of dried-back plants, tree leaves and grass, drinking through the Beaver holes in the snow-topped ice covering the river. Blue was still good at hiding his red and white patterns, practically invisible against the snow and earth patches, while Kotona began to develop a "snowy" butt and an "eagle tail," which to me meant she was carrying a girl horse, her natural "snowball" phase on top of her dark double roan extending far beyond the normal season.

Yakatche, on the other hand, stayed red but began to roan out and put on a darker red for a dorsal stripe, so I figured a little boy colt must be trying to come in through her, for Punk was a constantly shifting red, pink, copper, strawberry roan with a red stripe.

Both mares were due to drop their foals sometime in the late spring, having been with old Punk the previous June and never coming back into heat.

The winter had been snowy, especially high up, and so when we arrived in May to check on the mares they were far across the river up in the cliffs, eating the grasses springing out from where the stone faces warmed by the sun met the otherwise icy red earth.

But we couldn't easily cross the swollen creek which was rushing so hard it pulled out all the Beaver dams and fences— fences which Hanna and I set about repairing.

On our next visit the creek had mellowed into a mirror of root-beer-colored water reflecting blue sky, with a Blue Heron fishing and a Curlew, a Snipe and a Kingfisher all called by the little Trouts teasing them with the light of their metallic scales. It was the last day of May, gorgeous and drunkenly delicious with an array of every type of sweet and rank aroma of so many kinds of flowers busting loose.

Blue Flag was poking up throughout all the streamside grasses, along with Columbines, Purple Bellflowers, lots of Alfilerio, Red Penstemon, Asters, Engelmann Daisies and more. The Oaks hadn't leafed out for real yet and the Willows were still barely budding.

We had trouble locating any horses, and when we did Kotona was hiding right beside Blue who, standing as still as a mountain, peeked out from behind a tangle of ancient fallen Ponderosa trunks and Firs halfway up the cliff.

Yakatche was nowhere to be seen. We scoured the land up and down and still no Yakatche. Hanna and I split up, searching separately both sides of the creek up into the rocks and trees lining the canyon walls, but still no sign of Yakatche.

Mares raised in open lands usually wander away from their band when birth time comes. And no matter what anybody tells you, they give birth when they *think* to birth, not when it's unavoidable and time.

Each mare has her style, some preferring cloudy weather, others in the night, some prefer storms, others in the quiet clutter of hillside rocks. You may get to know them, but they time it so nobody's watching, not even another horse.

I pulled Blue to my truck with my scarf, pulled his saddle from the bed, saddled and bridled him, and from the height of my perch on his upper story we cruised around the land looking for his cousin's whereabouts. But we only found Yakatche when she nickered a warning to Blue from behind the shadow of a big tree on the river. She was slab-sided and her hocks were glazed with leftover birthing juices.

"She's had her foal it seems, but where is he?" I said to Blue.

There was no foal.

Had the Lions dragged the baby away? Had she crazily dropped him to drown in the river while birthing him?

We searched and searched for another hour but no baby.

Downcast and feeling deeply unliked by Fate, I reluctantly called off our search for the foal. Usually a mother horse is standing right over her napping baby and Yakatche was now standing in plain view in the shade of a big Elm tree that formed the north boundary of the magic land upon whose red earth and wild plant cushion I had so hoped my mares would lay their little ones, but there was no baby.

On Blue, Hanna and I rode back to the truck, where she pulled out our customary picnic fare and tea and we began moving down to the flat shady spot where Yakatche stood to comfort her for what we assumed was her lost foal, and because we did like eating right there on our past visits in warm weather.

Dismounting I unsaddled Old Blue Boy, threw his saddle and bridle back into the truck bed and set him loose to graze and go about his life. "What happened my friend, what happened to Yakatche's baby? She's obviously birthed the foal, it's been eleven and a half months, but what happened to the baby? Did the Lions get him?"

Blue wouldn't talk which was very rude and unlike him, as he was a lot like me and always had something to add, elucidate, or educate. He ambled off towards Kotona, still very pregnant, who'd just crossed the stream toward us, no doubt intent on scraping some more paint off my truck hood with her front teeth per horse custom as any open range horse-raising person can tell you.

A large meadow of salt grass and tightly packed white Yampa flowers spread elegantly out away from the tree, where Hanna was unrolling our Buffalo skin and blanket upon whose traditional cushion we liked to picnic.

She laid out a beguiling assortment of marvelous smelling soups and breads, roasted vegetables, drink, fruit and tea, all on a blanket in the middle of this meadow where ran a slight depression some ten feet across, thoroughly filled with very upright Wild Turnip plants whose bright flowers looked like a pond of yellow in the middle of a white Yampa field.

This wild Yampa plant was a wild-growing tuber that local people called a carrot for its parsley-carrot-looking flower. Yampa root has always been dug by Native peoples throughout the West, who sew them into long necklaces and hang them to dry. Many Spanish-speaking New Mexicans until recently did the same, their ancestors having learned from original people to only eat the root after it's dried and cooked in meat stews. The Ute people and especially their relatives the Numi were so involved with the Yampa root harvest throughout the mountain Southwest that whole divisions of their people are still designated as *Yamparika* or Wild Carrot Eaters, the word *Yampa* being a Numi/Ute term.

They are boiled back to size in the winter, sliced and stewed with any red meat and eaten as a very body-sustaining food during the cold winters. Some people even kept ornately braided strings of Yampa roots around their houses for the goodness of Life Abundance their presence attracted. I've seen this myself.

Blue was grazing happily nearby up on the rise behind us. Hanna handed me a bowl of rice and curried okra after I, having chosen not to sit on the blankets, plopped down into the closest profusion of Yampa flowers, whose exuberant growth came up to my chest to cushion my nonexistent rear end.*

*Real life New Mexico-reared males, regardless of race, culture or language, are famous for having nonexistent butts! Nobody knows the reason. Some say it's the chile, or the water, or the fact we are always moving. But whatever it is, it's a fact. You can tell a Texan male from a New Mexican man in a second. This however doesn't apply to the ladies because luckily enough, they are amply endowed.

I'd taken about three bites when I felt something thick and snake-like pull firmly out from under my right thigh. Fearing that it might be a rattler I very carefully leaned to the left and lifted my leg, then looking to my right expecting the worst, who should I see resting calmly under the canopy of yellow and white flowers but a beautiful little colt not four hours old whose coat matched so perfectly the hue of the Yampa and Turnip flowers above him that he was virtually invisible, camouflaged by the myriad little flower heads in which he was so peacefully ensconced!

When I reached to pet his silky flanks, he lifted his yellow head to look toward his mother who was quickly moving in on our picnic to shield her baby. Then he let out a whinny that startled us and made us laugh in delight 'cause it was deeper than his mother's, rumbling up from the flowers out of such a little horse.

Moving off a bit we watched as he worked his wobbly self up onto his big well-made legs, with which he strutted on over to Yakatche, under whose thighs he began suckling unabashedly loud not three feet off. Misty eyed and laughing, we all had our meal together. Of course I named that stud colt—the first child of Punk, the only child of Yakatche— Yamparika, Yampa for short. To this day he still matches the land he was born to, and this was the beginning of a color lineage matching the genes of the magical Beaver-land that camouflaged his first hours.

Chapter 12

A Wild Plum Tree Foals

It's always best to search for the afterbirth when a foal is born, so you can find the foal's spirit "twin" to make a fetish to add to the "herd" of horse fetishes in a horse breeder's ceremonial bundle, for this keeps the mother and baby safe. Often times you can't find the placental twin, so instead with a piece of the umbilical cable, after preparing it identically with the same Native jewels, same songs, and protective parts, you can "make" a twin for your foal. These fetishes are the "little spirit horses" in the bundles that when fed ritually can be called upon to collectively heal wounded horses, sick horses, horses having lost vitality or horses made ill by witchcraft or the bad thoughts of enemy humans. The together-spirit of so many horses' soul-fetishes—both alive and passed on—has the power to reboot the general timbre and overall wellbeing of the entire gathering of any animals. Fetishes of famous horses long dead were even more precious, and when combined in the bundle with those of new foals and living adults, a living horse herd's natural wellbeing could be maintained even from a remote place.

But Yampa's belly button cord I could not find. The afterbirth seemed to have disappeared into the rough and tumble of the Natural World. I was fairly certain that Yakatche had not eaten her afterbirth, as do cows, buffaloes, goats, antelope, wild sheep and other ruminants. Wherever she left it, its whereabouts remained for only her and the Earth to know.

Where I grew up, in and around the strictly maintained, solid-adobe-living-Native-Pueblo-ritual-mind, the vague interrupting done by the Euro-American colonial mind whose arrogant assumption of its complete takeover of the world as an inevitable event, did nothing but peripherally damage the unperturbable ingenuity and constantly renewing self-vitality of the local Indigenous presence. Therefore, not to be deterred, when I couldn't find Yampa's placenta twin, I relied on that same ingenuity by taking one of Yampa's shed "slippers", and once fed, wrapped, jeweled up and sang over, this slipper would become his twin in that bundle with my spirit herd.

All hoofed animals at birth have each of their sharp little hooves covered in a rubbery whitish slipper, thoughtfully supplied by the Mother of Life (Nature, if you must), which protects the delicate womb walls, vaginal canal and vulva from being dangerously torn or cut by eight hooves (in cloven-hoofed animals) or four little horse feet as the young horse makes his or her way toward air and light to drop onto the red sand and grass of the herd's house.

After being born, these little slippers take forty-five minutes or an hour to melt and fall away into small, curled up, nondescript, unimpressive organic husks, exposing a beautiful, brand new, hard little hoof of the type needed to run and survive on this earth. Prematurely born fetuses who don't survive usually arrive in this world wearing only these little rubber shoes with their hooves not yet developed. Either way, the mother survives better the scratching and knocking about of the little creature's legs as they struggle to enter this world.

It would be entirely remiss of me to leave the reader to assume that each of these bundle fetishes "represented" a living horse, or that the bundle "represented" the whole herd like some silly symbol or as spiritual senators in a congress of horse souls. That was white-man thinking and spiritually distant from the fact.

These fetishes are *NOT* "symbols" representing horses as per anthropological/psychological canon.

Like all the bundles and spirit fetishes of Natives and Indigenous Peoples throughout the world before and now, these fetishes are beyond life and death and are literally the vital twin of the horse they come from; these fetishes are horses who are fully alive in a world that also exists as a parallel twin inside the land over which his other self roams.

If you actually understand this and cherish the difference, then you're not really a "white man." But if you do understand, then do yourself a favor and don't try to tell anybody about it because they'll either beat that comprehension out of you or shame you into self-doubt, which is why most Natives without an uninterrupted tribal cohesion no longer truly understand this either.

Whereas everybody on this Holy Earth at some time in their history could understand this difference and participated in it until civilization to rationalize its presence felt compelled to convert all Nature into an inanimate resource. By enforcing this conversion through language that defines all Nature's functions as purely chemical or mechanical causes and effects, this left the ages that followed as sad orphans of a magical past who by developing rational technology to survive in a non-magical world has only furthered the presence of civilization's characteristic depressive alienation from our real Indigenous natures. This syndrome has literally polluted with poison all the waters on the Earth, our own arteries, dulled the stars and made people and all living things mentally and physically compromised by the toxic waves and nonmetabolizing by-products of the inventions used in civilization's frenetic pursuit of a life far, far away from Nature's embrace. They now foolishly push Nature away as their primitive enemy and embrace technology as the friend of their untutored desires.

By all reckoning Kotona had been due to foal the same day as Yakatche, and she had been as wide as she was long when we found silky Yampa sitting so pretty in his namesake flowers.

I stopped short of camping on the land to be present for her foaling, partly 'cause we had so many other animals to tend at the house in south Ojo Caliente, but also on account of a maniac who'd burned down at least fifteen barns full of hay within a twenty mile radius of us and whose fires seemed to be getting closer and closer to us. Like everybody else, we had to stay vigilant in case someone tried to torch our hay sheds and animal shelters, and I didn't want my bride to have to confront an arsonist alone if it came to that while I waited one hundred miles away for a mare to drop her baby.

Mysteriously, one night a week later, a man was seen setting ablaze a stalled car on the high road entering El Rito, who when confronted by a Spanish-speaking lady from her nearby house, started shooting at her with a pistol. Unfazed, this woman grabbed her husband's shotgun and started shooting back into the dark.

After that no more fires were reported. What actually happened we'll never know, but a lot of tales are circulating to this day, not the least of which maintain that this fire-setting man was the Devil, who everyone knew had been living in a cave above Sipawe Pueblo ruins to the south of El Rito, on the Rito itself. The shotgun lady said she recognized him because she and her long-departed husband once had the Devil over for dinner one night so the husband, who was a good musician, could get the Devil to tune his guitar for him to facilitate his winning the music contest at the Rio Arriba County Fair, which he did.

Anyway, relieved that the fires had stopped we headed off to the magic Beaver-land to check on the wellbeing and fate of our second mare Kotona, praying that a Mountain Lion and her kits had not caught up to Yampa.

Blue and Yakatche were standing in the Yampa field, with Yampa nearby having a relaxing lie down, his beautiful little head barely visible above the flowers that matched him. Nothing is as relaxed as a baby horse napping, except maybe a housecat napping.

I pulled out my big binoculars, climbed a rise and took a long visual survey of the land to the west. After about five sweeps I saw something move on the side of the old early 19th-century hand-piled berm that had brought water diverted from the river by Spanish and Native colonists of the area to irrigate Spanish wheat fields to our south, no longer visible, but which had gone to make bread to feed the American soldiers stationed at Fort Union guarding the American takeover of the Southwest from Mexico.

I grabbed Blue, saddled and bridled him up at the truck and rode to where I thought I'd seen some earlier movement. Kotona, if that movement were her, most likely, like any mare, would be naturally protective and testy about anybody getting close to her baby if she had one. But Kotona, unlike Yakatche, was not particularly friendly in the first place, much less broke to ride, which was funny because both Blue and Yakatche were reasonable enough although both of them had been born on the wild range, whereas Kotona was born in a stall in populated Minnesota alongside the San Croix river.

Riding Blue, Kotona's uncle (Blue's father was a famous horse from my home range and Kotona's grandfather), I felt I might be safer and able to get away quick enough if that Blue-Corn Roan should decide to take me out. She was really fast, capable of jumping over the moon and liked to bite hard.

When we came to the place on the slope of the *acequia*, we found Kotona standing grazing under a single, old, landraced, feral Italian Plum tree. But no baby.

I rode around and around. No baby. No afterbirth.

But Kotona had definitely dropped her foal somewhere 'cause she was only half the size and had the signs of birth all along her hocks.

And just like Yakatche I couldn't find the foal anywhere, alive or dead.

Kotona seemed relatively calm, so I got off Blue's back and set him to graze and as I turned back to Kotona, intending to ask her where her baby was, I noticed the very end of a dangling piece of umbilical cord hanging up in the tree right over Kotona grazing beneath!

When I looked overhead to find the origin of this arboreal umbilical cord, there like one of Salvador Dali's melting clocks, a twenty-pound rag of mucous and filmy flesh of the entire afterbirth was draped up in the thorny tree, bouncing heavy on a branch above my head!

This was rather out of the ordinary and peculiar to say the least. I'd heard of winged horses and I didn't think she was a flying mare, but then how could an earthbound mama horse flop her heavy afterbirth overhead into the air to hang it up in a Plum tree? And why?

I was stunned. Smiling but stunned.

Stunned and stumped, I stood considering, utterly bemused that I'd found the afterbirth before I'd located the foal, and that the afterbirth was inexplicably dropped from the sky onto a tree!

Kotona wouldn't leave her post, which was strange as well because mares out in the bush leave their afterbirth far behind as soon as the foal is ambulatory, getting as far away as is possible for the foal, ostensibly to throw off the olfactory trail for any pack-style predators like wolves, in the old days when there were wolves, who would definitely eat a baby horse as an easy and traditional meal.

The baby must be nearby or Kotona would've left the area, but then again, how did she manage to drop her baby's placenta in a tree above my head?

I moved toward Kotona intending to get a closer look to see if her udders had been suckling a baby, but she threatened to charge me, and when I retreated, she whinnied and turned back to the Plum tree. Then a moment later from somewhere way up in this tree an impressively large squeal of desperation and a gravel-voiced after-whinny reverberated down to us from overhead. I looked up…

And there she was…

Kotona's baby, up in a tree!

There, like a beetle on her back, caught upside down in the crotch of the tree, nine feet above the ground, hung a beautiful cream-colored filly with agate hooves and dark skin the color of Plum tree bark. Her struggling legs dangled over her in the air, while her head desperately strained unsuccessfully to right herself, her every motion causing her to become increasingly more ensconced.

I couldn't believe it.

Kotona had her baby up in a tree! How could it be?

Whoever heard of a mare dropping a foal and her afterbirth in a Plum tree?

But I'd have to wait and figure it all out later, 'cause now the conundrum was how to get an eighty-pound newborn horse out of a tree and onto the Holy Ground without damaging her eyes or mine on the thorns, or busting a rib, hers or mine, while dodging a powerful fierce mama horse who, though she wanted her baby on the ground, didn't want anybody even touching her baby!

So I roped Kotona and with great difficulty hitched her big, beautiful, angry, mama-brained, thick-skulled head to the tree's main branch. After which I climbed up into the tree, where push by grunt and nudge by scoot I very gradually managed to move the filly just enough to drop her sitting like a teddy bear onto the branch system beneath us. I wacked off all the thorns I could with my gloved hands but both of us got a bit pierced and scratched in our descent.

Then with one great heave I dropped the foal slithering to the base of the trunk, where she crumpled into a long-legged spraddled mat with her head upright, the first time on flat ground.

Kotona was furious, kicking and stomping, pulling hard and fighting the rope.

I stayed up in the tree and watched until the foal thought to stand for the first time. Surprisingly she got to her feet not so shakily for not having practiced moving on solid earth during her first hours as a tree-living horse, and after a couple of bold tries, washouts, a few upright tackings and turns, she managed to sail on over to her mother, whose moorings I was now consigned to have to laboriously cut, for my "easy release" hitches were no longer "easy," having been so intensely tightened that they were beyond release on account of Kotona's powerful, frenzied struggle.

Reaching from the upper story of the branches where I was still perched to keep out of range of Kotona's immanent rage upon her release, I began gnawing on the heavy-duty lariat knot with my knife. When I had almost cut through the rope, in order to keep my distance from the vengeance of this nine-hundred-pound angry mom, I shimmied higher up the tree, hauling the end of the rope with me. From that height I yanked hard to rip the last hair I'd left in the cut, which thankfully gave way and finally released Kotona to go touch noses with her beautiful velvety baby for the first time. Predictably and to my great relief she pulled off angrily to get as far away from me and that crazy tree as she could, the filly following close behind.

From my vista up there in the tree I could see now how Kotona, the city girl, had dropped her foal while standing on the summit of the berm that ran above and behind the tree. This old Italian Plum brought by immigrants had grown since the nineteenth century in successive gnarling Y's, hugging the vertical slope of the old handmade irrigation canal. Immediately at birth the foal must've rolled off the top of the earthen rise, down the slope, flopping straight into the upper canopy of the tree that stopped her fall. Struggling to right herself, she rolled further and further into the tangle of branches.

Though she would eventually become our most incredible brood mare, Kotona, as inexperienced as she was, had within minutes of foaling dropped the afterbirth by the same method down the steep side of the *acequia* berm until it too caught on the outer branches where we found it as if it had been dropped from the sky.

When you think about it, Tosapi was pretty much born from the sky. She'd already lived four hours in a tree before she came to earth a beautiful, black-skinned, buttermilk buckskin girl Barb horse with a skunk-maned tail. Like Yampa we named her a Comanche name in remembrance of that amazing unsung confederation of Natives who for eighty years kept up an impressive nomadic lifestyle against all odds in the 19th-century Southern Plains. Without losing a beat, when faced with inevitable concentration and forced settlement on reservations, many Comanche parents, in order to hide their children from the hands of the American Military and keep them from prison camp humiliation, moved them square into the welcoming homes of sympathetic American, Spanish-American and Pueblo family friends, also leaving their finest Barb horses to support them. Though this is a story always mistold in books, there's nobody on New Mexico's eastern plains today, whose family has been there over a century, who doesn't have a Comanche/Numi ancestor and horses with Comanche Barb horse blood. Horse people of the very best, their horses were these horses like Yampa and Tosapi.

Tosapi was a horse born on top of a tree.

Yampa would be Punk's only male child and his logical successor. Tosapi was the beginning of a long line of Punk's famous fillies.

Born in and from Wild Carrot flowers and Plum trees, Yampa and Tosapi were Punk's first babies. The herd had begun to reappear from Punk's chest of dreams.

Chapter 13

The Demon Horse

Raised and enclosed in a stall or even in a manicured paddock, a mare has no chance to birth her foal in the way her horse soul wants her to. That's because in her heart, a mare doesn't carry a pregnancy to birth a foal to make horses for people, but to birth an addition to her herd, even if she doesn't have one.

There are two basic kinds of natural horse bands. One's a group of mares run by an older mare, with a resident stallion who is the father of all these mare's foals and no direct relation of the mares.

The second band style consists of all young male horses being governed by a mature stallion with no mares or fillies. These young stallions are educated by their older peers but are always on the lookout to gather the fillies run off from the mare herds by the resident stallion, in order to establish their own new band.

In the mare herd, the stallion usually alienates all his offspring as soon as they become fertile enough to breed, forcefully running off the boys first.

This way, sons avoid breeding their mothers. These run-off sons become a separate band of their own or join an already formed stallion herd and spend their days in face-fighting and sparring contests of one-upmanship between bouts of grazing and searching for water.

The life expectancy of wild stallions is very precarious and most don't live to breed. The few crafty beauties who do end up ruling a herd and breeding are quickly exhausted from their endless pacing, jealously patrolling up and down to keep all in order. Fights with intruder stallions as well as the wicked love-kicks of their wives during breeding, result in so many broken or worn down teeth (they are incredibly vicious with their wolf teeth and incisors), that they can't eat in a way to absorb enough nutrition to truly thrive, making it so a stallion over twelve years old in a natural setting is very rare. Some lucky ones make it to fifteen, occasionally to eighteen, but by then they are a wandering bag of ribs and as wheezy as a worn out accordion. Living solo with no herdmates and barely able to eat, they eventually die of starvation, or more usually in a healthy wild land, are killed by predators—Lions, Bears or Coyotes—and eaten back into the belly of Holy Nature.

Mares, on the other hand, live together and some can live a long time out in their wild herd life. The oldest ones, past fertile childbearing years, become the admirals of the fleet of younger mother mares and their babies, making sure everyone feeds their babies, settling cat fights, and leading them all to grazing grounds known to her from her own youth.

In a wild Mesta band, when a pregnant mare is ready and "chooses" to drop her foal, this will most usually be at night and invariably the mare will drift away from her companions with the intention of losing herself to their view.

Finding some out of the way place, hidden between some tumbled slabs of stone with a gnarled, wild, bent, barely-living

Juniper for shelter, during a rainstorm or a spring snow, this wildish mare will birth her young one far from the maddening crowd and her herd.

Experts are fond of assuring everyone that mares do this to hide the birth from predators, but the safety of the herd would seem to be a better shelter from an enterprising pack of Coyotes, who could more easily kill and eat a lone newborn horse before the mother's up and kicking. Mountain Lions, Bears, and previously when they still ruled the land, Wolves, could always find a lone horse to be easy prey. So the reason for separating from the herd—beside the mother horse's very good and obvious desire to be undistracted during labor and to be able to focus with her entire being without the banal interruptions of other mares or their curious foals during the constant standing and dropping to the ground, the intense straining and struggling that incurs for birthing female mammals—is to avoid the attentions of the band's resident stallion.

Most people don't realize that female mammals, especially herd mammals, are capable of conceiving another child within seconds after giving birth. This includes humans. A mare with a newborn foal on the ground would be instantly mounted and bred by any stallion who found her.

This is a rude and unwanted situation as you may imagine. Not to mention that if the foal is not already up and running by the time the stallion, irrationally maddened into his erotic intentions by the smell of birth, shows up to mount this baby's already exhausted mother, it's very likely the foal would be trampled in the process, maybe killed or worse his legs broken, or traumatized in some way.

So to avoid the unwanted attention of a stallion's instinctual need to instantly renew a mare's pregnant belly, the mares wisely go off and away for a day or so until both mother and child are moving well enough to rejoin the herd, the birth smell much reduced by time.

Ironically, when her baby is first born, a mother horse is usually pretty calm about anyone holding her colt or blessing them both and singing to the silky new baby. This lasts about four hours in some horses and maybe a day in others, but then like an unexpected thunderstorm, if you even intimate you might be intending to gradually edge yourself into the vicinity of baby, you'll find a mare blocking your way, standing sideways between you and your intended goal in the gentler types, and a charging, open-mouthed-ready-to-bite, equine crocodile-woman in the more protective mothers.

Be careful. In a herd, truly protective mother horses mean business.

Soon though, the foal can run more swiftly than the adults and are a beautiful sight, coursing along smooth like a flock of swallows but with a gangly rocking motion like an African Okapi.

Whatever jumps from Nature's womb has its place in life's neural net-line where together all living things help snag reality out from oblivion into material view in this existence. Anything that hatches and develops fast does its part and dies fast after leaving eggs or spores, seeds or hibernating cocoons. Other things take millions of years to coalesce into Nature's big-mind making. We humans are too small to truly feel the gradual geological bulges and outbreaks of changes most things of the world do to grow and develop exactly as they should, not pushed or strained to reach a synthetic goal of any arrival, but grand at every stage, causing life's song to surge in its giant symphonic motion toward even more music.

Barbs raised on real wild arid highland grasses, on uncultivated land, drinking snowmelt water full of mica, gold, silver, iron, copper, selenium, the electric vibes of Salamanders and Beavers, and the constant thoughts of wily Trout, grow bones twice as dense as a chemical-dependent stall-bred Arabian or Thoroughbred. They grow hides three times thicker, stronger and more resilient than any other horse on the American continent.

Punk's first babies, Yampa and Tosapi, grew up at their mothers' sides and in their mothers' tracks, grazing, wandering up into the cliffs, down to the river to drink, splashing running through the water, scaring up the Swallows and Kingfishers, Herons and Curlews, then crossing to the canyon slopes opposite to graze the powerfully protective herbs and grasses from a totally different era.

One side of the river was ancient clear-water-made red sandstone, while the west side was utterly black with volcanic rock made by fire, the river slicing between the two, chewing both opposing ages and their distinct minerals, mixing them sparkling under the rush of her waters where they settled harmoniously in her bed.

The two foals flourished from their beginnings, as did their mothers now rematriated back into their ancestral homes. Blue of course felt he'd accomplished it all and took his job watching out for them very seriously. The magic land loved all five of them and gave them life.

To continue with making more babies, I had planned to buy more mares like Yakatche and Kotona whenever I came across them. But Punk stymied my efforts by refusing to setup housekeeping with any other girl horses except Yakatche and Kotona!

Every mare I purchased, he'd run around honking and making all the stallion motions to be their king, but breeding never happened. He was only in love with Yakatche and Kotona and that was that. And that really was it.

We had a lot of horses now but only Yakatche was the love of his life, whom he couldn't wait to see when I brought her back to visit. She felt the same way too, both of them grazing and living together. Kotona was the second wife and she loved Punk just like he loved her. But it wasn't the cosmic, forever, in-the-bone kind of love like it was between Punk and Yakatche.

They hated me when it came time for me to separate them at the end of each summer, as I sent Yakatche back out to the magic land with Kotona, both hopefully bred with new Punk foals in their bellies. But whether they had foals or not, both were always happy again the next summer, when Punk and his wives took up where they left off.

They were anciently romantic fools like their owner. Punk refused all others. So did Yakatche, but she never did make another Punk baby. It was mysterious, very mythological really. Like all those wonderful Mongol horse stories of Nomadic

Chieftains whose prized red mare every summer would birth a foal who would be kidnapped by some untamable force that arrived in a dark cloudbank. When it lifted, the foal would disappear with the storm.

With Yakatche it all came very tangibly into our view early one fall morning when Hanna and I, now expecting our own first child, drove to the magic land to drop off Yakatche, Kotona and our other mares, along with Blue and Tosapi, for the winter to grow their bellies on the good grass and snow melt for next summer's foals. Yampa wasn't with them of course, for I'd separated him. He was now living not far from his father by our home because he was getting to be a young breed-hungry stallion.

We parked our rig and let out the little band of six mares and Blue to the misty day of tinkling birds and the quiet roar of Nature with no machines. After saying hello to the land and getting ready to pull out our picnic, to feast along the river per our now established custom, a big fearsome male horse stormed up from nowhere along the fence line to the north, and wasting no time, threw his very un-Barb-like self at the barbwire fence with his chest, busting two of the lines, then slicing himself up on the remaining four strands as he rushed and dragged them to get into our land, where he began to rear, fully intending to mount and breed Yakatche. It was a blitzkrieg attack on an otherwise peaceful day and we were all caught unawares, but the intruder found himself confronted with Old Blue, who, though he was now twenty-eight years old and no physical match for this seven-year-old mal-brained screaming behemoth, was undaunted and took him on.

After a couple minutes of heavy skirmishing, the big white-man horse had torn open a patch of skin and fur from Blue's belly about ten inches across, with his teeth leaving it to flap and bleed as they went at it fang and hoof, screaming all the way.

Utterly unimpressed with my rope or our human presence, and leaving Old Blue behind like he was some ankle-biting Chickadee, this crazy horse turned and ran back down to fleeing Yakatche, again forcing himself onto her, cruelly crushing her to the ground solely with the violence of his weight and front hooves.

Limping, Blue continued to try but I caught him and separated him from the fray to save his old noble self from further damage.

Kotona and the remainder of our mares had successfully fled up into the cliffside.

In a scalping banshee rage, I scurried and fetched my old .30-30 from the truck, cocking it into action as I ran back fully intending to kill this horrid creature raping and maiming my Yakatche and destroying my precious Old Blue. Every cell of my ancient Irish Celt-Cree-Mohawk soul wanted to instantly drop that demon bastard horse and I would have most certainly done so, and was even legally vindicated to do so. But my bride's stricken eyes stopped me. Though she spoke not a word, I was sensibly warned by her tender vibe to please not do any killing. Frustrated and weeping, this look brought me to my senses, for of course even by the rules of my Native upbringing my killing of that big asshole stallion would have created death fright, which would have magically jeopardized the wellbeing of my wife and the birth of our coming child.

It was a test.

And that test took all my resolve and a whole layer off my molars, as gritting my teeth I uncocked my gun, put it back in its sheath and got us all safely into the truck, loading Old Blue back into the trailer to sew him up later at the house, and after beating off the intruder to the best of my small human force, I reloaded Yakatche who was pretty torn up as well. And in that post-battle condition we drove back home.

That strange demon horse was never again seen.

The next summer Kotona had a beautiful Punk baby, a roan filly. We called her Ishta. The other mares remained unbred. Yakatche gave birth to a sad little filly, not Punk's but belonging to the big demon horse. We kept her but she has always been pretty lost in the head.

Yakatche never made another baby. One amazing boy child—with all the wonder-filled details of his mother's magic and all his father's power, brilliance, romance and nobility—and his crazy half-sister were the only lives she ever made. But Yakatche was from another World and another time and she had come to do a magical thing and did it. What Yakatche gave us was more than I deserved, for Yampa would become old Punk's legitimate replacement.

Punk always has loved Yakatche and she him, and together they still gaze at one another and graze like an old married couple 'cause of course now they are. Yakatche tells him what to do and as always he does it gladly. They still breed but only spirit babies are born.

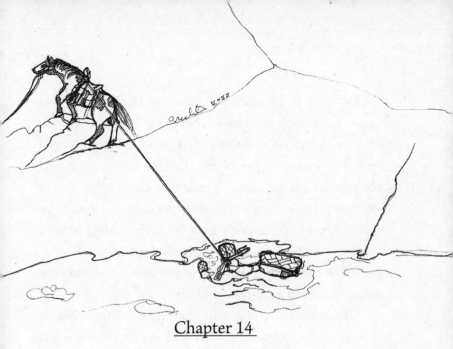

Chapter 14

They Just Go Up

"Hey!"

Somebody was yelling at me.

And there scowling and bowlegged, practically walking right on the outer sides of his use-softened riding boots, a strong little man came hobbling through an endless stretch of nodding snowballs of trumpet flowers from the rainy late summer's profusion of Sand Verbenas, whose fragrance owned the air with their always surprising, delicious, narcotic density thick enough to spoon with a shovel.

Pretty sure who he was, though I'd never met him, I knew he was allied with a certain land-wrecking banker, a mining-mogul monster whose very low opinion of my ways and presence in the area would probably make this visitor an enemy by association.

I was out at my morning feedings of Horses, Goats and Cows. Everybody for four to five miles in both directions knew everyone else's routines, when and where they emerged from their houses in the morning to tend their animals and fields, or not (in the case of people who drove off to jobs in the cities). Unless you were family, no one ever thought of going right up to someone's front door. That would be seen as confrontational. Courtesy demanded you stay in your truck until somebody showed up or the dogs announced your presence and someone came to check.

Like everyone, he'd already studied my habits whenever he went out looking after his livestock, as his grazing rights bordered our land. Now looking fierce and ready to argue, the little cowboy came up grumbling. He headed straight to my Yampa's corral, where pushing back his hat and wiping his brow, he leaned up against it to wait for me as I too was heading that way with hay to feed that now very stallion-y yellow roan. This way, the tough little old rich cattleman and I wouldn't have to even look at each other, but talk through the fence as if we were both chatting with Yampa, who listened fairly well to both of us while he clipped the hay I'd just thrown to him inside.

But this time I had all the cards. Because no matter what his political leanings were, like me this man was a rural New Mexican. After negotiating all those sweet-smelling Sand Verbenas, combined with the heady aroma of last night's long-hoped-for rain on the desert's grateful dust, the edge of his grudge would've been embarrassingly softened because in

New Mexico the return of rain not only took precedence over any bad feeling but the smell of rain and desert flowers made you forget what you were mad about to begin with!

Still, he was prickly and set in his mind.

"Hey!" he yelled again. "Why do you have all these damned horses? All they do is eat hay. They're gonna make you poor!"

"Nooo... they are my wealth. Because I have these beautiful Horses I'm not poor."

The forehead wrinkles below his potato-chip summer hat rose up in parallel arcs, and I think he almost smiled but tried hard not to. Resuming his hard voice he rasped out: "You mean you sell them?"

"Nooo... never, then I'd be poor. I'm rich 'cause I have these beautiful Horses."

"You know my dad's dad used to have horses that look a lot like these ones. I haven't seen these kind since he died."

"You're right! These are those same kinds. These are the ones, you know, the kind everyone used to have—Indians, Spanish people, everyone. Even a few Americans."

"You know, that's true 'cause my grandfather's mother was a German. Have you seen my cattle brand? The old German letter for *S*? But he married a lady who was a Jicarilla Apache. Me, I'm pure Spanish, and those horses are the only kind we ever had."

"Yeah, it's a shame they let them all disappear. You should've held onto them. Anyway, I'm trying to keep them going, the few that I can find."

"Ohhh…" he smiled, poking me hard on the chest with a very work-hardened, calloused finger. "So that's why you have all these horses because you *love* them, *¿Que no?*"

"That's exactly right. I love them."

"Well then that's the best reason," he laughed, shaking his head sideways looking very relieved. "Me too, that's why I have all these cows and horses of mine too," he added.

The Swallows dove and sped through the Verbenas by the hundreds, their faint chuckling twitters adding to Yampa's scream to the world. Then silence.

"For how much will you sell me that horse there?" Pointing to Punk and Kotona's third filly.

"No, I'm not selling any horses really."

He punched me on the shoulder and acted like we were done talking. He started to walk off but turned back, and smiling, kind of whispered like I was just being a horse trader trying to drive up a price, something he understood and respected: "Look Martín, you sell me that mare there in a couple of years. She's just exactly like my old Grandpa's, but I've got an old mare I've ridden for twenty years. She takes me everywhere, chasing cattle, everything. But she's getting old; when she passes on, I'll come for that mare there, I'll train her and she'll take her place."

"So you use horses to chase your cows? You haven't given over to those horrible ATVs?"

"No, I hate those things. Too noisy, smelly, they throw out exhaust, tear up the grass. I'll never use one of those damned machines. I'm using horses 'till the last card is played in the game. I'm in this way of life using horses, raising cows on the open range the old way 'till the last card is played."

"Alright then, I'll keep this mare for you, best I can, but I won't sell her, I'll trade you for hay!"

This man's family had piles of wild mountain grass hay.

"I can't take her now 'cause the other horse will be heartbroken. You know how they are."

And I did.

Away he hobbled on the sides of his boots. The rugged little Jicarilla Apache-German-pure-Spanish-New Mexican horseman climbed back into his truck and drove off to catch up with his life where he left it.

A couple of weeks later in early fall I met the same fellow, but this time elegantly seated in the saddle on his mare, while I on top of Old Blue was just returning from the wild land to the west across the river, through the bosque, where this same man who had the grazing concession there was checking on the welfare of his cattle hidden in the tamarisk thicket along the creek.

"Hey! Martín, I wanted to ask you if you could give me the phone number of the guy that shoes your horses."

"Well sir, actually, I don't shoe my horses. There's a guy that comes and trims their hooves every couple of months."

Pointing with his lips New Mexico style he answered, "Well I've seen you go up and down the sides of those rocky mesas over there. How is it you get up a thousand feet up those rocks and *barrancas* without falling if your horses don't have horseshoes?"

197

"They don't need shoes to get up there, they got hard old hooves, the horseshoers don't even want to hammer nails into them."

"I've never been able to get up there on my horses. How is it your horses go up there? They don't get lamed?"

"No, they do fine."

"How do they go up?" he asked.

"They just go up," I said.

"They just go up?" he yelled incredulous.

"Yeah, they just go up."

Scowling he swung his mare around. "She won't go up, she can't grip the ground. What's your secret? Nobody can get up there."

"They just go up."

"No wonder my grandfather would ride nothing but Indian Ponies. They just go up?"

"They just go up the side, ride all day on top, and we come down the same way we went up, come home and eat. Come on, let's ride to our house and go eat, I just came down."

And we did.

A year later, Old Blue was now about thirty years old and his eyesight started showing signs of creative invention. Blue would think he saw another horse and let out a whinny of greeting, but it might end up being a cow or an arrangement of tree trunks he'd seen. Sometimes while riding on a high ridge, his powerful legs still agile and worthy to climb and negotiate dangerous terrain, his eyes would fail to distinguish the edge of a precipice for which if I weren't vigilant enough to guide him away from onto more solid ground he'd have lost both of us over some five-hundred-foot vertical drops. This was a new phenomenon.

It would take me a long time to allow my better judgment to prevail, until one day I forced myself to put the thirty-one-year-old warrior, still powerful, still proud, still a good eater, in with the mare herd back at the magic land once and for all, and to stop riding him.

But not quite yet.

As we were just thundering out for our last real ride back up the "unassailable" mesa, after cantering through the creek, splashing up the water and scaring up the Mergansers, Mallards and Teals, a great racket of an overspun motor, loud swearing, and the nostril insulting blue smoke of a burning clutch came rushing up to our senses.

Once we were halfway up the hill, I stopped Blue on a vertical part of the trail, and shifting in the saddle I surveyed the valley below to see what was the source of all the ruckus. And there beneath us a couple of men were sloshing in the creek trying to dislodge an ATV stuck in a famous quicksand-like mudhole by an underwater spring right in the river.

In the rainy season or spring runoff there were several known places where if you accidentally walked or rode your horse you'd sink up to your ears and be hard put to extricate yourself. These guys had got stuck in one of the best known of these seasonal traps.

Everybody was wary of this beautiful confluence of a deep arroyo runoff spot into the Greenstain River—the Ojo Caliente.

By the time Blue and I rode back down and over to the spot we already surmised that the "last card must've been played" because it was none other than my old bowlegged scowling friend and his older son, who were raising such an exuberant exhibition of expletives and terrible imprecations in several languages.

"Hey," I yelled. "I thought you said you'd never use one of these infernal machines and were riding horses to chase cows 'till the last card was played?"

"Hey. Don't tell me that! It wasn't me," he lied, smiling. "It's my cousin's ATV, he got it stuck here."

"Stick with horses I say, friend," which was unfair, of course, 'cause lots of horses have been unwittingly ridden into deep mudholes by people not expecting New Mexico to be full of dangerous quicksand and horse- and cow-eating bogs.

To vindicate himself the old guy pointed to his horse, who was tied up at a tree up on the bank, a long calf rope stretched from the saddle horn to the handlebars of the mud-mired bike. "We tried to pull it out with the mare but this piece of crap is stuck worse than a cow." Cattle were always dying on account of these mudholes when no one could extricate them. Even when they succeeded getting stock unstuck, often the cow was so undone and exhausted they died anyway. It was a sad thing. These holes were a danger. Always bow your head to Nature.

Just then I heard Old Blue whisper in my head: "I can do it, Martín, let me pull that thing out with that silly little grass rope of yours. Let me do it."

When I asked permission to give it a try, the old man brightened up and agreed, but the son, an advocate of technology's superiority, disgusted, already wet and muddy, moved off across the river incensed that he couldn't dislodge the machine that was going to take over from horses.

"I'm going for the big truck with the winch," he mumbled and away he stomped.

I roped the handlebars with my little grass lariat, then we ran the mare's rope under one of the front wheel axles, turned Old Blue around, climbed back on top and moved off, tightening the ropes on the horn.

Blue, good old thirty-one-year-old Blue strained; good, big-footed, cliff-climbing Old Blue strained and strained and almost moved it.

We stopped pulling, moved back, tightened the ropes, and before the bike could sink again, Blue stood firm, resting against the taught ropes.

Then he pulled again, then again, then...

Pershlup.

The hind wheels lifted in the air and the son who'd never actually left ran out from where he was hiding in the thicket, cranked the key, turned the engine, and while Blue pulled, pushed the gas pedal and the crazy ugly machine gradually lumbered onto the more solid ground at the side of the creek!

Blue had done it! He did it!

No one could believe it. Not even me.

No come-alongs or truck winches had succeeded where ancient Blue, who I was afraid might have damaged his withers or knees pulling so much weight, had popped that hopelessly mired ATV out of the river mud. For Blue it was personal: at least one small battle in support of the beauty and ability of the old-time Spanish-Native ways over the dead nature-compromising weight and ugly presence of modernity's so-called labor-saving devices had ended in our favor!

That was Blue's last great deed before he was sent back out to "guard" the mares, to live out the remainder of his very worthy life. He and I had been riding for twenty-three years. He was always a show-off even after the last card was played.

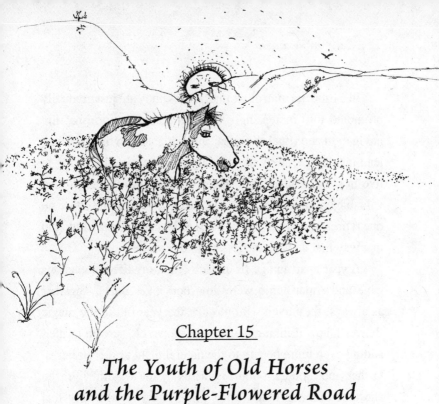

Chapter 15

The Youth of Old Horses and the Purple-Flowered Road of the Autumn Sun

To stay healthy and to continue layering beauty onto one's overall presence, Horses, just like people, have to be useful to something they love and believe in, at any age.

In the latter phases of their lives Horses and people don't need to *feel* useful, for that's a horrible insult: old Horses and people have to *be* indispensable and useful to something they believe in that believes in them. It takes a lot of spark and energy to be old in a way that feeds life. In New Mexico people are fond of saying "you need to be young enough to be this old!"

In a tribe, no man or woman retires, they are just gradually promoted into increasingly knowledgeable positions of life navigation and ritual expertise, and while still in the field they lead the charge, show the way, trying to inspire the young to live in some manner as to learn what it takes to get old and valuable enough to lead the next layer of people. In Nature no one retires, their functions are just redefined and they function in a way that's utterly necessary to the whole.

A year apart in age from each other, my life companions Blue and Amarillento were now both over thirty. Together as always, they lived wild most of the year out in the magic Beaver-land, drinking highland snowmelt stream water, adding even more beauty to the natural plant scatter of herbs, bushes and mountain prairie grasses by the way they grazed and stood among them. Their pride intact for the very real jobs they did protecting our herd of pushy foal-carrying Barb mares from predators, storms and horse thieves, they were both deeply immersed in the youthful season of their old age.

Whenever a mare out on the magic land seemed ready to breed with the stallion and make another baby, I would bring her back to our Ranchito with her yearling foal.

After letting the adolescent out with our growing free-grazing herd of youngsters, Kotona or one of the other mares would go to live with Punk in his "mansion" for the next three months, after which, back to the wild herd of girls in the magic land she would return, where together they moved freely about, eating and drinking, negotiating the weather.

I knew if I didn't put them back annually with Punk or Yampa, any or all of them would be driven by the natural urge to breed and leave our land, ending up as feral mares searching for a stallion, which actually did finally happen some years later, and I lost some horses, though one returned with a yearling baby after two years.

Whenever it was time to bring all the mares to Punk or Yampa, I'd let old Blue and Amarillento ride with them back to the house, where I'd attend to their feet, ride Blue around close in for old times' sake, and then set them all loose again for the winter with the older geldings guarding the girls in the wild land.

Blue loved flowers of every kind: Chokecherry flowers, Gooseberry flowers, wild flowers, Wild Roses, Wild Irises, Cota, Wild Oregano, Desert Marigolds, Guaco, every kind of flowers.

He didn't love to eat them or necessarily for their smell, but he loved "existing" in flowers, especially if they were buzzing with wild Bees and Crickets.

Old Blue not only knew how majestic he looked standing up to his belly in patches of plants packed with flowers of any type, he dug standing there. It was his high. With his Rhino-wrinkled lips, wild blue eyes and mottled markings like some tropical fish, Old Blue buried in flowers could blend right into the waving blossoms, looking very prehistoric in a Pleistocene kind of way, a living fossil of a long-ago unpeopled moment.

One fall after a summer of rare humidity and the blessing of daily rain, our whole Ranchito on the Greenstain River decided to flower butt to beak with three- to four-feet-tall Christmas trees of solid purple Asters, in such a crowded holographic brilliance that traffic on the little highway running up the valley in front of our place ran slow while people tried to catch a glimpse. Drivers would stop their trucks or cars, jump out to savor the view or photograph twenty acres of solid purple with Blue, of course, standing right in the middle holding up traffic for a while.

When I went to vote that week, the entire bureaucracy of local ladies dutifully "manning" the gauntlet of stations before and after the voting booths each wanted to be the first one to hear from me how we'd managed to actually grow such a choreographed patch of gorgeous flowering weeds, that even obeyed the corners of our land, filling it perfectly and evenly, with not one of the Aster plants jumping under the fences onto the neighbor's lands.

It really was a miracle. Northern New Mexico's purple Asters grow everywhere in the late summer but they are biennial, the first year growing in a very weed-like, nondescript form like hundreds of other plants without flowers. Then they die back all the way to the ground in winter, staying dry and gone until the next midsummer, when they poke up again but this time flowering into bushy stands of purple stars. With fall frosts they spread purple-tinged fluff everywhere, and then *whoosh*, they're completely absent again.

But they never grow where you plant them, when you plant them. Sometimes they can wait twenty years to grow their first flowerless year, then flower in their twenty-first, but only one plant here and one plant there, and always in conjunction with the very dependable, very golden, gummy, sneezy, broom-like flowers of the very fixed perennial Chamisa bushes.

For three weeks one fall we had a big twenty-acre square of purple Asters and a mythic blue-eyed Paint Horse who just stood there in the very middle, drunk on the miracle! The Asters never returned in that organized profusion again, reverting to their accustomed pattern, and practically disappearing altogether from our land when a few years later Blue himself went on.

We had resolved to build a big adobe Sacred Hall, a little like those palatial mystic halls of the ancient Margiana Oasis cultural phenomena way back in the Dream Temple days, a little like a rectangular sixteenth-century Native-built adobe church, and a little like a gigantic Lenape *Ngamwing* Big House. I designed it to be the Hall I'd always wanted to teach in.

It was exactly at this time that the miracle of these purple flowers happened, and it was exactly in the middle of that miracle of bright purple stars where I had decided to build the Hall that would rise from the feldspathic sand of our home along the Greenstain River and her valley.

So in the dark morning of the twenty-second of September, on the Fall Equinox of 2006, I saddled old Blue, put the bit of his favorite bridle into his rhinoceros mouth, and after pulling the heavy silver over his cheeks and ears I fastened the throat latch, and climbed into the saddle holding two sets of offerings and two stakes.

People were always surprised how in those days I always tied the horses while I saddled to an old Poplar tree in whose trunk two gigantic tribes of hybrid Bees lived, buzzing in constant profusion over and under my horses, coming in and out of the hives on their eternal missions of summer nectar, sap and construction supplies. Never once did they seem unhappy for our presence and no person or animal was ever stung.

The bees were already up and about in the Asters, the entire land buzzing like a dentist drill when Blue and I rode into the flowers searching for the location of my big sacred building.

Realizing that the Asters were stars and the land was the sky full of stars, and our Hall a universe inside the land of flowering stars of the sky on Earth, together with my cloud-spotted sky-horse Blue, we searched for constellations amongst the flowers to show me where to put my magical school.

Certain tribes of Ants had made large gravel piles in amongst some very old stone shrine piles, all right there in the sea of flowers.

I rode slowly through the flowers to one of those piles, having surmised for years that the arrangement of rocks was the earth surface equivalent of an Indigenous star cluster in the sky, which included what in English is called Orion, other piles corresponding to Algol and Sirius in the south. These very stars were just now returning to the sky at the Equinox. Riding carefully forward of these piles, Blue and I turned to face the coming Father Sun whose rising would be the hinge of time between the Sky and the Earth like the hinge on a Clam. Stars in the sky. Stones and flowers on the earth. Light in the seam.

Just like its equivalent on the horizon, this place where Blue and I stood that morning in the sea of purple stars would become the doorway of our new Hall. Once the Hall was standing that doorway would then become the world's Fall Equinox. The entire Hall would become the universe measured according to angles determined by the rising and setting of the Sun at the Winter and Summer Solstices at her corners.

That first morning though, there was no visible adobe Hall, only an invisible one made of spiritual prayer dimensions that I spoke into being which stood there for only the spirits to savor. The entire purple-flowered ground extended out to meet the gradually dawning sky whose increasing light ate the stars of Orion out of the night, but not without first leaving their daytime selves on Earth as this Antpile of gravel stars and its small upright stone shafts whose coordinates would dictate the position of the entrance to our new Hall.

When the Sun Father assumed the eastern horizon, I gave him one of my handheld offerings and a sound offering of an old delicious prayer from my singing voice. Dismounting, I placed both into a hole I dug with one of the stakes, then after pounding the stake into the hole, I remounted.

Standing with Blue right to the west of that stake, facing west with the Sun Father behind us in the east when the Sun was full upon us, a great long shadow of Blue and I stretched straight across the very top of the two- and three-foot-high sea of purple Asters rippling in that mild breeze of morning. Following exactly that shadow, Blue and I rode very slow and measured. Right on top of the Equinox morning's shadow we sprinkled cornmeal and pollen onto the trail of bent down flowers we left behind us. Like a carpenter's measuring tape our shadow rolled back into us as we proceeded, the shadow transforming into a trail of bent down flower stalks behind in the Dawn's light. When we had traveled seventy steps I stopped Blue, dismounted and right under his Rhino head I sang another prayer and dug another offering hole into which I placed a different offering (this one for the evening Equinox sunset) and pounded in the second stake. This would be the central spirit window of the rear wall of the Hall.

This purple trail of mashed Asters of the Sun's shadow of the Fall Equinox became the dimensional and sacred spine from which all the practical surveying of the foundations upon which a very fine, large, sacred adobe Hall would rise, a Hall inside of which the twin half of the universe outside sat like a horse's twin spirit sits inside a running horse. It was here, in just such a structure that I'd always wanted to teach, for the structure's dimensions were half the teachings.

The Sun had shown us the trail with Blue's dawn shadow. Blue had tramped his shadow into a flowering road, and I had marked its front door and back wall with offerings. Later that day when the foundation foreman and crew came, they would determine the whole building from those temporal goalposts of the Sun's Ballgame and commence to dig the footings.

Blue rode the stars of the ground, his old cloud-spotted beauty made it all happen.

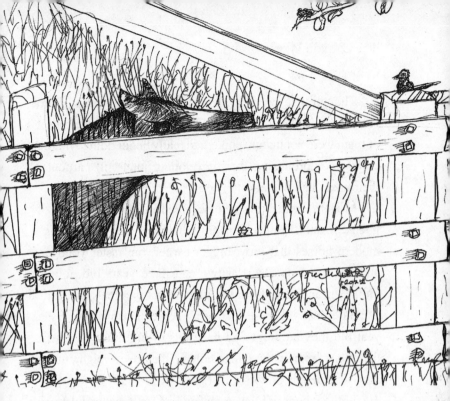

Chapter 16

Bubba

When Blue's last forays against modernity's literalist efficiency at our house were over: his animal majesty arrogantly rescuing a smelly mud-stuck machine, and his mystic measuring of the new building site with his shadow in a never-before-seen profusion of flowers, it was time for him and Amarillento to ride the big green trailer behind me and the truck back to the magic Beaver-land to watch over the band of Mares for the coming winter and spring months.

Though there were a pile of handsome new young Barb Horses at the Ranchito, all children of Punk, even the oldest of them were not mature enough to really begin riding without unduly compromising their developing joints, in particular their knees and withers.

Modern civilization's horse breeders, in the interest of intense financial gain, claim they have succeeded in "creating" modern horses that grow bigger earlier, run faster younger, and can be ridden hard at two and three years old, totally unlike the ancestors from whom these poor animals descend.

Sure enough, these "modern" horses get big fast. By a year old they are huge and have lots of big muscles. But... their bones remain too thin to hold up their own weight, much less carry people on top of that!

Without bones of the corresponding stoutness and density needed to carry so much increased muscle power and height, these poor horses' physiques will already begin to atrophy, break down and shatter at a time when a natural horse raised slow is just entering their prime years. These modern breeding "wonders" may perform and look good early on, but will only live to suffer terribly.

It is a tail-chasing conundrum because in order to fuel such overgrown megamuscle and performance, they are fed overly high-octane processed food with all sorts of artificial additives, chemical nutrients and farming byproducts combined in a way that actually overloads and ruins the horse's ability to absorb and metabolize the necessary heavier nutrients needed to grow bone. These performance wonder-horses' digestions are horribly imbalanced, to the point where if stressed by early use their joints collapse before they can ever fully develop properly.

A horse's bones must be able to grow first, at least at the same rate as the tendons and muscles. To be strong, bones *cannot* and should not grow too fast, no matter what nutrition is available. Though horses move rapidly across the Earth, they grow up gradually and live gradually.

With a natural horse, if you let them develop at their own speed, it will be slow, but then you'll have bones thick like ivory. For this to happen foals have to suckle at their mama's udders for a good while, not just a month. But this also means the baby has to have a mom who has been raised right too, and having developed slowly has those nutrients extra to give in her milk as well as a digestion that can feed two! While growing, both mamas and babies have to have good grass to graze and water with plenty of chelated minerals flowing in it. Young horses can be suppled a little to get them accustomed to the idea of eventual work, but never with weight on their backs, and more importantly never pushed to constantly run in repetitive tight circles. Horses are not meant to carry or pull any weight whatsoever. They aren't machines. But in our love of being allowed to be carried on their backs like the wind, we must at least give their fetlocks, knees, flexor tendons, hocks, hips and spine time to fully form and harden. The leg and shoulder bone assemblage of a horse are free moving and not socketed to any vertebral bones, so the magnificent arrangement of microligaments, tendons and muscles which do hold and cause a horse's powerful frontal movement must be allowed to grow, flex and encase the withers area without any added weight and with only natural turning.

Even a real horse raised right will begin to fail early on if not allowed to develop full bones, joints and mind before being put to hard effort. But if given the time, good chow, good water and allowed to move naturally, a Barb Horse, not just left to grow confined, can be ridden easy from five to six years old, allowed to run free a year, ridden hard and consistent from seven to nine years old, put back with the herd for a year, then ridden really hard from eleven to twenty-eight or twenty-nine years old; all of this with no arthritis or joint problems except maybe a teeth-float or two depending.

Anyway, modern horses are bred to grow muscles too fast, but can't grow bone to catch up to their bodies. Their joints remain adolescent and begin to grind down when forced to do adult work and carry adult weight so these animals' bodies are often used up by the age of fifteen, or if they miraculously last longer they usually live on cortisone shots. Especially true in the case of expensive breeding stock. But why breed horses to be dependent on drugs to survive?

Bad. No good.

It was impressive though, on the Rez where we had no vets or supplements, how long so many of these old-type horses lasted, even when ridden technically too young. This was because they had their mama's milk, had light riders and wild, open riding without constantly contained tight maneuvers, only seasonal hard use with off-season herd grazing.

At age thirty, Blue and Amarillento could still ride forever on the harshest terrain; their joints, bones, muscles and umph were still 100%. But their eyesight and crazy brains made it so I finally had to stop riding them out in the bush. I therefore redefined their jobs and promoted them to be the royal guards of Punk's mares and foals. Because of this, and because I had to wait until our dozen new young up-and-coming Barbs had grown mature enough to ride, I found myself singing the normal horse raiser's lament: "Horses, horses everywhere, stallions, mares, geldings and young foals, but not a single beast to ride!" Though surrounded by beautiful Horses, once again, I was left afoot.

So until the young ones could be ridden, as some temporary relief for this ridiculous situation, (but against my better judgment), I fell into the pit of buying even more riding horses! In my desperate hopes of finding just one that remotely fit the bill, I bought "trained" registered Barbs and Spanish Mustang geldings, whose papers claimed similar ancestry to those amazing animals gracing our corrals; but in every case they were troubling, or troubled, single-colored, and all looked like Quarter horses. Weirdly enough, they had morphed over two generations into strangely prejudiced "white people" horses no longer resembling any of the characteristics I associated with the little Native Mesta-raised Spanish cowboy horses we were raising.

One by one I gave these horses as gifts to people who fell in love with them, mostly riders who found themselves horseless. Life sometimes quietly conspires to make you keep your promises: as a twelve-year-old I used to tell my mother that when I grew up I would have a lot of good horses and I would give them to people as gifts, especially to those who loved horses!

One of these horses came to me advertised as a rideable Barb mare, but this animal was better known throughout the registries for her topaz yellow eyes, rare cremello-isabella color, and her propensity for dropping foals of equal color.

Touted as a well-trained riding horse and reputedly a good brood mare, like a lot of horses who were the "*n*th" generation of horses culled to obtain pastel-colored designer foals, Yeshi was a monster. A couple had bought her for me as a gift for conducting their marriage ceremony in the time-told tradition of giving horses to people to honor them. This would have been a wonderful gift.

But with the increased accessibility to designer veterinary pharmaceuticals, unscrupulous horse breeders and dealers had recently adopted the common ruse of drugging their unsellable problem horses, selling them as tame, and dropping them at the buyer's ranch. When the sedatives had worn off, you were left with an unhealthy depressive demon the seller wouldn't take back. And then nine times out of ten the victim of this procedure, unwilling to lose their cash, turned around and did the same thing, trading these poor beasts on down the line till someone finally had them destroyed.

I had a policy of always quarantining new horses for a minimum of two weeks to make sure they were well and not carrying some transmittable sickness, but in my excitement I very foolishly put this new mare in with Punk right away to see what he thought about making babies with this fancy, pretty-looking, uptown lady. He kept sniffing her, parading off and around, coming back, trying to see what she was like or get her to admire him. She just stood there dead in the water. But by the next day she was more lively, when the mood-masking pharmaceuticals had worn off, and she instantly broke Punk's right jawbone and snapped his sternum with a vicious assault out of nowhere.

It was a horror. Punk would heal and live on, but when I moved that mare into a pasture beneath, she kicked to death one of my other mare's foals.

She was acting very un-Barb-like and was a bona fide monster, dangerous to every person and animal. She'd been a "color creation" of those foolish type of people who cross and back-cross mares and stallions to develop a genetic equation whereby certain pastel-colored animals can be predictably bred from certain mares to be sold for a hefty profit. In this inbreeding process they lost the sound bodies and sane minds of whole bloodlines of otherwise relatively good old-time horses. Breeding for color is mostly what ruined the old Barbs that had been so hopefully gathered up and made into registries. For a while they got colors but in the end lost the horse. The natural Barb did have beautiful colors, but their appearance should've been the sole domain of the Goddess of Horses, not greedy polyester-wearing, gene-manipulating humans.

Nonetheless, I bravely worked with this crazed mare and after a time I could actually ride her, but it was not a joy or a grand together-thing. She continued with a strange dangerous mind and she had to live separate from all our living beings. And that's how it was.

Then one day the next spring, a man called me from somewhere in western Missouri trying very concertedly to talk me into selling him this crazy polar-bear-colored mare with topaz yellow eyes. He didn't care that she kicked, bit, killed, charged, and though rideable had a gait like a stainless steel Giraffe. His wife had fallen in love with this crazy mare a year past at some festival when she wasn't yet for sale. Mr. Missouri wanted to buy the horse as a surprise birthday gift for his sweetheart.

Unwilling to be yet another purveyor of undesirable horses in a revolving-door syndrome under a smokescreen of lies, I explained a hundred times to this nice person how it seemed to be with this horse and that I couldn't possibly sell to him what I myself would never knowingly buy, but he was adamant and in the end he ground me down.

He proposed a trade: he would give me one of their Barb-type horses, a Paint that his young son had trained to ride, in exchange for this strange yellow-eyed mare. That way no money was exchanged; I would have an animal to ride and we could be the ones giving his wife her dream...'cause she just loved this "monster horse!"

With the crazed fat mare in our green trailer hitched behind my very legal white Ford F-250, we drove through the incredible one-hundred-plus-degree heat of July, crossing the Texas and Oklahoma Panhandles, the state of Kansas and into Missouri sounding like a gigantic lowrider as Yeshi dented the sides, pounding out her funk rhythms with her angry hooves the entire 900 miles!

Everywhere it seemed possible I'd pull up to a water source, slosh the mare down to keep her cooled and offer water to drink. She was ungrateful but dutiful to her character by booting the bucket as far as she could and kicking at me, thankfully never connecting.

The next day was even hotter. After ascertaining the whereabouts of this charming mare's new home, as we pulled quietly into the midday Cicada-buzzing tree-shade of a Missouri farmhouse, I looked around for horses and saw a little steel-blue horse with his head nosed into the corner of a pasture *way* too lush for any horse to be set out on, up to his withers in long green grass. When we drove up he came instantly out of his stupor to whinny high and long, his black, black eyes instantly catching mine before we'd even come to a halt.

The denizens of this house had not yet emerged but the sweet aroma of frying bacon did, and eating a couple of strips, a twelve-year-old barefoot boy popped out of the same tall grass with a little dog, somehow gliding over to our trailer where on his tiptoes he peeked in and whispered a whistle, raised his black eyebrows and made a face.

"It's a good thing you're letting that one go," he quietly mumbled while swallowing his pig meat.

"Yeah," I kind of mumbled my agreeance while climbing down from the truck, seeing that the dog was calm, "but they said they wanted her so here we are."

"My dad's giving her to Tanya, my stepmom, she'll be fine with this mare."

"What horse is that one over there in the corner?" I asked, pointing to the grulla in the grass.

"That's Bubba."

"Bubba?" I laughed.

"Yeah, he belongs to Tanya; he stumbles a lot; my dad just uses him to haul cases of beer to their parties in the woods. He's gentle but doesn't ride too well."

"What kind of horse is he?" knowing full well he was something akin to my own, it never hurts to ask 'cause you always learn something.

"He's from South Dakota, but his mom is one of those Arizona Havasupai Barbs and his dad is one half descended from that famous New Mexico mail horse and the other side's a Banker pony they say."

I thought so, almost one of ours, minus the Island Pony. The mail horse was Kotona's grandmother.

"You guys are the ones gonna take Dream Catcher away?" Like some kid out of an old Mark Twain novel, this young man so free and able had a big sadness badly hidden in his slouch.

"Is that the Paint your dad wants to trade me for this crazy mare to give to your mom?"

"Well yes, except Tanya's not my mother."

"This Dream Catcher, is he, like, your horse?"

"Well, my dad said if I trained him and he sold him, he'd give me the money so I could buy my own saddle."

"Why don't you make yourself a saddle? Find you an old beat-up saddle nobody wants, tear all the leather off, pay attention to how it's made and find new leather and cut it to size and remake the old saddle. That's what I did so's I could get a saddle to fit my little old-time horses."

"That's a really good idea. I could do it too, I know I could."

"I know it too, 'cause any person who could train that powerful wild-eyed dirty paint over there would certainly be smart and able enough to figure out a saddle. The leather will cost you something but not as much as a saddle. That way you don't have to sell your horse!" I said, without really knowing the situation.

The smell of cooked bacon became so permeating I turned to look and heard Hanna talking to someone on the other side of the cab.

"Oh, well thank you very much, this smells so delicious," Hanna said to a lady handing her a very large platter half-filled with a pound of fried bacon and an equal amount of green beans fried in bacon grease, covered in salt and pepper.

She had one for me too, and while a man gave both of us cold soda pop and invited us to sit, this big lady peeked into the trailer which hadn't thundered at all since we parked.

"Oh my God, I don't believe it. Look honey, it's my dream horse. Where did you get her, oh my God, what's she doin' here?"

"She's all yours Tanya, happy birthday."

Except the wonderful boy and my little Hannita, nobody we'd come across in this rural neighborhood could be accidentally regarded as slim. This was no surprise considering their faithful compliance to the local consensus on what constituted "proper nutrition," which specified that bacon should be a part of every meal, and that a pound of fried bacon with some deep-fried vegetables was a perfect twice-a-day between-meal snack!

And though Tanya was definitely an adherent of this food custom, she was strong and quick, generous and full of affection. After hauling off to fetch her saddle, pad, and bridle and plopping it all next to our trailer like it was an empty laundry basket, with a halter and lead in her left hand she opened the rear gate and walked right into the trailer sweetly talking all the time to her new "beautiful girl" and unhitched that mare.

In my apprehension of what violent outcome might occur I almost stopped her, but stopped myself. Neither the mare nor this woman had missed many meals and when Yeshi backed out of the trailer she could've easily crushed to death her new owner. But when Tanya jumped to the ground with her horse the world could feel the thud and they were both smiling and upright.

Yeshi's ecstatic new owner was basically the same color as the mare: same hair and mane, same pale cream skin and coat, both with topaz eyes, both handsome and ample. Holding the halter lead in one hand, Tanya never stopped talking sweet while with the other she flopped the saddle pad up and into place, then with the same single hand effortlessly tossed her very heavy, gigantic, brand new squeaky western saddle as if it were a bag of feathers up onto that normally jumpy mare's back. I don't think I'd taken a breath for a half an hour, waiting for something terrible to transpire; I could feel the bacon and green beans fighting my tight diaphragm trying to edge their way into my digestion.

But Yeshi just stood there, legs spread so Tanya could buckle her rig. Once the halter had been dropped and her mechanical hackamore (I hate those things!) had been pulled into place over the ears and fastened at the throat latch, the lady of the house took the reins, and after perfunctorily pulling them over the mare's little moon-colored ears, the horse stood perfectly stretched out, like in the breed books preparing for the impact to come. Tanya then grabbed the horn with one hand, shoved her left foot into the stirrup, and looking like a couch shot from a cannon, jumped straight up and expertly landed square into her saddle causing the horse to reel and stagger a bit (Tanya had a lot of ability and there was a lot of her to have it in). After the lady got her right foot (flip-flops and all) positioned into the stirrup side-opposite, away the two of them oozed.

Tanya still sweetly conversing and overflowing the saddle, Yeshi overflowing the road, right down the middle of which they together calmly rolled, they eventually disappeared from view as I looked on in complete wonder.

We were tired, it was hotter than the devil's rear end, and our nerves had been in a holding pattern for two days, not knowing exactly what horse explosion might be waiting to erupt. That crazy horse had been a real toxic roughneck at our place, and though I felt a bit small and chagrined, questioning all I felt I knew about being with horses, it was a huge relief to see these two "big" beings so perfectly matched and at home with each other, as unexpected as it was.

Still, I didn't start really breathing again till Yeshi had reappeared forty-five minutes later with a very elated Tanya still on top directing. She dismounted as graceful as a ballerina and started issuing orders for the preparation of dinner, which turned out to be two-inch-thick broiled steaks smothered in bacon and fried green beans with watermelon for desert and a lot of cold beer and lemonade.

These people were kind-hearted and generous in every way, but they were like a den of giants who never expected anything to go wrong, and when something did go haywire they just ignored it as normal.

But when Papa commanded his son to bring around the boy's Paint horse, the one he'd trained as the previously agreed-upon trade for Yeshi (who on the market would've brought at least eight thousand dollars from color-breeding horse types), I saw the grief-stricken eyes of this respectful barefoot kid as he dutifully slouched off to retrieve a young dirty Paint with marble eyes.

The boy rode up with no more than a halter rope on this horse's muzzle—no bridle, no pad, no saddle, just the boy and the horse, and the horse doing everything the boy suggested as if the horse were the boy's own breath.

The nobility of that kid's posture while mounted I'd only known in my childhood Native friends, never in an "American," as the Indians I grew up with called "white" people.

Full of steaks, bacon, beans, potatoes, watermelon and beer, and feeling some shade-like relief from the blazing Cicada-driven-evening's slight drop in temperature, the father said I should saddle this boy's horse and "try" him out for myself.

Having brought what for these Missouri people was a wild New Mexican Indianized saddle, I complied, mounted, and felt the tense unhappiness of this horse's dislike of anybody but his childhood sidekick. Deliberately taking advantage of this, I put my heels into his fifth rib, causing the desired result of a pretty stiff series of crow-hops and one midair buck with a legitimately showy kick-out, after which he landed square legs locked and obstinate as if not planning on doing anything I asked. The boy was standing close-ish with his eyes piercing my soul, livid that I had caused him to look like a bad horse trainer when we both knew it was my own doing, though he didn't know I knew and figured I was just an asshole.

So in an attempt to assuage his proud heart, not the horse's—who was just fine—but the boy's, I swung the pony around to face the young man, and where nobody else could see I scrunched up my face and winked at him with one eye, which made him kind of almost smile.

"To be honest folks," I intoned through my very baconed breath to these sweet people, "I think there's too much horse for me in this animal and I don't think we're really a match." As I climbed down the horse cooperated by acting out his part in my ruse, skittering wild all over till the boy, grinning, grabbed his head. I unsaddled.

"Well sir," the father sounding very worried, "how much do you want for the mare 'cause I can't let you have her back, she's Tanya's dream horse for her birthday."

"What about that little fellow over there?" I said, pointing with my lips to the grulla who still had his New Mexico head glued in the corner of the pasture fence. "Would you consider him as our trade?"

It was all human silence under a blanket of loud cicadas, then the sound of a lady's voice yodeling in from the road: "Are you guys ready?" This was the neighbor who had come to deliver the health and transportation papers on the Paint horse they had assumed I was soon to haul away in exchange for Yeshi.

"Do you really want… Bubba?" Tanya painfully sang out. "My little Bubba, but honey, Bubba's our friend. Can we let him go? Plus he stumbles, he's lame somehow on his front. He only turns to the right, and what horse are you thinking of strapping your cases of beer onto in your forest rendezvous with the boys? I'm telling you we're not giving Yeshi back, she's mine!"

"Sir, she's right. This horse, as pretty as he is, is clumsy and dinky and wouldn't make much of a horse for you. I'm so embarrassed about the Paint bucking on you right out, but how can I send you home with such a messed up little horse and look myself in the mirror?"

"To me," I replied, "that little horse is just the right color and he's right for me, plus there's something about him that's hard to put your finger on that I like. He'll serve just fine as an even trade for Yeshi as far as I'm concerned."

And that part was accurate. At our place Yeshi had made herself a dangerous unwanted mess. Here, for these generous bacon-people, Bubba was a barely tolerated, kind of friendly mess. So I figured with this trade I not only didn't have to feel guilty for trading a "bad" horse to an unsuspecting recipient, since Yeshi and her new owner were so happy together, but also I was pretty sure what was good about Bubba would begin to surface once he was rematriated back in our mythic existence in dry New Mexico. So the trade really was pretty even!

The neighbor turned out to be the local vet who simply changed the name on the papers, and with Bubba, who was very tame, away we drove in the dark, trying to get past the sparking flint plains south of Kansas City by dawn where some people we knew said we could bivouac a couple of hours, let the horse out to graze and sleep before driving home and to digest a lot of bacon.

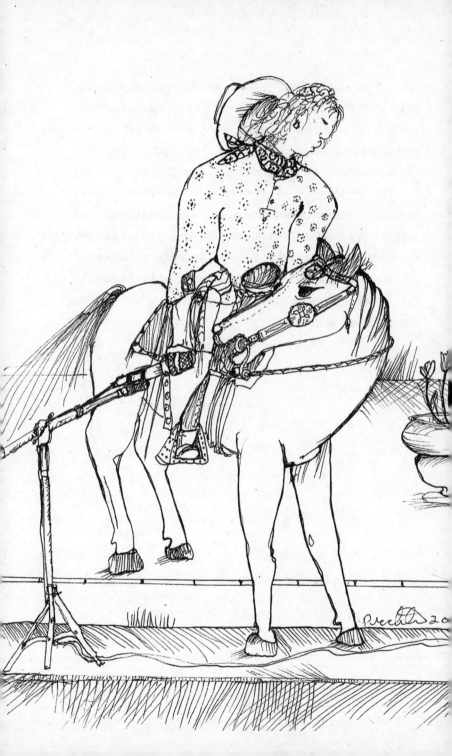

Chapter 17

Mohino

The antiquated mystic ornateness upon which the lyricism of my natural-born soul thrived would most likely have avoided deliberately naming any horse of mine… Bubba.

I knew the first motion toward healing this horse's lameness had to begin in finding him a life-promoting name, one that wouldn't keep him down. Bubba was a trivializing Redneck name, no doubt intended as an ironic pop comment on the big personality in his little body. But it was a cheap pickle-and-bacon-eater's name that made me wonder if this little seven-year-old horse hadn't been some kind of hardheaded "terror" in his past, thereby inspiring some less courageous person to brand him with a handle of diminution that would give the cowardly more courage to "handle" him.

To the drone of the truck and trailer wheels as we hauled our way across Kansas, Oklahoma, Texas and the eastern New Mexico plains, I sang out a liturgy of my favorite horse names, especially those I'd been saving for years in my mental archive for horses as yet unborn or unmet: Delbito, Chanate, Chaquegue, Cuzco, Beto, Ramoncito, Rayo, Yupe, Ilano, Matzin, Waymuk, Pancho, Paco, Percy, Piki, Pando, Zango, Elbeg, Dashik and a hundred more, but none of them would stick. By the time we were back in New Mexico and the little grulla was safely standing in his own corral eating our hay, the name Bubba was gone but he was still nameless. In desperation I almost named him "Nergui," which is a common Mongol name meaning "No Name"! But he didn't like that one either. We waited.

Then true to the form of all my other horses (to none of whom he was more than a very distant relation), by the time the first snow fell he'd faithfully grown out a beautiful fall coat and color pattern very distinct from his equally handsome summer outfit. Before the morning snow on his back melted, at a distance he looked for all the world like one of those small black basaltic mountains just north of us, each of which bore a dark ring of Piñon and Ponderosa trees at the cliff base, giving way toward the middle of the hill to a thick growth of tall golden grasses all the way to the peak, but with dark volcanic ground all the way up, matching this horse's winter colors exactly.

The wooded lower parts of these hills stayed dark all year round, but the big body-like mound rising out their dark ring changed colors with each season.

By springtime their new grass was blue green on the sides and top, which corresponded exactly in color to this new horse's summer coat of reflective steel blue. With his four dark steely legs and dark muzzle in the summer he looked just like one of these mountains in summer.

The winter colors of the mountains' grass-covered upper zones turned to a glistening golden straw growing out of a black ground, while the base remained an unchanged blue-green of evergreen trees on black basalt.

As a boy I always thought of these hills as gigantic animals, the humps of Grizzly Bears or Golden Buffaloes rising out of the earth, inside of which most of their royal selves waited quietly underground to eventually emerge rumbling at some later geological moment.

The New Mexican Spanish name for this particular color phenomenon in a mountain's annual appearance was *mohino*. In Spain, *mohino* originally referred to the bluish-green-goldish patina that bronze took on with age, which also accurately described this little horse's coat colors.

Since it's only right to ask someone if they want to be named this or that, I asked our new little horse:

"Hello new little Horse! Would you like to be known as Mohino?"

I was sitting on his back in the saddle when I put it to him. Like a brat he faked me out, feigning the demeanor of a beat down horse he lethargically turned his head as if to reply, then in a flash bit my knee and stared back at me smirking.

It was then that I remembered the other related meaning of Mohino, which when pronounced "properly" without the *h* sound was a term used by local mothers for their very young, whiny, unreasonable and spoiled children, especially when they were biting everything while cutting new teeth!

I interpreted this ambush of rude knee-biting as his smartass way of saying he was in agreement. So Mohino he became and Mohino he is to this day.

Old Blue had been the only horse I'd ever known with whom I could actually converse. Very talkative and quite a good thinker, he spoke mostly in dreams, but spoke also directly in my heart.

I'm sure everyone has known horses who were competent communicators in one fashion or the next. What I took for a "yes" from Mohino was not a yes, but just turned out to be his real rascally nature, for he was a rascal, just as able as Amarillento had been early on.

But Mohino *did* talk. He was raised in South Dakota and was of that particular school of Nordic communication which dictated one should never speak until spoken to, and even then only with a lot of consideration and single word responses. He was a sparse talker, but he did talk.

I remember conversing on a phone once with a famous cowboy from South Dakota, a horseman.

"Emmet, can I have a moment of your time?" I asked.

Long silence. Then:

"Why not," he said

"Do you think it would be alright with you if my wife and I came over to your place to look over a couple of those fillies you got up there by the Tower?"

A long silence, then:

"Sure."

"What would be the best time for you?"

A little silence, then:

"Anytime."

"How about midmorning?" I asked.

"Good," he replied.

Look forward to meeting you sir, we can't wait."

"Right."

And that's how it went in person too. He'd get very expressive at the sign off:

"Make sure you close all the gates," he'd expound.

"You bet," I'd reply. You had to really watch out 'cause this cold-country speech pattern was infectious.

Well that's pretty much how Mohino communicated. You had to keep your senses awake 'cause if you zoned out for even a second, you might miss what he said. Plus you had to frame your question such that it could be answered in one word or so. He was perverse like that but he was multilingual like Blue, and at least I had another horse that could talk.

"Mohino naq abanoum?" (Tzutujil Mayan for "What ya been up to?")

No reply.

"Mohino, nish na waj shin n koba pta 'yu?" (Would you be inclined to ride up to the shrines on the hill?)

Silence.

Then smiling, Mohino would very slightly twitch his head to the right, which meant "Hieach" (Tzutujil for "yup").

This little bronzy grulla was easy to catch, saddle up and bridle. Mohino loved all my silver, especially his own Diné-style silver bridle whose heavy bit he preferred. In the winter I always warmed the bit in my armpit before easing it into his soft little mouth.

But like they said, he stumbled a lot. It wasn't that he wouldn't turn to the left, he couldn't turn left 'cause it hurt him. He must've been injured in some way up in his shoulder or withers that healed in a way that made turning left too precarious, and if forced caused him to tumble to the ground.

In my homegrown notion of trying to slowly change this situation, I carried a hoof rasp in my *alforjas*, and every time before I rode him I very slightly trimmed each hoof in a way that forced his front feet to sit at new angles, which seemed to cause his one crooked front foot to break over differently and land in such a way that slowly, over a year, the tendons up and down his legs had adjusted enough that this foot seemed to no longer cause him the pain that had made him unable to turn to the left.

Though I trimmed all his feet in a way no experts advocated, gradually and gently I could get him to turn increasingly to the left and right, and he stopped stumbling altogether at a walk or trot. A canter was great fun with him 'cause he was very sparky and pretty agile, but every once in a while he'd wash out completely with no warning, and more than once we both ended up rolled upside down in the clumpgrass. So for the most part we took all the trails at a fast "Indian shuffle," for which he was the perfect expert of all time. We rarely ran except in emergencies, but that was truly nerve-wracking.

When he got strong enough we "just went up" the sides of the big mesa surrounding our little Ranchito. This was not lost on the rich little bandy-legged cowboy whose ATV Blue had rescued from the midstream mudhole. Turned out he was actually a former racehorse jockey and a very good rider, and earlier in the year he'd seen me on Mohino, stumbling on the slightest sandrise in the arroyos. True to his form this tough little man now wanted to borrow my hoof rasp, as if it magically had something that made horse's feet heal and "just go up"!

But like I intimated to Mohino's former owners, what was extraordinary about him was difficult to explain to people of today. The little grulla's most precious qualities were not in his riding and probably wouldn't command the respect his abilities received at our place. The modern "settler-culture's" definition of what horses are supposed to be and do has mostly to do with winning something, recreation, or money, not the Divine. And although a lot of what Western ranchers did on their horses was often impressive and pretty diverse, it mostly all came under the heading of "work or exhibition."

The truth is I never actually just "went for a ride" on a Horse. I always had a purpose beyond just riding for the fun of it. Where I grew up, anybody who looked like they were out taking a walk, if asked, was gathering herbs or hunting to provide meat (nobody *ever* hunted for sport); in the case of sacredly involved officials, they were giving offerings, making prayers, or gathering what the village needed from the wild heart of Nature to do their constant calendar of important ceremonies needed to spiritually maintain the people's relation with the Holy in Nature, a rather vast subject.

The same went for horse riding. Though we kids, once out of the scrutiny of any elder, definitely went tearing around joyriding on whatever horses upon whose backs we ended up on, we were still always officially out on some mission: to bring cows, water livestock, check fences, or certain sacred errands, but technically we were never "out riding" like purposeless, rich English gentlemen taking their cobs for a casual skedaddle up the bridle path to relax. We were taught to be proud of our work, to love our lives doing our work. Natives didn't work to amass a fortune so they could stop working a job they hated, and then go about doing nothing but relaxing. We relaxed by doing the work of being Native. We were admired for our abilities, not for our ability to escape having to work. Granted, our work was beautiful.

Like horses of any type, Mohino could very easily fall into a rut of daily routine habits and trails. If one day I had the audacity to vary our routine, it was always a fight to get him pointed into the new idea. But on the other side of that, this very trait made Mohino the best number one A-OK prayer-making horse I'd ever own 'cause he had a memory that took in the subtleties of sequence like no other creature I'd ever met.

Signed on years before as a spiritual man, I have always given and continue to give offerings to feed Deified Time as the Holy, feeding the spiritual heart of life-giving natural places. The first time I went mounted on Mohino to deliver my prayers in a river shrine for the health of the world or people, Mohino remembered my every move exactly. The next time when we arrived at these sacred precincts I no longer had to dismount to pray. I could remain in the saddle and while mounted have the free use of my hands to do whatever I needed. Mohino would stand as still as a mountain, then after listening to my prayers, without any prompting go automatically to the next exact spot in the sequence, and at the exact right interval turn to the next exact direction in the sequence. When I'd finished in a certain precinct I could just rest the reins on his neck, and he just by listening to the next set of prayers knew exactly when it was time for us to move on to the next precinct. Mohino paid so much attention to the subtleties of the motions and types of gifts I always gave in every shrine that with perfect timing he knew just when to proceed to the next place or when to go upstream or down! Mohino was a great help to me in the Church of the Holy in Nature and quite astounding to see.

The little grulla Mohino and I were a team of prayer-makers who could be seen up and down the hills or desert, in the stream, over the ice, all year long coming and going on these spiritually motivated missions. But we were never out just riding. That was beneath our dignity. But we did enjoy our work together. That's the way it was with us for a long period.

He was not a racehorse, or a great Cow Pony really, though we did herd some cattle for a while till my bull snuck around us one day while we were separating some of this bull's heifers, and picked Mohino with me on top up in the air with his hornless head, intending to toss the little horse square onto his side. This he almost accomplished, except Mohino, staggering from the blow, miraculously recovered and landed without stumbling. Mohino hit the ground running as we hightailed it out of that grumpy bull's territory with the bull in close pursuit.

Mohino was not so adamant about cattle work after that, so we stuck to praying. Blue had been the Cow Pony of all time.

Though not so good with cows, stumbly at a run, a rascally and irritating escape artist and a fine prayer horse, where Mohino uniquely excelled was anything that involved people. Rather harsh to other horses, he loved humans. It was spooky how quickly Mohino could discern one type of person from the next as far as their motives went. This talent was of great assistance while we were building our big adobe school hall on the Ranchito land.

When the big three- to four-foot-thick adobe brick walls of the old-style communal hall (a place for the people coming from all over to hear my lectures and learn ancient hands-on knowledge in my recently established school) had risen to over nine feet of the intended twelve feet and it was almost time to set the enormous vigas for the roof, we required more and more people with good hearts to place the adobe bricks, mix and haul the mud mortar, cut straw and more.

No human-made ruckus fazed Mohino in the least. No yelling, loud claps, hammering, chainsaws, dropped tools, tossed shovels, gunfire, car engines or tractors; nothing that spooked other horses threw him off.

The one policy I tried to maintain with everyone who was hired to work on this beautiful building was that they did so with a good heart. I didn't want any bad feelings or grudges to seep into any part of this Hall. It had to be made of good memories. If a conflict arose between workers, I wanted peace to be found before the work resumed. I didn't allow someone who disliked me or my family who ended up working on the building just because it was a "job" to continue unless that feeling was ameliorated. Only goodness should enter the work. If a worker thought this was a ridiculous demand, they didn't need to work with us.

Each day after Mohino and I had returned from feeding the Holy in the hills, we would wander down to the building site and ride right into the structure to check on things. For some horses this would have been a nightmare: a table saw would be whirring, a chainsaw or two buzzing away, cement mixers clanging, the thud of a floor tamper bumping up and down, hammers whanging and people yelling; then all of a sudden a stone saw would start up, slicing some quartzite flagstone with an ear-splitting, grating whine. Mohino as calm as a fossil clam would just saunter along without any flinching. People would ask me if he was deaf. He wasn't deaf at all, just a horse intent on even-headedness as an art form. Rare and wonderful. And very useful.

We'd ride up and chat with the different leaders and foremen to make sure they had what they needed and to see that all was peaceful. It was during one of these daily visits that I discovered Mohino's intense capacity to detect a false heart and hidden enmity in a person.

While walking along the still sand floor of the Hall whose walls were only a week from receiving their vigas (the crossbeams whose size would make the Hall one of New Mexico's unique structures), almost forty dedicated men and women, most of them facing away from us along the big walls, were laboring assiduously to raise those walls in time before the fall frosts, when traditional adobe work must cease.

As always I gave little Mohino his head and let him walk where he would. Of his own accord he'd stop behind each person, walk again and stop behind the next person, assessing each person's heart one at a time. As we passed the back of a young man in shorts with a beat-up Australian hat working eight feet up on the south wall, ten feet from the southeastern corner whose position Blue and I had measured in flowers, Mohino refused to proceed. Standing there like a block of marble he would only be moved to the right, which brought his cute little muzzle directly to the back of this hairy fellow's knees.

Mohino decided he should snort, and when he did he sent his breath point-blank tickling the back of this man's hairy legs.

Apparently this guy had no sense of humor, which I guess was the point Mohino was trying to make, for when he felt my horse's hot blast on the back of his calves, he spun around in an ugly mood ready to fight, hurling the mud mortar piled on his hawk right at Mohino. It exploded on Mohino's forehead, splattering all over both him and me. Undaunted, the little horse moved even closer.

"Sir," I asked calmly, "do I know you? Have we met?" I made it my custom to have spoken and shaken hands with every individual who'd signed up to work and I couldn't recollect ever having seen this mud-slinging character previously.

Out spewed a lot of uncreatively strung together obscenities whose burden of meaning exposed the fact that we hadn't hired him at all. He'd just wandered in, biding his time, plotting to get back at me in some way for something he claimed I'd once spoken during some radio interview.

"Come on sir, let's make peace. I don't allow any fighting or hatred in this hall whatsoever." But he didn't want to.

"You lazy asshole, you really think you're something riding around doing nothing up there on that stupid horse like some—"

"Sir, let's go take a walk outside the hall and discuss this, plus this horse isn't stupid at all and I'm not sitting 'up' anywhere; he's barely fourteen hands tall... Come on, let's go and talk about this somewhere else." He didn't want to move. He wanted to fight. But he did finally leave. He didn't want peace.

Mohino was smiling.

If ever two people were getting ready to blow, Mohino could smell it and we'd find them and stay until peace was established. After a while Mohino became the guarantor of calm 'cause when anyone saw him coming they made damn certain they were digging the work or Mohino would joyfully smell the pheromones of their bitterness and single them out! Plus nobody was ever sure when we might make a visit. Because of Mohino, our Hall was made by good-hearted people and had only Love in the walls.

Mohino was cute but not really a good ride. Unlike Blue, Mohino was practical, not exactly a mystic, but for me he was plenty magical, a horse of the most practical kind of magic.

Of course it stands to reason that after years of living as "little neglected Bubba" with his snout in a fence corner, foundering and lame from lush Missouri grass, once he was a desert hero he started to get a big head. Like Amarillento he'd get a wild hair and out of the blue let every horse and cow out of their corrals, mysteriously managing to open snaps not even I could open in the freezing weather, and after locking himself in Punk's corral, he'd stand there looking like an innocent victim of some prankster, which of course was none other than himself.

But it wasn't until our Hall, "The Lady" as it is called, was built and students, after parking their cars in a little place we'd cleared for the purpose right between our horse- and goat-filled corrals, came wandering down to sit and attend classes in the Hall that Mohino would develop his crowning talent!

It was not until the foundations were poured; the thick walls piled high; the viga roof beams laid; the latillas herringboned; the windows built and installed; the doorways made; the hinges, hasps, door handles, sleeve bolts and spikes hand-forged and clinched in; the cattail insulation piled in the roof; the dirt floor laid, pounded and polished; the wood stove welded and hauled in; the handmade rugs laid out; the sound system strung; the sound person seated behind her faders; the stage made ready; the chairs set; the sheepskins spread; and one hundred eighty people were sitting expectantly waiting for me to begin teaching that after hearing Mohino speak the biggest sentence of his life: "Martín, what do you say, let's ride together right into that big room and jump up on stage and you teach from my back"—I had the audacity to saddle up and do exactly that.

I'd made all four doors along medieval feasting hall guidelines, with big wood doorjambs, handmade goat milk and azurite paint, with doorways wide enough for a mounted person to ride through.

The "Equinox" doorway, however, was even big enough for two horses ridden side-by-side.

The great learning from riding all dressed up into the Hall, both Mohino and I in our silver and best togs, was the fact that most of the people sitting there didn't even notice there was a man on a horse riding down the aisle right next to them!

Nobody saw us. We weren't invisible—Mohino unlike Blue couldn't do that.

They just didn't see us!

My Hall was magical in a hundred ways and made especially so a horseman could ride in and back out, just as the old-time feasting halls and spiritual places had been for at least several thousand years in Europe, the Mediterranean, Africa, Central Asia, North Asia and Indonesia. People had registered to learn what I wanted to teach them in that Hall. But to do that they had to learn to see and hear and be right where they were. For that to happen they had to learn about themselves by learning about the incredibleness of the world. Most often the grandest learning came from things that are right in front of us waiting. But... if we are so dulled by modern life to only see what we are taught should be there, and bored with that, then we see nothing of the majesty of what's standing right there waiting.

And Mohino with me on his back were right there in front of all the people waiting, all the new students chitchatting, "networking", impressing each other, yet nobody but two or three saw us, and they were standing one foot out the door, jaws dropped, eyes wide, terrified!

When I directed Mohino to jump up onto the low-lying stage, before I could even turn around, just like his grandiose self had been waiting his whole life to do, Mohino very loudly introduced himself by screaming louder than he'd ever screamed before, right into the M80 mic whose sound through the PA made even the window glass shudder, blowing the complacent assumptions of one hundred and seventy-seven people right out of their pores. Some were scared, some chagrined, others delighted, but most were amazed at themselves for being any of the above, for not having seen what they didn't expect to see.

• • •

That was the first lesson I taught in the Hall.

Mohino just loved being in crowds of people, and really, really liked having his own stage with everybody watching. But what he really, really, really, really, really liked was having his own microphone and yelling and scaring everybody.

After that, every once in a while we'd go to class together, not to scare people but to reassure them that the world was still a live place and not all of us were conquered, contained or virtual projections. Mohino, who was so calm and cute around people, was also, like his rider, a fierce little king in love with the indigenous beauty of all our souls, which have no respect for modernity's menu of mediocrity and life viewed on a screen. Unlike Blue and his relatives, Mohino didn't act, but he loved being himself on stage.

Unfortunately, there were those with no sense of humor and charm, people with unbending definitions of what's what, who couldn't see the gift of the lesson much less receive it, who thought Mohino and I were just acting to get applause in some choreographed, self-aggrandizing pop spectacle for effect.

At least I was flexible enough to learn, for after that I refused to allow any of my Horses to get their souls singed by coming too close to those who weren't yet ready to understand the heroic epic souls they were actually seeing, who didn't yet see with the eyes of their own Indigenous Souls; and for that reason I am now consigned to teach in our beloved Hall alone on foot.

But, Mohino, still today always asks if I think the people have learned enough so he can come with me to class again.

Blue loved cameras, Mohino still misses the mics.

Chapter 18

Punk Straightens Out a Tractor

Punk's mansion, his roomy six-foot-high welded-steel stallion pen was the first corral you drove by whenever entering our Ranchito from the little highway.

This big corral was really only a suggestion of where I preferred Punk would keep himself so as to avoid any collisions with drone-brained drivers zooming down the highways, as had so often happened with other local ranchers. The bow-legged cowboy and my friend Apolanario had between them lost at least five mother cows and seven riding-horses that year already due to tourists crossing their lands who neglecting to close the gates behind them, allowed animals to wander up onto the dangerous highway, where, crossing that thoroughfare in the night, they were killed by semi trucks.

"Suggestion", I say, for every breeding season Punk routinely smashed to pieces a corral panel or two made of three-inch welded-steel pipe as if they were orange crates just because he was wound up and needed to do his job: something important like breed, fight, lay down the law; something fierce, forceful and noisy—all necessary stallion things to his thinking.

Except for myself and my family and Marilyn, Punk, who was almost thirty years old now, regarded most other humans as barely recognizable life forms. Punk didn't initially dislike people; after all, there were several hundred students driving right past him the whole year long.

Punk didn't see people as people but as an ubiquitous aspect of all the metal vehicles that rolled down the highway and in and out of our land. People were some soft-skinned, detachable organic inner component of the beetle-like cars and trucks that could exit their stationary shells at will, chirping and laughing, then wander about independently of their carapaces doing aimless bug-like things, until eventually, re-entering their husks, they buzzed off and away.

He didn't even bother to look at them much because all Punk really cared about were girl horses. If the breeze carried so much as a hint of the perfume of a mare in heat somewhere in the county, Punk would pace his fence line for hours thinking about girls, forgetting to eat, marching himself skinny.

Punk knew those of us who were his people like he knew the other horses or dogs, or the mocking ravens or the wind. He didn't know us as parts of cars! We were part of his living everyday world. Punk had no particular suspicion or loathing for all the vehicles or their people, for he knew they were also part of some world somewhere, so in the beginning he tolerated them all. But the articles of his amnesty to vehicles did *not* extend to our red tractor. Punk had it in for the tractor. He could wait, but someday he knew he would kill our little red Kubota 3430.

Of all Punk's peculiarities this was one of the strangest.

At first I thought it was the rattle and rumbling roar of the tractor that set him off, but he didn't like it sitting still with the engine off either! Then I thought maybe it was the red color, or the shape, or the size, and maybe those things all contributed, but Punk's reason for his need to battle the tractor turned out to be a completely logical Barb stallion's reaction to a situation whose intricacies made me love these old-time horses even more, even if it had become life imperiling to drive "our" tractor anywhere near pushy old beautiful Punk!

Like everything else in the Natural World, whose mysteries you really want to get close to and maybe understand, with Horses like Punk you have to first empty your head of all you think you know, then be willing to watch patiently forever while keeping all your Nature-supplied senses awake—your ears, your eyes, your nose, your intuition—and with your sense of wonder try to learn to recognize what you're seeing when it happens or you'll miss it. And of course you must be able to laugh, especially at yourself.

I remember one summer when crews of students were generously coming in to "re-mud" with red clay the Hall, now a couple of years old, which like all *real* adobe buildings needed a fresh layer of beautiful adobe layered over the cracks caused by rain, snow, freeze and winds, a big Red Racer Snake fell in love with me somewhere and kept finding her way into our house and into our bed and into my pillowcase, laying rolled up all calm waiting for me to show up at night to sleep! The Natives where I come from know all kinds of animals fall in love with people, and mythologically the Racer had originally been a jilted young woman who in her rage and grief had turned herself into this elegant Snake. And this one was determined to sleep between me and my wife!

The Racers we have in our area are not represented in any guidebooks or scientific monographs, for ours are mostly pinkish and golden sand colored with maroon bands the width of adult hands cinching their bodies every eight inches or so, alternated with plum and ochre bands. They are blessed with ridge-ribbed bellies whose pronounced rings look like ladders, and when they glide across the sand they move very swiftly, they "race", the friction of their belly scales on the earth emitting a unique Dopplered whistle loud enough to even startle the horse you're riding. They don't like to be seen and can nip a pretty good gash into your hand with their rows of little razory teeth if they assess your motives to be hostile to their welfare, but this lady Racer was calm and determined to steal me away from my wife.

Racers can climb adobe walls and trees to raid bird nests high up. They also swim and hunt in water, which is amazing considering they are desert dwellers.

They get moving fast from the get go, jumping right out from a lie-down—when they move they don't undulate back and forth like Bull Snakes or Rattlers, but shoot straight ahead like whistling arrows.

I'd already deported this lady Snake at least five times using the pillowcase as a convenient transport, seeing as she was already in it and just loved doing things with me. After releasing her way out in the bush, within a day or two she'd be right back in my bed!

I'm not sure how she did it or how she entered the house 'cause we kept the doors firmly tight to keep out rodents and to avoid the same situation with a visiting Rattlesnake.

One of my students, William Robichaud, a gifted biologist who at that time specialized in studying Southeast Asian mammals, in particular rare Rhinoceroses, was a member of the crew of students who'd generously volunteered to re-mud our Teaching Hall during the same two weeks I was continually hauling my would-be Snake paramour to release out of my pillowcase into the bush.

"Hey Martín, what's with the pillowcase, what do you have in there?" Bill yelled from the tables where the mudders were feasting on the food Hanna had cooked in our mud ovens. He could tell I was toting an animal.

Not wanting a crowd, I called him over and explained I had a Racer Snake who wanted to be my lover, and was planning on releasing her next to a shallow Cattail-lined Frog pond that lay on our Ranchito toward the Greenstain River.

"I've never seen a live Racer, can I see her?"

"Not now, these snakes are too fast, she'd get out!" I said. "Come with me, when we get to the pond you can see her as I let her go into the water, but don't blink or look away or you'll miss seeing her; they're really quick."

In the times when and where I grew up it was considered necessary to make jokes and I was always joking, but this time I meant what I said. But Bill was laughing as he followed us to the pond's edge, which was actually barely within sight of the mudders' delicious picnic.

"Now keep your eyes on my hands and this sack and don't take your eyes off of it."

I lowered the pillowcase, and just as I was preparing to open it and release the beautiful Snake, someone yelled to Mr. Robichaud, asking if he wanted some tea up at the feast.

He looked up for a nanosecond to reply, and when he instantly resumed his stare the lady Snake had already shot into the water and utterly disappeared. He'd missed it!

He started swearing at himself, amazed at the truth of that snake's rapidity. He knew the naturalists' reports said they only move at five or six miles per hour. But that's nonsense, these reptiles can really move.

Calming him and pointing to my ears I signed for us to listen instead, and within a second a lot of bird screaming came from inside the Reeds toward where we crept. Bill got to see the Racer snatch a Red-winged Blackbird fledgling and dive like a sea monster back into the drink to emerge side-opposite, whistling into the Cottonwood thicket.

You blink. You missed it. You blinked? Alright, keep listening and you'll hear it, as the old men would always tell us. You gotta supple your mind, refine your hearing, start to allow the world to teach you.

* * *

Punk's first surprise attack on the little red tractor came when a good-hearted fellow who worked for us had decided to use the tractor to clear the manure out of a seasonally occupied corral adjacent to Punk's palatial stronghold, where the Mares lived when we brought them in from the Beaver-land to breed.

This mares' corral was big and used only a couple of weeks a year, and I'd never felt the need to disturb the mares' little ridges of road apples. Most mares, unlike stallions, are very democratic about where they lay their manure, but my Mares were wild-descended Barbs and they made ridges. Punk made pyramid piles; the Mares made manure ridges.

Because Northern New Mexico most of the year is dry, there is no urgency to clear large corrals of horse manure; it dries on its own to form a sweet-smelling fibrous blanket that can easily be gathered three times a year to make compost.

Except for those times we were on the road, Hanna and I since forever tended to all our animal's needs by ourselves: feeding, watering, trimming hooves, riding, deworming, repairing fences and corrals, cracking ice in the water troughs during winter, separating mothers and foals, chasing off wild dogs, and of course cleaning corrals.

But because the school now needed my presence and books needed writing that had publishing deadlines and children were born who needed our attention, hired hands, most of them wonderful, took up doing some of our chores.

When I was cleaning my own horses' corrals it never seemed prudent, kosher or even necessary, and definitely not kind, to move Punk from his corral kingdom and haul away the sacred stallion piles he so deeply coveted and whose construction he so ardently labored over for so long, so I never cleaned his corral. Plus, when you looked at it "his" way, his corral was "clean" because all the manure was already perfectly stacked!

I felt the same way about the adjacent mares' corral. Though at first it seemed to me to be a more casual issue, I'd never bothered to haul off any of the mares' ridges as they blended so thoroughly with the sand and winds.

But the new helper that month was a bit of a "neatnik" from the city trying hard to be an alternative "cowboy" if you will, and he was bound and determined that by the end of his first two weeks on the job all the corrals would be manure-free if it was the last thing he ever did.

And by most definitions of a "clean corral" this fellow had achieved exactly that, minus the mares' presently unoccupied breeding pen and Punk's adjacent mansion which I'd told him to leave for me to do later, though I only said so to make him feel good about how much he'd accomplished, and so he could move on to other more pressing chores.

But to achieve a "sense of closure," as he later told me, he went ahead and, disregarding my directive, without bowing to King Punk or asking his permission, this silly man opened up the panels of one side of the mares' corral big enough to drive in one of our trucks, and returning with the tractor proceeded to unceremoniously slice into the mares' bank of accumulated manure from the last six years with the front-end loader. Bucket by bucket, he commenced to dumping whatever he excavated into the truck bed like he'd done in all the other corrals.

Punk didn't like this one bit and began circling his corral madly, screaming and battering what steel pipe panels stood between him and the man on my tractor diligently cleaning away.

When Punk's complaint had no effect, Punk ran harder and harder, and finally flopping his two front feet over the top rung of his six-foot container, just like when he was a bratty little stud colt, he wiggled all of his thirty-year-old self completely over the fence, landing square and able. With teeth bared Punk immediately charged the moving tractor just as it was approaching the truck to let off its sixth bucketload.

Rearing up, Punk landed one hoof on the tractor hood and the other onto what would've been the driver's lap if he hadn't had the adroitness to see what was coming and dive from his seat to roll onto the ground, where he got to his feet and ran to find me, shaking and bewildered.

I was on stage in our big mud Hall, talking away to the crowd, teaching as always, when someone brought me word that Punk had escaped and was busy strutting and screaming and pummeling my tractor all to hell.

Punk woke from his trance a bit when he heard my voice, enough so that when I opened his corral gate and firmly suggested that he return back into his own "house", he eventually complied.

Afterward, no matter what, if Punk could see or hear that innocent unassuming tractor anywhere, he would rile himself into a mad rage. This was all very strange because up to that moment he couldn't have given half a Sand Cricket fart for that tractor. Now it was his enemy *#1*.

None of this would have been more than the emergence of yet another in the repertoire of Punk-specific quirks to remember when dealing with this mature stallion, except for the reality that now I couldn't find anybody willing to brave the cleaning of our corrals for fear that powerful, crazy old horse would come dangerously storming out to kill them.

In reality Punk was only a danger if he could see the tractor. And he had no beef with the driver, just the machine. Nevertheless, this still left a dozen other corrals whose needs anyone could have addressed without Punk getting after them, but nobody would do it.

So after tying up Punk to a big, thick, ancient Juniper post buried six feet in the ground, I took care of cleaning all the corrals within his view, leaving the mares' corral and his home mansion untouched. This worked out alright, but it was all a fascinating turn of weirdness, this overnight anathema Punk had for tractors after thirty years of relative tractor peace! I just figured it to be one of those mysterious obsessions geriatric horses take on: seeing enemies only they can see but nobody else can, or living in another dream world of wild events, etc. Modern people care more about humans than animals, and so their old folks are more famous for their old-age mind quirks; most horse people, on the other hand, never see this in their horses because they euthanize old horses when they're past "useful" age, or they keep their quirky old animals stoned, just like they do old people in nursing homes! Bad. But at our place all our "old" horses got to live out their quirky old trips by being useful to the herds.

All that being said, it turned out I was mistaken about the tractor and His Lordship, the great King of our new herd, Punk, and it was on one of our visits to check on the welfare of the big-bellied Mama Horses and Blue and Amarillento, living the good life out on the wild Beaver-land, that Blue woke me up to what was really happening!

Though his eyesight had become compromised enough to cause him to have to interpret what he thought he was seeing instead of recognizing what his cones registered, Blue's smell and his ears became even sharper and more dependable, picking up where his blue eyes had left off.

His thinking remained as clear as dew drops dripping off the Juniper branches at dawn, and together we could still converse in each other's hearts, better than ever.

Blue was going on thirty-three years old and had, as you might imagine, never given up his ability to make himself invisible. For the joy it gave him to see if we really still loved him, lately whenever we visited the wild Beaver-land, knowing perfectly the sound of our truck arriving for over a mile away on the unnamed dirt road, Blue would hide himself or even drive his whole "herd" somewhere hidden, knowing we'd be desperately running around trying to find them, afraid some terrible fate had befallen our horses when we couldn't locate any of them.

On this occasion we found only the "girls" and Amarillento. Blue remained at large. But after several hours of searching, tracking, sniffing manure (not to brag, but like a horse I knew them all by the shape of their feet and the smell of their droppings), we feared that the old Horse had finally died, been taken down and eaten by Lions or shot and his carcass lying somewhere as yet undetermined. Though we'd come hungry from home and were famished, we were so sick at heart at having lost Blue that none of us could eat the incredible picnic Hannita had spread out.

Then, after a few moments of sad moping sitting on the feast blanket, right next to us from behind a short stand of riverside Red Willows, Blue's proud scream reverberated through the canyon and out he shuffled, his hooves grass polished, his mane encrusted with burrs and a big smile on his face. Blue just wanted to be sure we'd really missed him, as if he were really dead. He never quit; it was different every time he did it, and after hours of fruitless searching we always fell for it. I'm sure he actually was invisible until he was certain we really cared!

After he'd drunk a cup of tea with us, I tied my big red silk scarf around his neck, behind his funny red ears, and dragged him off a ways onto the flat, away from the river so we could converse to the intermittent tinkle of a Bobolink.

When I asked him about Punk's all-of-a-sudden need to ambush the tractor, Blue said nothing at first, but then smiling like a Grasshopper on a cabbage leaf, he spoke:

"Don't be an idiot, Martín, you've been hanging around too many cyber-brained people. Think like you used to, back when we together made that big white mule that Civil War reenactor impersonating an officer was riding lie down with the angry "officer" still in the saddle, and go sound asleep till the next day." (Another tale for some other time.) "Remember how you did it?! With what?"

"With magical historical smells in Deer tallow I rubbed on his face." (The mule's.)

"Right," Blue snorted and smiled, remembering his part; how he'd talked to the mule while "Colonel Sibley" read me the riot act about interfering in their "war games" by pulling up their tent stakes while they slept, which I had no hand in, but of which I was fully accused without trial. It was Conrad Purdy who'd done it and told the "soldiers" it was me. I guess they didn't have anyone to reenact a sentry!

"Well, with Punk it's the same thing," Blue intimated.

"How is it the same thing?"

"History by smell, that's what I mean!"

I sat down on the edge of the bluff's red clay soil, Blue's big hooves next to my thighs, and thought a while.

"You mean that by digging into and hauling away manure from that little ridge of the mares' droppings from the last ten years of Punk's breeding of mares in that pen, we were inadvertently hauling away Punk's history, destroying his past?"

Blue cocked his head a centimeter toward me, giving me a look of contempt while rolling his eyeballs: "Christ Almighty, Martín, I know we are all romantics, but don't be such a maudlin ninny. No… your worker wasn't hauling *away* Punk's history. By digging in those manure ridges you guys were *opening up* Punk's history, causing all his history and some of yours to actually reappear right here, right now in our lives. I'd think of all people at least you would've understood this."

In his old age Blue was more exasperated by human dumminess than ever.

"You know full well that Horses, especially "our" horses, can "see" with their noses peering right into times past. That ridge of mare manure was a bank of smells, smells perfectly filed in chronological order, filed in stratified layers of the annually accumulated droppings and urine that mares pee and poop during their heat cycles to signal to the stallion their readiness to breed and the exact state of their approaching moments of fertility. You know 'cause you arranged it this way, for that corral was for all those years only for mares getting ready to be with Punk, who was waiting to enter from the adjacent corral. So every little stratum in that manure ridge that formed in there not only had each mare's olfactory signature, but the historical smell of Punk's urine "reply" to each mare's pheromonal urine message soaked into that layer and buried, preserved with the next layers accumulating on top in the following seasons.

"Horses read the world with their noses, *especially* stallions. By digging into that ridge of perfectly stratified fertility-sequence manure made *only* by Punk himself and *his* Mares over time, your naughty little tractor was making all of what transpired in those past times rise back up out of the ground, to come alive again in Punk's soul and body by the powerful effect of their smells on his mind.

"Those smells were all in the tractor's bucket, each mare's heat, his own stallion musk from those times emanating from the tractor.

"Now my cousin Punk, as wonderful as he is, just like the time he thought he saw an enemy stallion in a window and attacked it when it was his own image all along, doesn't recognize that the ancient stallion aroma coming from the tractor's lift bucket is in reality Punk's very own ancient stallion aroma. Punk thinks that whatever the tractor actually is, the tractor smells like a legitimately dangerous stallion interloper stealing his Mares in heat, whose ancient smell is also emanating from the manure in the tractor bucket!" Blue snorted, squinting his wild old eyes. He continued:

"Well, try to see the tractor from Punk's eyes. The tractor does have four limbs: his tires. The tractor is pushy and like a stallion doesn't listen when confronted. The tractor smells like a younger stallion, Punk himself. He has a head—the bucket—and like a stallion the tractor scurries around all over with a guy sitting on him riding him like a stallion of some kind. So the tractor, while making hideous, antagonistic rattling and rumbling noises, is kind of stallion-like and even smells like a stallion. Therefore?"

"So as far as Punk is concerned that tractor *is* just a weird-looking stallion, an asshole invader into Punk's territory."

"But check it out: the tractor doesn't have Punk's smell today, but his smell from years previous, so the way Punk reads all this makes his present-day jealous self pick a fight with his own historical self! Punk is defending Mares of the past by fighting his own self from the past in the form of a noisy little red tractor!"

To make sure I understood Blue rephrased it:

"By sensible stallion olfactory reckoning, to defend the Mares he smelled in the tractor-hauling-manure mix, Punk was ardently fighting the tractor as his own historical self as an invader from the past!"

Amazing.

I felt so silly to have misunderstood my beautiful Punk. How many other Horse's actions have been grossly misconstrued in this world? Humans were better off floating elegantly in their cultural boats of ancient magic stories than sinking foundered from following the simple-minded navigations of civilization's lost boat of rationalist assumptions.

Chapter 19

Musashi High Up in His Cave

From the very first, having chosen and accepted Punk to be the Father of our emerging herd meant we were agreeing to cherish and shelter a force of Nature from a time long before our own.

I knew that somewhere there had to be people who still lived close to the Earth, who retained the more original, ancestrally intact human mind that continued to understand that memory doesn't actually live isolated as something mechanically stored in any "brain". There had to be people somewhere who still remembered that memory lives only in constant electric motion, in a back and forth pulse of simultaneously renewing plasmic echoes between our entire body's nervous system, including the brain, and the equivalent myriad memory places in the Earth as a body, with all Her "life remembering" creatures. Punk could not be the only creature left on Earth who needed to be understood in such a way.

When Blue opened my head and heart to understand what Punk's nobly originated vendetta against our tractor really was, I was also able to then recognize how Punk's continued agitated demeanor, even far away from the tractor, was not any kind of surprise development in Punk. For Punk had not actually changed at all and was still made of the same handsome and principled substance.

Punk hadn't changed all of a sudden, but his situation had changed because our life's situation had changed, with the recent influx of hundreds of students, supply vehicles for the school, and our own children being born.

It was I who hadn't noticed how we had caused Punk's daily reality to change.

Punk wasn't aggravated, he was agitated. Like any wild herd stallion he was trying to find a way to protect me and my family and all the horses of his herd from what he perceived as an outside threat, in the form of all the students, to the former peace and wellbeing of our little Ranch.

What had to change was my ability to better see and admire the natural logic of how Punk's thirty-year-old, always honest, Pleistocene-derived stallion mind negotiated his first exposure to the ruckus of modernity's smells and sounds coming in with the hordes of students and their cellphones, their city vibes, their strange city-style-body motions, perfumes, cars, beeps, tweets, yells, chatter, laughter and general oblivious disregard for the presence of our "animals" as anything more than a decorative retro-prop, like an Amish wheelbarrow planted with petunias. They could not see Punk was very real, fierce, alive, dangerous and the literal "King" of all the horses.

Most of the students were citified or suburban people who still needed to be dunked into the Earth-living reality of their own forgotten ancestral mythic past—a past from which their own people would not even have survived to become people today if not for the ancient prominent presence of large animals in their own ancestral stories and mythic existence. For most students, animals were at best a minor detail of life. The people who had come to learn from me had forgotten that they descended from cultures for whom Horses were their central concern. These students still needed to first learn how to recognize the deep reality of real Horses, then learn how to be around real Horses, and then maybe how to be *with* real Horses.

The students, of course, had no idea what a threat they had become to Punk. But Punk didn't pity them, he was standing guard anyway. What can you do? I loved them all. It couldn't be helped.

To avoid any mishaps, every couple of months while the school was in session I took the precaution of hauling out all the horses, minus Yampa, Mohino and Punk, to graze and temporarily live with the rest on the magic Beaver-land.

This was better for the welfare of the horses, who like natural humans easily fell sick from people's untutored stares treating them like objects or zoo animals. Our curious foals were more susceptible to damage by being fed odd byproducts of people's lunches, including carrot shavings, kombucha marc, cough drops and barley sprouts. I don't know who teaches city people that Horses are garbage disposals or some kind of peasants' pigs that should eat their table scraps and throwaway crud like their lap dogs do. Horses eat wild grass, herbs, plants and some bark.

Until students learned how to be with the animals, I figured it would be safer for both the horses and humans if I kept the horses far away. Especially for their little kids, all of whom for the most part had grown up "watching" Nature behind a TV screen or at arm's length in a manicured park, and for whom the world was still some animated cartoon irreality. Our place was a very real, beautiful but dangerous neighborhood, both culturally and naturally. It not only amazed me how far modern humans had slipped away from true natural awareness of both their surroundings and themselves in their surroundings, but also how proudly they served the banner of their alienated drift away from Nature as if their ignorance were a sign of "progress".

They didn't know they didn't know that none of my horses, cows, goats, dogs or barn cats were hobby animals put behind fences as exhibits for their viewing pleasure. My Barb Horses, as handsome as they are, were not part of a petting zoo, but mostly unbroke, half-wild, hard-headed little broncs, who could bite, strike, eat the upholstery off your car seat or kick out a headlight just for the sound of the tinkling glass.

After a couple of years, many of these new students would fill with vision and rewire themselves with spiritual nerves enough that even if they had no ability with the animals surrounding them as they walked into the enchantment of our land, they at least would learn to see and respect what they might not yet truly grasp, and maybe even finally bow their heads to Punk and know why.

But for now most of the horses were always out and away until the school sessions ended, at which time Hanna, myself and the family would retire to the creek's edges in the magic Beaver-land to unwind from teaching, have a little feast, and then gather the "home" horses into our trailer and bring them back to live at the Ranchito until the next class was scheduled at which time we'd haul them back out again. Except, of course, for Blue, Amarillento and the breeding mares, who were now more or less residents of the Magic land.

Of all our horses, Amarillento was now the eldest, and though we left him with Blue and the Mares on the wild land, he lived his life off and away from the herd, grazing and drinking on his own, always on the east side of the stream.

Amarillento was almost thirty-four and had crazy eyesight. I think he could actually still see pretty well, but preferred to roll a different vision of life inside his head, way behind his eyes causing him to see things nobody else could see. The same went for what his cute horn-like ears heard, adding in the sounds and sights of a world only he and the Goddess of Horses could perceive into those of the world we all lived in.

The old yellow warrior's body was in good shape, but at times he'd suddenly face strange directions, listen, then run like a maniac for a quarter mile, where, after arriving at a little hollow of red earth covered in Cota flowers, he'd take on the ground itself, raising a cloud of dust, pounding and nipping, bravely fighting some demon on the land none of us could see.

He'd generally wear out the phantom, and when the dust had cleared, without blinking go back and pick up where he'd left off grazing.

Because you could never really predict when one of these demons might pop up in your trail and a skirmish might ensue, we no longer found it prudent to saddle Mari and ride him in close around the land like I still did with his sidekick Old Blue.

Whenever we came out to the Magic Land he'd generally be off in the flats on the bank opposite, standing, unmoving, thinking. We'd call his name till it echoed continually off the cliffs behind him, but Amarillento would never give us any attention. He'd always been that way: pretending he didn't hear you, but then during our picnic in the Yampa swale he'd inevitably thunder right up to us, just at the moment Blue came pulling into view as well finally emerging from the shadows where he had predictably hidden himself just to see if we still missed him!

Then we'd all have a good visit, giving each other a lot of hugs and advice, and after both horses had drunk up all our tea they'd saunter off, each in his own direction. Amarillento would gallop splashing back through the creek, while Blue pulled himself up the bluff to where all "his" Mares were occupied carving the smooth blue paint off my truck hood with their lower incisors, probably more for the "crunch" and "squeak" of doing it than the taste.

By the following spring and on my subsequent visits, I couldn't locate Amarillento anywhere. Maybe he'd been killed by Lions, for three times in his life I'd found him deeply raked by the talons of a Lion trying to drop him, and now in his old-age-youth maybe he'd finally fallen prey to a family of Lions.

I didn't want this to be the case 'cause I loved circling arms around the neck of my companion of our crazy earlier exploits, but still I hoped that when Blue and Amarillento had to die they would do so heroically, on their own terms on the wild land, merging into the Earth that birthed and fed them with little suffering. If Lions or a Bear ate them back into the belly of the Wild Flowering Earth, then they would've been elegantly served by Life for all their devoted service to me. Many vets had suggested putting them down to avoid either from slowly starving to death, but both had so far remained fat and able.

But the problem was, every time I came and Mari was missing, his tracks, which were unmistakable for their shape and size, emblazoned the mud the entire east side of the creek by the big Beaver dams. So it seemed he was still around somewhere, but where was he keeping himself?

That following summer while driving out of the canyon on the unnamed dirt road, I encountered Mando and his dogs "fixing" a fence to let his cows into someone's land to graze. When I asked him about Mari, "Your little butter-colored Mustang? Yeah I saw him yesterday, he was standing right there by that big square boulder."

"Really? I can't find him anywhere."

"He comes down from those cliffs, I think, every two or three days to drink and eat and goes back up somewhere. Who knows."

The following autumn, while leaving off our herds from the Ranchito in preparation for the influx of students, we were still unable to locate that wild-brained, old yellow hero horse anywhere on our magic Beaver-land.

The resident Mares were all at home and calm, their beautiful bellies starting to look almost pregnant. Blue, off a ways as usual and getting furry for winter, was busy carrying out his appointed jobs of being a "formidable presence" and grazing the rare thigh-high Grama after a summer of endless moisture.

271

Amar-ee-yento-to-to-to…

We called Amarillento until his name echoing from our side of the canyon's cliff also echoed off the canyon's opposite walls in a continuous back and forth rolling music. All our yelling was just our need to express out loud our immense love for the missing gelding, not from any hope he would actually appear, for unlike most of our Barbs, for his entire life Amarillento had never once responded to his name!

All ranchers in the West keep binoculars in their trucks and saddlebags. My big ones were slung from my seat in the truck, and with these my eyes searched every visible cranny and slope in the canyon walls.

From the buffalo robe on top of which Hanna and I lounged, boiling up tea and eating our picnic, I swept the lenses very methodically to survey every altitude of complexity of the vertical stone of the canyon sides, looking hard for the crazy little gelding.

The endless herds of ever-morphing clouds that ran up and over the capstone, in certain light and speed, often caused the clouds to stand still and the stones to take off running and undulating like a huge stone snake. It was wonderful and mystical, its unexpected wild motion forcing most people to close their eyes to keep from falling over dizzy and disoriented.

But the shadows of any kind of clouds on a sunny day or a moonlit night always caused all sorts of previously unnoticed formations of rock, caves, ledges, or vertical spires to jump out from hiding, then vanish again into the background.

The improbable growth of a one-hundred-foot Ponderosa or Fir anchored right into the stone of a bare capstone spire would leap out, or a cave you'd never seen with a Scrub Oak–choked entrance all of a sudden appeared, then two minutes later, blend right back into the magic matrix of what was usually visible.

Endless changing shapes morphed way up there on the miles of the east rock wall as well. Faces, heads, eyes, hands, giant Mountain Sheep horns, Gods of every kind. In one of these very ephemeral revelatory mutations of ever-shifting shapes in the sweep of my field glasses, I thought I might have for a split second, from the corner of my vision, seen what seemed to be a kind of detached horse's head poking unnaturally, almost weirdly square out of a gigantic slab of solid sandstone way up in a vertical wrinkle on the canyon side.

I spoke low and excited. "Ah Tza' Aht gowa." (There you are! Is that you?)

Hanna took a look.

Neither of us could really make the big horse head match up to what we knew of Amarillento, and we both doubted our imaginations until the head pulled right into the rock and disappeared before our eyes!

It was as if a kind of spirit aspect of a Horse had his head poking out of the matrix of solid stone.

Blue yelled out, then Kotona, then six mares yelled.

After which the smell of a fish-eating Bear came in on us, along with the tinkling clatter of scree sliding and slabs of rock thudding and groaning.

Always there were Bears here.

Then right from where the timber left off at the base of the cliff, and the prairie middle ground of Wild Oregano, Estafiate and Grama Grass took up, a horse screamed—and out popped Amarillento, nose in the air, crashing down the remainder of the slope, galloping like his former self; where after disappearing into the willows and then the splashing sound of a horse cruising through the creek at a run, there he was "sliding into first" right in front of us, just in time for tea!

Amarillento was definitely still here.

Though alive and always around somewhere unseen, when he was seen, he never again entered the company of the herd. When Amarillento would appear, he and Blue might touch noses but that was it, off one of them would thunder, then the other, Blue to the herd, Amarillento to where only the Holy knew.

Among animals who in the wild customarily live in groups, like Coatis, Elk, Bison, Camels, Horses, Gorillas, Prairie Dogs and many more, the very rare old age presence of any truly old male who has survived life and predators is usually lived out in an utterly changed existence off on his own, away from the group. They eventually die of starvation or just from general equipment atrophy, finally providing a meal for all the Eagles, Vultures, Magpies, Mice, Lions, Coyotes, Foxes, Badgers, Bears, Beetles, Porcupines (they like the bones) and others right where they fall.

That Amarillento was actually living out his old age following this ancient romantic tribal tradition made my heart full of gratitude to the Holies and Life Fate who made it so my old horses could do what they were meant to do, just as nomadic people and their horses have done for thousands of years. The people of today are so proud of being lost. No need for us to stay that way.

All of this was grand for Amarillento, and though he was definitely still here, that day after he'd finished his tea, as I watched him mosey back to the creek, stand in the middle up to his knees, stare off into the south, take a big long drink and then, water dripping from his jaws, turn and run like a Leopard disappearing back into the timber of the natural canyon walls, his crash and tinkle being all we could discern of his ascent until that too melted beneath our audial detection into the groaning chant of the canyon's eternal breeze, I don't think what he was up to had yet entered my consciousness.

When we had seen in the binoculars what we figured was his head way up in the rocks and saw him after he'd descended (which took a lot of youthful ligament and muscle), I had just surmised that he lived wandering about, moving on his daily whim to go wherever he thought to go. It never occurred to me that Amarillento was actually living in a cave!

There were legends about horses living in caves and some scholarly surmising's about wild Equines surviving deep Ice Age cold in Europe's caverns. In a lot of places bandits always lived in caves, bivouacking their horses and booty there, successfully avoiding detection, but I'd never met a horse who lived alone in a cave.

Yet, there it was: my own horse Amarillento had become a horse who decided to live out his old age in a cave.

It took a while to locate his cave, but even so I could never manage to get up to it, which was amazing to think that he could. Like Blue, Amarillento had always been a great horse to be riding when taking on huge treacherous stretches of mountain scree and ridgetop riding, but where he was keeping himself seemed to get farther and farther up the cliff the closer you got. And steeper...

Who could determine how many holes, ledges, caves, caverns or inner labyrinths were scattered and Swiss-cheesed throughout the upper reaches of the magic Beaver-land's canyon walls? Where Amarillento was living was where all the Eagles flew in and out of, entering the side then flying out the roof!

Many smaller holes and caves were nests to Vultures and Golden Eagles from spring to summer.

Amarillento's cave also had a nice flat front deck, an appealing stone veranda fenced with Raspberries, Gooseberries, and Scrub Oak bushes. Whenever we'd really get a clear far-away glimpse of His Lordship, it would be when he was outside sunning himself on that west-facing veranda off the main gallery of his mansion.

I'm fairly certain Amarillento had water up there in a pool inside the cliff 'cause he only came down to drink once a week, and for sure there was something to graze as well. What? Where? How? It was all his secret and I let him have it. Modern people seem to have contracted an unfortunate sickness that is passed congenitally to their offspring, and that is the constant restless need to make every mystery into a trite nothing, to make every folktale into a mushy story, every tribal mythology into an entertaining fiction, every cave into an invaded private magic.

So his mystery I left him. I didn't need to penetrate his cave and I'm not even certain if he lived in only one cave, for there were many. How he got up to any of them without flying, I will never know, for I certainly could have only gone just so close. But he lived in a labyrinth of caves in another world, overlooking his brother Blue's herd of beautiful Mares and Foals and our own selves when we visited.

I often wondered if Amarillento's end would come somewhere up high in the maze of those practically unassailable cliffs.

The little horse once named Amarillento, forgotten by the world, renamed Sunny, then refound and renamed Amarillento, I now renamed Musashi, after the infamous Japanese sword fighter. For not unlike that zany, strangely put together, low-born, despised, homeless, swordless Samurai of old shogunate Japan, who after so many legendary exploits, not the least of which were his notorious duels in which he single-handedly vanquished a string of Japan's most famous and mighty trained Samurai sword-fighting aristocrats and their armies of retainers using for a sword the handle of a canoe paddle against fancy razor-sharp steel swords, who when he finally retired undefeated went up into the hills to live as a hermit, isolated from the world in a cave where he said he would learn to be a Samurai whose sword was now an Ink brush, and who wrote books and painted pictures describing what he thought "real" warriors should come to understand, beyond the art of "vanquishing men."

Amarillento from his lost early years as a thrown away, malformed despised little horse became an incredible, courageous and zany accomplice in our legendary attempts at maintaining a heroic presence of honor and beauty in a time of smiley face fascism and lost epic culture and the natural dignity of man and beast, now instead of retiring had also very naturally grown right into the hidden world of stone mazes up in our cliffs to become a cave-dwelling hermit King, presiding over something bigger than his well-adventured past, making even his own ending something equally heroic and unique.

Thus Amarillento became Musashi in his high-up cave. Word got around, and for passing locals it became a challenge, a kind of friendly competition to see who'd seen the rarity of a horse's head barely poking out of a cave way up high.

He would still come down at times, but he lived up in the cave. Sometimes we'd see him, but mostly we wouldn't, but you could feel his warm yellow horse soul inside those yellow rocks. It was good. And that's how it was for most of that year.

• • •

One evening in mid-March Musashi came down the cliffs, crossed the river still edged with late winter lacy ice, walked up and over to the flats where Blue and the Mares were grazing, then very calmly laid down facing towards his cliff wall in the east, and prepared to die.

He never could right himself again.

I wasn't there when he laid down and didn't rise, but was in the Hall one hundred and ten miles away teaching. Mando had seen him walk down the cliff and then later again, alone lying there dying 'cause Blue had taken the Mares north.

It seemed to take years to drive the 110 mountain miles after Mando called me, but Musashi Amarillento was still alive when I arrived, flat on his left side waiting for me, watching the shadows creep up the canyon wall, from the early canyon sunset of late winter.

When his eyes looked to the side and saw I was there kneeling by his beautiful old head, like all the great old animals I'd ever known in their last long stretch of suffering, Amarillento tried hard to rise, to will himself to stand. My dying friends always wanted to be themselves standing well again, knowing I would want it too; and sometimes, very rarely, a deeply loved Horse or Cow or Goat on their last, struggling to die, who unable to stand, if you give them the magic just right they can sometimes receive sufficient juice in their life-cables to get re-energized and reconnected enough to stand and live one more year, at which time they then die for sure.

But Amarillento Musashi was dying, he told me so, and the deep sadness in his eyes was not for the trouble of dying but for his missing forever the joy of our lives, his running, his delicious existence where his skin like an Eel felt every natural smell and every change of weather. Amarillento had been a big heroic tongue, tasting life to the fullest.

I put my best Chief Joseph Pendleton folded under his head to cushion his eyes and we conferred. We agreed that I should send him out of this life running on an old song, "Hozholgo Nazado," to catch up with the next dawn's stars of Orion and to loosen his Earth soul as a tempest, and in exchange he agreed to bring rain and storms every summer.

This was his next big job.

So I sang and sang, until the old mischievous smirk ruled again his face, and when swishing his tail the fear left his eyes, still singing, I shot him square and well and he died instantly, his soul running straight toward the cliffs, up the sides and into the sky; and no sooner done than a great dust-impregnated straight-line wind descended from there driving me into my truck cab, where the tears made mud of my dusty still-singing face; all the other horses were forced to turn their living bottoms and squint against the force of Amarillento's soul-wind to avoid suffocating in the incredible blast.

And then as quickly as it came, it died down and he was gone.

Amarillento was dead.

I cried for a billion light years every sunset.

He was the fastest, most courageous, inconvenient little horse to ever take on the world and he died well, as he knew he could. His body would come apart and disappear like the night stars do at dawn, but the epic of his having been here would keep running. Unlike all my other animals, I buried him with goods and planted tons of wild grasses on his low mound.

For ten days after I got home every mechanized thing on our Ranch went haywire. Lightbulbs exploded, the well house pump blew up, one of the truck engines blew, the tractor's tires went flat, the trough heaters started boiling water; for a week every time we tried to make a local phone call we'd wake up somebody in India, in New Delhi, Fez or Singapore.

I got to meet a lot of nice people. Ceiling fans started twirling that had never worked and never worked again thereafter, and on and on. We were New Mexicans; we all knew this was just one of Amarillento's other souls doing what he did best, that way we knew he wasn't really that far away. His rascally ways helped us with our grief.

Chapter 20

Still as a Mountain

Even more than human beings, Horses everywhere hate being forcibly separated from the company of their lifelong sidekicks.

With his old friend gone, Blue now basically lived on top of Amarillento's grave. Brilliant and always in charge, standing there as still as a mountain, every once in a while Blue's head would cock to the side and then he'd lower it all the way to the ground, ears perched as if he were listening to something talking to him from beneath the mound. Blue's lips would twitch and he'd stand straight again as if asleep.

It was pretty clear to me that Blue was bossing around the underground bugs, roots, worms, mice and bacteria, telling them how they should separate Amarillento's hard old bones in a way that would feed the horse-sustaining grasses that grew on the mound in the coming years!

Amarillento's grave was now Blue's office, his center of command, so to speak. For it was from there that he directed all the Mares by remote, gyrating in place to face south or north or anywhere his big furry head thought "his girls" might be grazing. His eyes, misty now and no longer really discerning the details of his herd's whereabouts, since Blue was glued to his friend's mound he more often than not shot off the rumbling screams of his customary quasi-stallion, echo-locating directives in a direction quite opposite from where all of his charges were spread out down the canyon.

The girl horses didn't mind. They were comforted by the fact that their protector ran the world like a baseball pitcher standing on the mound 'cause Blue was still smack in the middle of their universe, a hub around which the wheel of the spread-out band slowly revolved grazing.

More than once, while driving into our valley at a distant height and still up on the steep hill to the south, I stopped to drink in the grandeur of that big mountain-edged universe of the stream-cut Canyon, along whose grassy reaches the little dark forms of our mare herd spread out like planets around the white and red spot of their painted leader elevated in the center brilliant like the Sun.

For Blue, Amarillento had been the other half of whatever organism their twenty-year presence together on this Earth had been.

Now that Blue's half of that organism was the only part still moving here alive in the Canyon, it was as if Blue had lost half his legs and couldn't move beyond his other half living under the Earth, buried in the red mica clay of the magic Beaver-land. Blue was stuck to his grief mound.

Of course, he was old enough now, just a year younger than his departed cohort who'd died at thirty three, to once in a while forget he wasn't whole anymore and he'd wander away from his grief on the mound to graze alone or with the girls, with whom he'd find his way to the muddy edges of the creek and drink the clean snowmelt water so packed with the spent jokes of the rascally native Trout that tried to tease him, but he missed the jokes 'cause he couldn't see them flitting about insulting him.

But like all of us he'd remember again, and the next time you'd see him, Blue would have taken his lady charges to graze up by Mari's prairie tomb and he would be standing back on his mound, happy to be closer to his friend.

In reality Blue was halfway in the other world already, for as anyone who knows Horses or even just a little about life, unless great spiritual precautions are observed, a horse like Amarillento was just as likely to haul Blue off to his new dimension, free of the body concerns of equine life, as Blue was likely to try to die to follow his other half, his friend.

We all pretty much figured Blue would be the next one to leave us to join his old friend in the Pleiades.

What we didn't know was when or how.

While Blue often spoke in dreams, all he said was that he'd come to help us when we needed him, but for now he was needed elsewhere. Since Blue looked good, was not starving or suffering any pain, he could still move plenty fine, digested and lived well in his unique way, I left him to continue on with his assignment in the magic Beaver-land, watching over the mares, so the old Boy could die on his own terms close to the Holy in the Wild.

But he didn't die that spring, nor during the births of several new fillies the following summer. He lived on through the fall and even started getting shaggy for winter and looked well.

He finally quit mourning on the mound and pretty much just grazed at will, sometimes with the rest, but then mostly by chance 'cause he didn't always know where they were except by smell. Old Blue still cared about them, he was just off by himself a lot.

There roamed a little grulla Mare with our Mare horses who I never really cottoned up to. A Barb who by most people's reckoning would be considered a good ride, fast and friendly, but there was something she didn't have that all the rest did. Something more like an in-your-pocket spoiled Arabian mare, she was very edgy and hard on all the other horses. I'd purchased her back when as a two year old to breed with Old Punk, but it had never worked out because Punk didn't accept her as his wife.

Punk's son Yampa was now of an age to breed and he was all for breeding this little grulla Mare, but she just beat on him till he looked like a melon that had been used for a soccer ball.

One strange day a month before Amarillento died, this Mare contrived to pound her way out of her corral at our Ranchito on the Ojo Caliente River and somehow moved herself in with Punk without opening any gates. Stranger still was the fact that Old Punk (who was nearly thirty) now thought this was a good idea and the two of them seemed to be breeding.

This mystery was compounded by the fact that we had never had any Mares bred during winter months, mostly because their cycles were always in the spring or summer and, because foals take eleven to twelve months to make in their patient, ornery mothers' bellies, breeding in winter also meant foaling the following winter.

In the magic Beaver-land Canyon, December temperatures at night were regularly minus eighteen degrees Fahrenheit and sometimes as cold as fifty below, often with a blizzard of snow attached. This is very hard weather in which to birth a wet baby and keep him alive the first hours.

So this was something I would always try to avoid, like natural horses do, who have their babies starting in May through September.

But this crazy grulla had arranged to be bred to foal the December following Amarillento's March death.

I put her on the range with the others, with whom she was less than cordial, and for months she never looked pregnant. Then all of a sudden in the fall of that year this spoiled horse's belly began to grow exponentially, until when I visited in November she looked entirely ready to foal sometime in December. I hadn't come with the trailer or I'd have brought her home to the Ranchito to foal, so I watched the weather and waited because school was in session. I was teaching and figured to go pick her up on the break day so she could foal in more sheltered circumstances.

But the early morning of December second, right during my winter school session, a harsh confusing dream crashed over me like a wave waking me in a cold sweat of terror.

Unable to clearly recollect what had all transpired, I awoke with the smell of mammalian birth in my nostrils and therefore logically assumed I'd better head out to the Beaver-land.

After reassigning the day off for the students to give them a rest from my hard-driving way of teaching, I hitched up the trailer, filled my thermoses with hot beef stock and tea, loaded my blizzard jacket, blankets and water, and headed to the magic Beaver-land.

Nothing resembling any kind of emergency was in motion when I got there, but because the Sun Father went down at 2 p.m. in the canyon in late fall, it was already about ten degrees when I loaded up a very copacetic, pregnant grulla Mare in absolutely no distress.

"Well," I thought, "she's probably going to give birth this week and it's good to take her now, because once the snows get heavy we won't be able to drive in."

Before leaving to drive the icy passes to get back home, unload, eat, sleep and up early to get to teaching the one hundred and eighty expectant adult students in the morning, I intended to go down the land to find Old Blue.

But he appeared of his own accord, running the entire quarter mile to my truck like a two year old, screaming the whole way.

In his old age Blue had become very affectionate and always rubbed his big old Rhino head up and over your whole body till you fell. Always as furry as an ice age Pleistocene Pony in winter, hugging Blue in the cold was a wonderfully warming event. My arms around his neck, I wept and wept as we talked and talked about the most trivial trash, but in my heart I knew that it would be beyond all reasoning that my powerful old Pony could survive another cold winter and then he, like Amarillento would be gone.

I sang him a couple of his favorite riding songs, a Navajo song and a Mongol epic.

He just stood straight and grand as the day he emerged from the ice twenty-six years past, all thirty-three years of him alive, warm and my friend.

It was getting dark and really cold, and I had to get going to reach home before the ice froze on the steep mountain passes.

Pulling myself away from Old Blue seemed too hard. But I just kept singing, and as I did, pretended I was still holding him as I walked back to my truck, got in, turned on the engine, and with the mare in the trailer began to roll across the prairie towards our entrance gate, watching Old Blue in the mirror, still standing in the same place and the same position looking at me, as still as a mountain as I left.

When I got down to open the gate and drove through, I couldn't take it and I said to myself, "I'll go back and load up my old friend and haul him home with me. I can't bear to leave him behind thinking I may never see him again."

So I lifted out a rope from the backseat and walked happier back to Old Blue, intending to pull the loop over his big white and sorrel Rhino head and lead him up into my trailer, next to that grumpy self-centered Mare, lock the rear, and take them both back home with me to the Ranchito.

Blue was staring hard somewhere, not at me or the trailer up ahead, and when I lifted the loop and tried to slip it over his head, Blue was not warm, he was unmoving, not even breathing but standing as still and cold as a winter mountain in a storm.

Blue was dead.

Blue died standing!

I pulled the loop away and reached out to touch him…

…but his knees buckled and he tumbled to the ground with a big thud, very much dead.

Without knowing it I'd sung his souls out of him, it had been time, and Blue's spirit was already halfway to the Pleiades whose clustered herd of stars would be rising in an hour.

Blue *would* have to somehow outdo Amarillento, his companion in heroic greatness, even in dying, for part of their famous attachment to each other was their never-ending one-upmanship.

God I loved that Horse and I still do, but who the hell ever heard of a horse dying standing and staying standing after they were dead? Blue had spent a good percentage of his entire life acting like he was dead just to fake everybody out, lying on his side when he was really alive, in which role he was often too convincing. It stood to reason that when Blue decided to really die, it would be his call, and he would have to act like he was still alive standing even though he really was dead!

He'd done it. What a nut he was.

Amarillento became Musashi in his cave and Blue died standing.

Amarillento had been the absolute fastest, bravest Horse of all time.

Blue, he was the best and most merciful Horse even in dying. I had been so worried I might have to shoot him, but he died standing, staring bravely into the next world while I was there. You can't beat that for a good friend.

It was all a big, big plan, but who planned it? I had wanted all my loyal old Horses to have their choice to live and die with dignity on their own terms in the Natural Universe of the Holy in the Wild. That's true. So I made that happen to the best of my ability.

But that ornery grulla Mare had never been pregnant in the first place, and once I brought her back to the Ranchito, day by day she shrank back to her normal, spoiled, svelte, catty-self size. Punk wouldn't even look at her, and she thought he was troll poop.

It was all a ruse. A ruse to make certain I was in the Canyon when Blue died standing.

Blue and Amarillento were natural-born Hero Horses, and on their backs I could count on an epic existence.

We buried Blue next to his friend with goods and planted his mound with fluffy Purple Aster seeds I'd gathered and kept from the miracle field.

I still cry for both of them. Blue occasionally talks to me in dreams, but don't get too emotional about that 'cause he's really not as reasonable as he used to be.

Chapter 21

Do Rivers Sleep at Night?

Three and a half years old and my sidekick everywhere I went and in everything I did, my little daughter, sand shovel in her hand, sunhat strapped under her chin, her calico shift full of flowers and birds, early one morning in the glory of a late New Mexico summer, while standing side by side watching one of our two-year-old fillies artistically tackle the pile of mountain-grass hay we'd just lowered over the fence, needed to ask me a question, a big one!

"Papa! Papa?!" she yelled.

"Yes ma'am," I responded loudly. "What d'ya need little one?"

The Greenstain River was full of noises and crashing through the bottom of our land, having overflowed from yesterday's thunderstorms, so we were forced to lift our voices to understand one another.

"Papa, can I ask you a question?" It ran in our Prechtel blood that before we asked a question, we always asked if we could ask one.

"Well, of course you can, what do you want to ask?"

"Papa, do rivers stop running at night?"

Wow, what an idea.

"What d'ya mean?" I asked. It was also a family custom to respond to all questions with a question!

"You know when it gets dark at night we all go to sleep, all the animals go to sleep, the sun goes to sleep; do rivers sleep too? Doesn't the water stop moving? Then when the sun comes back in the morning, doesn't the river wake up again and start running?"

"Well," I replied. Being a trustworthy Papa I always told her the truth: "I haven't seen all the rivers of the world, and to tell the truth, of all the rivers I have been close to, I've only been around a few of them at night, and those ones seemed to be going along pretty steadily just like in the day, though they all sounded different at night."

"No Papa, rivers get tired of working all day and they sleep at night."

And that was that. It also ran in my people's blood to ask people a question, listen to their reply and tell them courteously they're mistaken no matter what they say!

The world smelled earthy and good, and we just listened to the horse crunching hay over the roaring of the river and a bunch of arguing Magpies.

"Papa! Papa!"

"Yeah baby girl, what d'ya need?"

"Can I ask you a question?"

"Sure, what do you want to know?"

"Papa, does the world go dark for you when I close my eyes?"

Oye, I had to think about that. Imagine the world going dark every time someone blinked! Maybe nighttime is just the world blinking.

"Well, little girl, I've never noticed that it did much, but why do you ask?" I inquired.

"'Cause I'm sure it must go dark for everyone when my eyes close 'cause it goes dark for me… but I keep trying to find out, but every time I open my eyes to see if it's dark for the others the world is bright again!"

"Do you think if someone else closed their eyes and the world was dark for them it would be dark for you too?"

"I can't tell," she said very carefully.

Just the sound of the river rushing and Punk and Yampa screaming up at the top of our land. This meant someone was driving in.

"Papa can I ask you a question?"

"Alright Topknots, what would you like to ask me?"

"Papa! Don't you think bugs would like to ride horses?"

Whew! Finally an easy question for which I confidently knew the answer:

"Oh yeah, you better believe it, little one, I've seen lots of 'bugs' riding horses. Horseflies love to latch on to a horse's neck or belly and ride right along with the horse, not to mention Mosquitoes, Gnats, Mites, Deer Flies; all kinds of bugs like to ride horses."

"No, silly Papa, not those kinds of bugs, those are flies, I mean real bugs. Do they like to ride horses?"

"What do ya mean? Horseflies are real bugs; what kind of bugs are you talking about?" I asked this well-dressed, pert, three-foot-tall, self-assured person down there to my left.

And after pointing with her "Dig" (the little metal sand shovel she took with her everywhere) to a big black Tarantula that had escaped my notice, perched on the sand right in front of us looking up at the munching horse's left front leg, she replied:

"Like that bug right there!"

All Northern New Mexican Tarantulas are handsome gigantic spiders, usually peaceful and almost always on a mission heading somewhere, tending children, or sitting waiting in weird, unlikely places to pounce on some bug, bird or lizard to eat. With a three-and-a-half-inch leg span and black as a moonless night, this Tarantula's obsidian bristles glistened like glass hair in the morning sun.

This was a truly impressive "Bug", who, utterly unconcerned about our human presence and standing less than a foot away, really did look as if she was sizing up the Filly for a ride!

Then, just as I was about to say something vacant like:

"Wow, look at the size of that spider..."

And before I could say it,

With all eight eyes flashing, this giant black bristling spider suddenly sprung sideways right onto the lacings of my daughter's left shoe and in the same motion scurried up under the little girl's calico smock, emerging out instantly from her neckline! Then running out to her left shoulder, the Tarantula shot up onto the brim of her sunhat, where bouncing up and down like a little kid on a trampoline, the big spider used the hat brim as a springboard to launch herself through the air, landing square onto the back of the horse, who, because it all happened in a nanosecond hadn't registered she had a three-inch-wide spider sitting proudly on her backbone, just kept on munching as if nothing had happened!

This audacious big-minded Tarantula sat there calmly thinking. Then she commenced to hop rapidly in place, rotating like the turret of a tank positioning to fire, which caused the Filly to definitely notice she had some big, bristly, live thing on her back.

Whipping her tail at the bug, the horse began spinning hysterically, intermittently stopping to stretch out and bend her neck and head back to nip at the spider or chase her off.

But this "Bug" was a pro at avoiding all the incoming tail-hair-whipping and teeth of the horse, shuffling crab-like to position herself always just a millimeter out of range. This really infuriated the young horse, but not as much as when the Tarantula managed to saunter up the Filly's back to arrive on top of her withers.

This is right where we all put our saddles, and this spider, facing forward, now looked like a jockey ready to ride.

Like a bareback bronc rider digging in with his spurs to start his draw to buck, this crazy "Bug" dug all "eight" of her legs into the Filly's withers, which inspired this normally prim lady horse to violently throw herself onto her side to the ground, where in a cloud of red New Mexico dust she rolled onto her back and squirmed to get that obnoxious bristly menace off her spine.

But like the air bubble in a carpenter's level, that Tarantula was agile and always managed to be on top and exactly where she needed to be to avoid being smashed or brushed off.

The Filly got back to her feet, shook hard to get the dust off and, assuming the spider had been eliminated, commenced to drift back to her hay pile.

But Mama Tarantula was exactly where she'd always been.

Now this time when that well-made, plotting, glistening, dark gigantic spider put her "spurs" into the Filly's hump, she gave the horse a good Tarantula bite and off and away they ran.

Looking for all the world like an iridescent cowgirl riding out a monster bronc fifteen stories tall, that spider was as glued to that horse as a beak on a bird as they tore on down toward the riverside thicket.

The Filly jumped, she ran, she bucked, swirled around, crow-hopped, ran and stopped again, then finally took off in a galloping terror, crashing right into several acres of Tamarisk tangle too thick to even crawl through, intending no doubt to brush that Goddamned Bug off her back with the branches.

The loud din of popping wood, slapping branches and horse-grunting echoed up the river valley, startling the resident Mallards and Mergansers up into the sky.

But soon the crashing horse, head down, sprang out from the tangle still running top speed with her determined jockey still firmly clamped onto the withers, the black spider smiling ear to ear with glee, her bristles bending in the breeze of their wild ride, whose last leg took them blasting right back to where my little girl and I were still standing.

Like two spectators in the bleachers at the local outdoor rodeo, my little one and I laughed in fascination as the spider and "Her" horse slid to a stop exactly where the whole amazing event had begun.

After the few seconds it took the thick dust to clear enough for us to see that the Tarantula was still mounted, and her horse was standing stock still afraid to even move without the spider's permission, it seemed to us that the Tarantula was hoping for some applause, so we began clapping and cheering, whistling and praising, and we really meant it.

Only then did that Tarantula drop to the ground beside the sweaty, panting, unmoving horse, where after raising her hat to the crowd, she dusted off her eight legs and swaggered south across the sand and into the arroyo, disappearing back into the matrix of her normal world.

I could hardly believe it.

"Whew, little girl, did you see that?"

"I told you Bugs like to ride horses," she said, nonplussed like some little old lady who'd seen it all a thousand times before.

"Well, I sure didn't know Tarantulas liked to ride other animals," I added.

"Papa. There's a lot of things you don't know."

"Thank God for that."

Miles to go.

Colophon

Of my original three Native Barb Horse companions, only Punk remained. Though the old stallion kept trying, after fifteen years of beautiful foals, no more babies came out of old Punk. And strange it was that of all the many horses he fathered over the decades with a couple of Mares, only fillies were ever born, except of course for Yakatche, who birthed only one Punk baby, period, and hers was the only boy, Yampa.

Now, Punk and Yakatche's yellow roan son, Yampa, fills the land with foals of the most brilliant old-time cut, but strangely, unlike his father, these have been mostly stud colts.

The old herd had returned.

The magic Beaver-land is still ruled by Beavers, in whose pools yellow-jawed Water Snakes bask, golden-eyed Frogs hide and native Trout still flash, taunting the Herons and Curlews. The place still smells of Bears, and the Lions have eaten only one foal in twenty years.

While at the Ranchito along the Greenstain River of Ojo Caliente, Ravens still line up on Punk's ancient back telling him lies about everything. He's a good listener; he's like their therapist.

Dragonflies still rest between Yakatche's ears, and the Canyon Wren still sings in both canyons.

And that's how it was, and that's how it is, and life goes on.

Here ends *The Canyon Wren*.

Here begins *The Snowdrift Foal*.

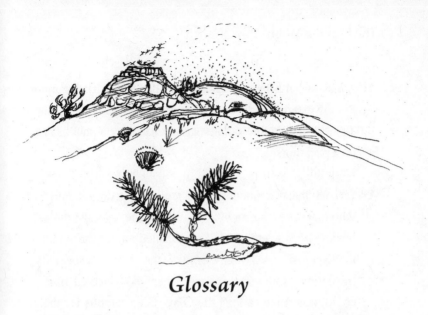

Glossary

Aleika (Native North American word from Chata people): the natural born aura, magic, plasmic emanation or charisma, of a person, place, object or animal, that gives them a life power beyond science's ability to analyze. Like the more common Haudenosaunee term "Orenda."

Afilerillo or **Alfilario** (Spanish): a type of wild geranium with beautiful little purple flowers that can form an acre wide mat of vines and flowers. Gathered for medicine in New Mexico, another related species is highly regarded as livestock graze, often called "Filery" by Anglo cowboys. The word Afilerillo means little seamstress' pin in Spanish in reference to the long needle at the top of the seed capsule. Anglo herbalists call the same plant "storksbill" for the same reason.

Alforjas (Awl-for-hahs) (Arabic descended Spanish): common Southwestern word, even among Anglo cattlemen, that signifies the double saddle bags spread over a pack frame on a pack horse.

Arriéro (Spanish; pronounced Ah-ree-err-o): a drover. Person who manages a string of pack or baggage animals: mules, burros, horses, etc. A well-established career throughout the Spanish speaking areas of the world, especially traversing mountainous areas where no wheeled traffic could pass. Like sailors, they have been famous for their songs, poems, stories, and their knowledge of knots and the stars.

Arrisco (Spanish): common term for a horse that is very alert, elusive and difficult to catch.

Banker Pony: colloquial Mustang/Barb people's term for the feral horses thriving on various offshore southern state islands; Asseteque, Chinqotegue and others, whose populations of equines are protected and periodically caught and sold. Reputedly old time Spanish horses variously surmised to have been either left there from Spanish colonial ships to propagate for their later use in taking over the area, or from horse-filled ships foundered in storms, the horses swimming to these islands. Some Barb people consider them legitimate Spanish Barb horses.

Barba quejo (Spanish): signifies the chin strap that keeps a rider's hat from flying off in the wind or the breeze caused by fast riding. Originally, this strap could be considerably adorned, made of ornate braided goatskin with a carved bone or silver slider for tightening under the chin. Literally a "beard stay."

Barb horse: at present day, a confusing term for more than one kind of horse whose meaning has been clouded by various European horse registries claiming Barb ancestries for horses that actually originated from Central Asian Nomadic stock, which are technically not *Barbs*. Originally, a Barb horse referred to horses historically belonging to any of the many diverse Berber peoples, both nomadic and settled, both inland and along the *Barbary coast* of Morocco, Algeria, Libya, parts of Egypt, etc.

    The famous Spanish horse of the Middle Ages and Renaissance no longer truly exists in Spain due to devastating horse epidemics during the Napoleonic Wars and the 19th century Spanish Civil War, but was originally a fine Barb-type horse. The original *Mesta* horses of the Americas, the Cow pony of the American Southwest, was often called a Barb by 19th century American cattlemen, and Moro (Moorish horse) by Spanish Americans, who very intelligently recognized these powerful, small, beautiful horses for what they were: a North African Spanish horse of mostly Barb descendancy that were brought to the Americas before they largely disappeared in Europe during the terrible horse epidemics.

Barranca (Spanish): A steep-sided ravine.

Bramadero (Spanish): from the word *brama*, meaning the fertile period or sexual heat in a female animal. A bramadero is a very sturdily built breeding pen with a stout post buried in the middle where a bull and heifers are brought together for mating. But in the Spanish speaking Americas, a bramadero more often refers to the post or *brake* where horses begin their training. See *breaking a horse*.

Breaking a horse: bad pulp fiction about horses has confused the notion of what breaking a horse actually means in English. A horse that is broken is not *broken* like a twig, but tamed to be ridden. While there are horses that have most certainly been wrecked, destroyed, their souls reduced to sulky bitterness, and this is all atrocious and uncalled for, none of this has anything to do with what people mean with the term *breaking a horse*.

Breaking a horse arises from an historical semantic mix-up and orthographic inconsistency. Originally the word *breaking*, as in breaking a horse, was written *braking a horse*, referred to *softening* or *suppling* something, as when softening an untanned hide to turn it into leather. *Braking a hide* was part of the old European leather tanning process and was carried out by two individuals who, from opposite sides, pulled a previously *cured* skin back and forth over the top of a smooth stake to soften it. Looking like a five-foot-high, gigantic polished baseball bat set deeply into the ground, this stake was known as a *brake* in German, Celtic, and eventually English. When hide tanners went about softening a skin, toward the end of the tanning process, they called it *braking a skin* not *breaking a skin* i.e., softening a hide on a brake. Training a *raw, green* horse properly, stage by stage, over a period of time, to slowly make a suppled, tame riding horse was likened to the many stages of courting a raw, freshly-removed skin of a large animal, called a *green hide*, to slowly turn it into a beautiful, pliable, strong, good smelling, and very useful piece of leather. The last stage of hide-softening and horse-gentling was also called the gradual *braking* or suppling of the horse, like a calf skin, into a pliable and useful riding horse!

While a *horse braker* was originally a person who could *gentle* a horse, a horse *breaker*, on the other hand, was a term invented by pulp fiction writers to designate those people who used rough methods to *dominate* strings of green horses for quick sale by bucking them out till they couldn't move and selling them as *broke*.

A horse tamer was a person who *bucked* horses out. A horse gentler was a person who softened horses and accustomed them to the saddle or harness. It's good to know your own history. But in the American West, a *broke* horse still means a horse that's been gentled, softened, and made pliable to ride, not a horse ruined and dominated into submission.

Bozal (Spanish; pronounced bow-sáhl): horseriding equipment. In the Americas, a braided leather or rawhide noseband set in a headstall. Shaped like the frame of a Native snowshoe, the *bozal* is used instead of a bit to train a horse to respond to being steered with reins by pressure on the nose, without the danger of ruining a horse's mouth. Usually, once the horse rides well on the *bozal*, a bit is added and a very thin *bozal* replaces the original noseband. The theory is that the horse learns to respond to very subtle rein cues without having to be cued by any direct pressure on the bit.

Cabestro (Spanish): means different things in different parts of the world. But generally it refers to some type of horse halter, a rig that fits over a horse or donkey's head, running from behind the ears to a noseband and fastens under the jaw. In some places, *cabestro* refers to a headstall. See halter.

Chaquegue (Tewa Pueblo language adapted into New Mexico Spanish: pronounced chah-káy-way): this is a mush made of Native blue flour corn, toasted, then ground fine and mixed with cold water, then added to separately boiling water and stirred until cooked and smooth. The ancestor of the modern Italian polenta, which of course originated in the Americas under many different names. Chaquegue is one of the most ancient foods throughout the American Southwest, Mexico, Central America and South America.

Served variously as a base of many sauces and protein. In Northern New Mexico this is the traditional breakfast, often served sweet with honey and goat milk, or savory with chile and eggs.

Chimajá (Spanish from the Native Keres *Ch'm'aa*): referring to a dwarf, wild-desert celery whose leaves and roots are locally prized and eaten fried, fresh or dried and crumbled into all types of traditional food among all old-time New Mexicans: Pueblos, Diné Navajos and Spanish speaking. Also used to make famous *digestivo*, a kind of liquor. By soaking the fresh leaves of this plant in *mula* (native corn moonshine), the resulting liquid, after a year, is used externally as a liniment for contusions and sore muscles, and internally on Christmas and New Year's Eve, where a small *shot* is consumed by each member of a family to insure good health.

Chicken snare saddle: in the old American West the word *chicken*, in settler-English and the corresponding *gallina* in post-colonial Spanish, did not always refer to a domesticated chicken, but more often than not to some species of grouse or prairie chicken. Thus, even on a map today, the Gallina Mountains, Gallina River, or Gallina Canyon, Chicken Creek, etc. all refer to the wild galliformes, not Leghorns or Barred rocks. The early Spanish and the first Anglo-Americans in the West learned to trap and eat these wild ground birds from the original Native peoples of the area they invaded. One type of these traps had two bars connected by two bent branches and a net stretched over the whole that would snap shut like a clam when tripped by a bird trying to eat the corn with which it was baited.

The *quick to make,* rawhide-covered, antler and wood-slab saddle made by many tribes for riding or packing was likened to a prairie chicken snare: thus the name chicken snare saddle. Very useful, actually difficult to craft, and with a good furry sheepskin or pelt, not too bad on the bottom. Native American women's saddles were for the most part exquisite works of art and, although made of elk antler as well, they were very tall and a different thing altogether.

Coloratura (Italian, Spanish, English): opera singing term for the improvisational trills and ululations at the ends of phrases in old Italian operas.

Coscojos (Spanish): little jinglers or tiny silver bells hanging from curb chains in tiers, sewn onto men's pants, or suspended from *anqueras*: the hip straps that run under a horse's tail. This very ancient horse adornment descends from the Caucasus, Central Asia and North Africa. Many medieval European knights had these sound makers all over their outfit. Very rare nowadays, but still a standard part of Native bridles in some places.

Cota (New Mexican Spanish from old Tewa): a wild perennial with small petaless yellow flowers, which along with its grass-like leaves and thin stems are highly prized for tea by everybody of every culture in Northern New Mexico. The wild plant is also good medicine and makes gorgeous dye colors for wool and also cotton ranging from pale mustard to deep yellow to coral red. Commonly called Indian Tea.

Coursing: an unofficial term for a very official horse gait. People think that saying a horse is *coursing* over the land just means the horse is galloping fast, but *coursing* is a particular way to cover land. Some people think horses have only four gaits: walk, trot, canter and gallop. But horses around the world have all sorts of gaits associated with types and breeds. There is the tölt, paso fino, amble, marchalarga, walk-run, the rack, not to mention unfortunate, synthetically enforced gaits, to name just a few.

While individual foals are often born with extra gaits unknown to the parents, for the most part in my neighborhood, our horses move in the following gaits:

1. A walk, which has a two beat rhythm.

2. A trot, which has a single alternating staccato beat.

3. An Indian shuffle, which is a cross between a trot and a rack that is a smooth motion through sand that rocks from side to side.

4. A lope is a slow canter in three beats, lovely and fast enough.

5. A full canter, a fast three beat motion, the best gait of all.

6. A gallop, a fast four beat divided into two.

7. A run, a smooth very fast, reaching gait.

8. A *course*, just like a Jackrabbit or Leopard runs, by reaching forward past the ears with the hind legs and pushing powerfully forward, while reaching way forward with both front legs and powerfully pulling forward. Once well established, its just like a fast-moving river and feels pretty much like flying, because the horse is in the air three times longer than his feet are on the ground. So coursing across the land, a herd of wild horses can look like a flash flood of flesh, fur, and dust. Very majestic to ride and see. Called a full career by the stuffy.

Crop (English): a thin, semi-flexible, short whip used to cue a saddle horse. A constant presence and fetish of status in northern European horse riding. Originally made of a thin piece of dried bull penis covered in braided black silk, but later made from whale baleen and braided silk, nowadays most are fiberglass and polyester. Any European-derived, saddle riding tradition is always done with a crop, often a symbol of gentry, imperial domination, and European cavalry. While all horse cultures have some sort of riding whip to urge their horses, more often they are beautifully adorned, more whiplike, and works of art in themselves. Worn more as a piece of tribal jewelry than a functional tool; compared to these, an English crop is a rather anal, puritan-looking, sneering twig.

Delicia (Spanish, Southwestern "English"): the lusciousness of something, the deliciousness.

Diné (Diné): a Diné word for themselves. Also known as Navajo. The actual meaning of the word Diné in Diné language is complex. It is now politically proper to designate any Navajo person as pertaining to the Diné tribe. But the word Diné doesn't actually imply Navajos, or humans. It refers to the living form of anything. For instance, Lightning Diné, or Fir Tree Diné, or Corn Beetle Diné, or Rain Diné. Different tribes are *Paiute* Diné or *Taos* Diné, *Mexican* Diné etc. To distinguish themselves, the Diné of today generally say *Ta'á Diné* to signify their particular *Navajo* Diné.

Dinétah: old Diné word for their tribal homeland. A euphemism sometimes used by non-Navajos for the landscape where one *belongs*.

Disco (colloquial New Mexican Spanish): for the ever popular Northern New Mexican custom of making roadside get-togethers that feature various meats deep fried in a deep round-bottomed steel pot (Disco) over an open wood fire, plenty of beer and people singing with guitars or accordians. The name "disco" comes from the original use of a bolt-plugged discarded disc from a disc plow set over the fire and used to melt pig fat and deep-fry meat. Nowadays most use a heavy cast-iron round bottom frying pot created especially for the purpose still called a "disco" and available in many New Mexican feed stores.

Doings (Native American English): signifies an important ceremonial ritual with a large communal attendance.

Dorsal stripe (English): a type of horse marking, used to signify the dark narrow line (red, black, grey) that some horses exhibit that runs from the mane down and over their withers, right on top of their spine, to the tail. Considered by veterinary science to be a primitive horse coat pattern from before the Pleistocene era.

Draw: in rodeo contests all the Bulls and bucking Horses that bronc and bull riders end up riding are determined by pulling the names of the animals out of a hat which is called the luck of the draw. Many Bulls and bucking Horses are famously difficult and have particular motions all their own. The "draw" eliminates any favoritism.

Ergot (Latin/English): the strange English language term for the little bony protuberances at the rear of the fetlock on a horse's foot, which, along with the *chestnuts* found on the insides of the horse's forearms, constitute what remains of the original three other toes of the pre-historic horse ancestors of our now single-toed horses.

For a lot of tribal horse people worldwide, these ergots and chestnuts are considered to be very powerfully charged with medicine.

Gallo and *gallo horse* (Spanish): The word gallo (pronounced gah-yo), means literally a rooster in Spanish. But a *gallo* is also the colloquial name for an ancient game played on horseback that has far-flung origins among horse people throughout North Africa, Europe, Central and North Asia.

When the Spanish colonial culture came to what later was called the American Southwest, they brought with them a lot of their animals, cultivars, tools, and methods for taking care of all that, their religion and a lot of customs. Not all of these things flourished in their new setting, but some things stuck and became so much a part of Native cultures and Hispanic post-colonial life that people sometimes forget their origins.

Horses, long-horned cows, Churro sheep, Angora goats, big red hogs, rabbit hounds, steel knives, axes, hoes, pulleys, shovels, pliers, scissors, nails, wheat, barley, grapes, peaches, plums, cherries, radishes, haba beans, parsnips, carrots, oats, peas, floor looms, spinning wheels, playing cards, chess, to name just a few, all combined with the amazing plants and minerals, tools and methods of other people the Spanish had overrun farther south; when all of these things merged in turn with the equally rich and capable cultures already in place in what is now New Mexico, the resulting culture became the unique phenomena it is today.

One of the things that really took off was the raising of chickens. With chickens, one doesn't only end up with eggs and delicious chicken recipes, but roosters. You only need a single rooster to breed forty to fifty hens, but with a lot of broody hens you end up with a lot of roosters. Just like horses, unless you castrate them, you end up having to deal with a lot of fighting males. Like stallions, roosters are very fierce and jealous of their females. A castrated rooster, called a capon, is an eating specialty of certain peoples, especially the French and Italians and formerly the English. They grow real big and taste very good.

But in our area, the yearly over-population of roosters was annually dealt with by their part in an ancient horse game, brought by the Spanish, which was then further finessed into Pueblo spiritualism. In our area of New Mexico, on the Saint's day of San Antonio on June 14, San Juan on June 24, and Santiago on July 24, great contests and exhibitions of horse riding expertise were carried out, called the *gallo*: the rooster.

In this game, after villagers donate a great number of live roosters, up to three hundred Native riders and their little horses line up to have a chance to pull a live rooster out of a hill of sand where he has been buried up to his neck. Riders canter past the rooster, just to the left, then without stopping, and leaning way over to the right, attempt to pull the entire flapping bird out of the ground as they pass. Most fail to grab the wily dodging head of the rooster, but when one is successful, this rider then grabs the bird tight so as to avoid the rooster's wicked spurs, and in the same moment, with a knotted cloth for a quirt, the rider starts his horse galloping as fast as he can, and in any design of motion to avoid the thundering mass of the rest of the three hundred riders chasing him and his horse and the flapping rooster, who are all dedicated to rudely wresting the rooster away from him by whatever means possible. At break-neck speeds, the riders dodge and hit, ride sideways, and do all sorts of maneuvers, the rooster often serving as a club to beat off assailants.

The flapping of the rooster only served to make all the horses go faster.

The goal, if you got a rooster out of the ground and got away, or succeeded in taking it away from some other rider in the thick dust and swirling milieu of horses, was to ride like hell to the house of the girl you loved the most and throw the rooster in through her adobe doorway, at which point the rooster was already dead, or killed by the lady of the house, and all pursuit was called off and the next round of riders went after the next rooster in the very long line of buried roosters. The *gallo* could go on in this way for eight to ten hours making it a test of tremendous endurance for both man and beast. The roosters thus distributed were plucked and stewed and taken, by the sweetheart, all dressed up, to the parents of the young man who had tossed the bird into her house as a kind of courting gesture.

In this game a lot of expert riding techniques were used, but riders often toppled from their horses, losing their seat while trying to retrieve a rooster. Newly proficient young riders, the heroes of the game, were always emerging to take the day, but a lot of big, rowdy, middle-aged Indians, veterans of many *gallos*, were the admitted masters. Church bells were rung and bugles blown every time someone was fleeing with a rooster. And after a while, all the previous winners had to ride single-file between two long poles, each maneuvered by two men on the ground. Between the tops of these poles a rope was stretched in whose center a live rooster was fastened. The idea was to stand up on your horse as you rode underneath this rooster that was held between the poles as he dropped and rose, grab the bird, jump back down into your saddle and once again run like hell to avoid a hundred riders on your tail trying to get the bird away from you.

To ride in the *gallo* you needed a really good horse and the short little *Mesta* Barbs were made for it. Like polo ponies, they had to be able to stand, but then respond in a flash, turn on a dime, move sideways and feint, stop and jump out, charge undaunted into other horses, and into a huge rush of animals, then light out, like a Hawk with a chicken, in a second without biting or striking, and never tire. It was extremely rugged, very exciting, and very heroic. There were a lot of broken noses, dislocated fingers, broken ribs. Sometimes riders were maimed in the fray and every few years someone was killed, usually dragged, caught in the stirrup, and smashed into a wall. But everyone riding in a *gallo* came out a little beat up and bloody, but smiling and excited. The horses loved the *gallo* with all the herd-like free-for-alls.

But a good *gallo* horse was always a prize animal. Funnily enough, when American-style rodeos began to dominate the *Western* scene, they were all called *gallos* by the locals, not rodeos. In some Native languages, such as Diné, a rodeo is still called *hoohai*: chicken. When I was a little kid it took me a long while to figure out why Navajos always called their much beloved rodeos the *hoohai* or chicken. "Hey, let's go rope at the chicken, Martín!" It makes sense once you think about it, for at least where I grew up, in a full-on *gallo* there was a lot more wild horsemanship involved than any rodeo or horse event. Anyone who's seen or ridden in one can attest to the accuracy of that statement!

Of course when it comes to the Native ritual aspect of the *gallo*, there's a lot more to tell than the Spanish bugles, the bellringing, painting of the horses, the communal gift giving, the feasting, the anger contest, and a thousand more beautiful components, but in my experience, all the charm and excitement that a large *gallo* inspires in New Mexicans and Natives seems to be lost on most modern, urban people, so I'll just leave it at that. You get the general idea. Anglos call the *gallo* a rooster pull.

Gelding (English): a castrated stallion. Supposedly devoid of the testosterone driven fierceness of stallions, and the unpredictable craze of mares in heat every twenty-one days; geldings are the world's most common form of riding horse. Most cultures geld male horses, keeping only a few intact stallions to further the line.

Granny gear (American slang): compound low gear in old-time trucks. Those vehicles had four forward gears and reverse. But first gear was so low and powerful, most people started their trucks in second gear, using first gear (granny gear) only for slow, very difficult terrain. Before four-wheel drive was common, granny gear was all we had.

Green horse: an untrained horse. See *breaking a horse*.

Grulla (pronounced grew-yah): horse color from the Spanish word *grulla*, or Crane, as in Sandhill Crane. Typically a kind of holographic coat that reflects red or blueish overtones with dark legs, dark dorsal stripes, dark tail, muzzle, and mane. Crane colored.

Guacamole Horse (Colloquial New Mexican): term to describe any grade horse of great sturdiness and sporting nature, ie. a horse that can really scramble into the rocks and brush without having to worry too much about cuts and bruises. A lot like a "wood truck" used to haul firewood, which is always beat up and dented but gets the job done.

Hackamore: is a Southwestern Anglo cowboy pronunciation of the old Spanish word Jaquima, which is presumed to be a North African Berber word.

Jaquima or Hackamore was originally a halter-like head rig for a Horse made of braided horsehair, or braided rawhide, with a nose band and an adjustable chin knot, still called a "Hackamore knot," which is also the Buddhist "Everlasting knot." This rig could be put together in a matter of minutes or made so ornately as to consume weeks in its construction. Throughout the world some form of this Hackamore was employed to break horses without the use of the bit, like that still in use that employs a rawhide Bozal noseband (see entry).

But in modern times, the word hackamore more often signifies a bitless metal hinge-like affair with shanks like a curb-bit where the reins attach, designed to put lever action pressure simultaneously on the horse's nose and chin with a curb strap. This is very different than the original Bozal/Jaquima/Hackamore and is generally used on horses with ruined mouthbars that will not respond to a bit (I don't like mechanical hackamores).

Halter: a horse's headgear made of rope, leather, or webbing. Goes over a horse's head, behind the ears, buckling at the throat, used with a tie-on or clip-on lead rope to guide a horse to where you want, and for tying up to hold a horse still while saddling. Not made for riding, just for moving a horse on the ground, though there are people who ride with halters and reins these days.

Hand: in old Europe, comparative heights of plants, animals and people were generally communicated by the human hand, in positions.

By lowering or lifting an extended handheld horizontally, palm up, the height of a young sapling, or a crop of wheat would be conveyed.

The height of one's children was shown in the same way, but by holding the palm down, to distinguish.

To express the height of a farm animal: a cow, or pig, a lamb, or goat etc., the hand was held sideways, and represented the animals head, with the thumb up, standing for the animal's ears. By lifting or lowering the hand, the relative size of an animal could be expressed to a person watching or listening.

A horse, on the other hand, was and still is measured by the distance of how many of these sideways hands, with the thumb held parallel, measured across the knuckles, it takes, from the front hoof, up the leg, past the shoulders, to reach the tip-top of the horse's withers. Four fingers equaled a hand. Thus a horse could be 14 hands and 2 fingers or 15 hands, or 13 hands and 3 fingers. Eventually the *hand* measurement was standardized in most of European countries to be four inches, and each finger an inch.

Thus a horse that stands fifty six inches from the ground, at the front hoof to the top of the withers, is said to be fourteen hands tall. A horse that stands fifty eight inches to the withers is said to be 14.2 hands, or 14 and a half hands high, etc. Thus a 16 hand Thoroughbred is sixty four inches tall at the withers.

Hashmarks (Western American cowboy slang): horse color term for any number of dark, parallel stripes that sometimes adorn the fur of a horse's forearm, like the chevrons on the shoulders and cuffs of military uniforms that signify rank. Along with *dorsal stripes*, *spider webbing*, and *smokey withers* or *cross*, *hashmarks* are thought to be throwback markings from prehistoric equines.

Headstall (English): the leather head gear that holds a bit in a horse's mouth, or noseband, in place. Used for riding with reins attached to bits or noseband.

Horno (Spanish; pronounced o´r-no): a wood-fired, outside oven. In northern New Mexico, horno signifies a large beehive shaped oven made of tufa or adobes plastered with mud; used to bake bread, biscochitos, cookies, prune and peach pies, to roast meat, squash, and sweetcorn. Everyone loves to eat what comes out of the horno.

Horsality (New Mexico, cowboy English): term used by horse lovers to signify the natural core reality of *horsiness*, where a horse's manner, politic, moods and reasoning don't derive from their generational exposure to human expectations. Where a horse's reactions and sense of self-respect retain all aspects of having a natural *horsality*, instead of the neurotic, boring, in-your-pocket, idiot horse who only has a *personality*!

Hozhro or *Hozho* or *Hozhon* (Diné Navajo): term that implies the condition of wellbeing where every being is living according to his or her Nature and all life flourishes. The deepest definition of health.

In hand (English): a common EuroAmerican riding term that signifies that a horse ridden, or horses driven, are responding to the signals of the rider, or their driver, by means of the reins held in the rider's or driver's hands: i.e., the rider is in control.

    The common spoken English expression denoting a situation that is out of control: things "have gotten *out of hand*," originally meant that a rider's horse was not listening and responding to the handheld reins, and the horse was therefore *out of hand*, going berserk, ready to bolt, out of control. Thus, things are *in hand* or *out of hand*.

Jinglebobs (Western American English): refers to two small iron, silver or brass pendants which dangle, free-hanging, from a hole in the rowel pin of a spur with a large rowel. An inheritance from Latin America and Spain and ultimately Medieval Europe, in which the spurs are made to really *jingle*. I don't use spurs, or like them, but I love jinglebobs on spurs to walk around feeling musical at every step.

Lance-side: an old English horseman's term for what in all of Europe, in their own languages, is the original designation of what today is called the offside on a horse: the right side.

Because medieval European knights, and earlier North African and Arab knights, kept their swords belted to the left, to be drawn with their right hand, and their lance-butts socketed on the right side in a sheath-like holder strapped onto the front cinch or stirrup strap, they always mounted from the left, holding onto the lance to get into the saddle.

While horse cultures worldwide taught their children, boys and girls, to mount and dismount from either side (a very good policy), European descended riding traditions mount only from the left, this being *the on-side*, and the right being *the offside*, all motions militarily derived.

Latillas (New Mexico Spanish; pronounced Lah-tea-yahs): the smaller poles or rough split cedar wooden slats that are laid between the vigas (see entry) in a traditional adobe house, that form the ceiling. Sometimes fitted in an elegant herringbone fashion, or other pattern, giving a wonderful royal feel to the humblest of homes. Traditionally the latillas supported several layers of cedar bark on top of which was piled a six inch cushion of dried cattail reeds, which in turn held a several inch thick dried adobe clay flat roof.

Mecate (Mexican Spanish; pronounced mek-ah-tei): from the Nahuat *mecatl*, originally an Indigenous Mexica term for rope or cordage, usually expertly twisted from the fibers of the blades of certain species of maguey or lechuguilla plants. But, in Spanish, it gradually gestated to mean a three or two-ply rope, one inch thick, made of the mane hair of horses, and about twenty foot long. When used in conjunction with the *jaquima* and *bozal*, it binds the whole headrig in such a way as to provide both a set of reins and a lead rope, all in one. American cowboys call it a McCardy.

But the word *mecate*, used casually, usually signifies a twenty foot rope used to halter horses *old style*, without a halter, by a couple of configurations, to tie up a horse while saddling and bridling, after which a loop remains around the horse's neck, and the slack tied up to the saddle while riding. This slack can then be let out while resting a horse, or tied to a tree while the horse grazes and the rider boils up some tea or coffee. Just like tying up a boat. I grew up with the *mecate* and not halters.

Mesta (Spanish): originally a co-operative of Spanish stock-raisers who graze their animals in common and take turns watching over them and come together to co-operatively round up, move the animals, doctor them, and train them in the case of oxen or horses.

A kind of ancient Iberian grange where members met and voted on leaders, and what to do with animals, and who communally shared expenses. Because the livestock was generally herded in wild-open areas and not held in fenced paddocks or pastures, some herders had to always be on the job.

Any animal raised in this style of open, wild grazing was called, in Spanish: *Mesteño*. The word *Mesteño* eventually gestated into the American English word mustang. But originally a *Mesteño* horse was never an unprovenanced, ownerless, feral animal, but a horse raised in a *Mesta* herd, watched over by *Mesta* rangers. Colonial Spanish horse raisers spread the institution of the *Mesta* to their colonies, and Native populations continued raising their cattle and horses in this same time-honored way after Spain no longer claimed the area. We still did so in my youth.

It is interesting to note that the word mustang, even in standard American English dictionaries up until WWII, signified a "small, narrow-chested, Spanish horse of great endurance and steady temperament from the American Southwest": basically identical to what a horse of the *Mesta* had always meant.

But mustangs as *Mesta* horses disappear from the American consciousness after the 1940's, and ever since any large clump of unowned, feral, American ranch horses, draft horses, and ponies running on public land have been called mustangs. Though some of these are interesting, they are not the same animal in the least.

Mare: mature female horse.

Oregano de la Sierra: a variety of Monarda, a mountain mint treasured by Northern New Mexicans for medicine.

Orenda: see *Aleika*

The Owners: As it occurs in the *Stories of My Horses*, the Owners refer to various wealthy, white families and individuals who for several decades, starting in the 1970's, were those who purported to be rescuing the Spanish Barb horses, the Native Mesta horse, from extinction, but whose practical motives were more deeply vested with the sizeable federal tax exemptions their horse-saving operations garnered for their inherited money.

To do this, these Owners joined a registry dedicated to the preservation of this famous American horse. This registry predictably schismed when several quarrelling Owners, each of whom *owned* sizeable bands of horses with particular traits, claimed that only their animals had the real original traits and therefore the original bloodlines. This in turn caused many registries to sprout up, each with their own breed of wealthy founder: i.e., Owners.

There were a few sincere people, both wealthy and not, who loved and rode these horses, who purchased horses from these Big Owners, but the gene pool became so absurdly reduced by all the fracturing into quarreling camps that it became impossible for regular people to keep their interest in this beautiful animal thriving without getting immersed in a pointless war of high school factionalism in which they had no vested interest.

When the federal tax laws were changed in the 1980's and again in the 1990's, all these tax shelter registries and all these Owners disappeared into the ether. Their horses were still around, but as a recognized breed they fell into total limbo and were scattered to the winds.

All the Barb Spanish Mesta style horses these Owners had ever *owned* were horses originally gathered up by a couple of old-time Westerners way before these Owners ever existed, mostly from Native Americans and Reservations.

When the Owners first entered the scene, they felt they alone possessed what was needed to save Native horses, and felt that they alone had the funds to do it, and that all the lesser non-monied people should be thankful to contribute to the cause in the capacity of laborers and advisors in the actual *work* of feeding, trimming, breeding, doctoring, gelding etc. to maintain the Owner's tax shelters. A kind of feudal mentality.

All the Native Navajos and Pueblos with whom I grew up have the time-honored tradition of developing nicknames for people based on some overriding trait, or something they might resemble in their folly. This is a fine science among most Natives and ends up becoming the name people know each other by. In this tradition, we facetiously called these wealthy people the Owners.

In *Stories of My Horses*, a specific division of the Owners is meant by the use of the word the Owners.

Our particular, local branch of the Owners, having no real experience with hands-on ranching or horse breeding to begin with, themselves fell prey to many *helpful shysters* whose *cost cutting* schemes resulted in a number of bad decisions made by the Owners, i.e.: badly designed barns, corrals, training pens, purchases of substandard hay and feed etc.. Entrepreneurial opportunists can always be found on the fringes of any family with money, and one of these dreamed up a way to use miles and miles of conveyor-belting discarded by some failed assembly line facility. After convincing at least one *horse authority* on the more *humane* stretchy qualities of pens and corrals made by stringing heavy, three inch strips of rubber conveyor belting between creosote-soaked railroad ties, also discarded by the train companies, several wealthy horse people adopted this form of horse housing. Following suit, our particular Owners made so many runs and pens, including a double-story barn, of these materials that their horse operation was locally known as the *conveyor-belt horse facility*.

Unfortunately, the fiberglass and nylon-fiber-reinforcement-webbing running through this conveyor-belt rubber was always stripping off, causing colts who accidentally ingested these to experience severe intestinal obstructions and colic. The multiple accidents to frightened horses trapped into the stretchy fencing, combined with the constant exposure to heavy metals ingested by the horses chewing on the rubber, mostly lead, not to mention the arsenic in the treated railroad posts, caused tremendous health problems, several deaths, and a general unsettled character to all this would-be *horse rescue*.

What most people who just loved these particular horses didn't grasp was that the Owners throughout the country didn't actually want to have viable businesses with these horses. They wanted to have a money-losing operation that allowed a few of them to look like saviors, while saving taxes for their families, thereby *making money*.

Unlike the beautiful Native Spanish Mesta Barbs, the Owners were a specific breed of people who are still very easy to find and certainly don't need rescuing. The horses they said they were keeping vital have practically disappeared, yet again, back into the matrix of the world.

While there are people who still love, keep, understand and ride these animals, most have learned to lie very low and maintain what they do hidden away in their own unflamboyant existences. Ironically though, many of us in New Mexico, not so very long ago, grew up riding these exact types of horses on the Reservations. After the horses evaporated into the incoming *white American* lifestyle of the 1950's and 60's, in order for any of us to gather up even just a few of these old-time animals in the 1980's, we had to turn to these same rich people who were ruining them by claiming to save them for their tax write-offs, because, by then, only the Owners had them!

Picaro (Spanish): someone mischevious, sparky and always looking for an opportunity to get away with a forbidden activity. From the verb *picar*, to sting.

Picketwire mountains: Anglo settler rendition of the earlier French settlers name for the beautiful peaks of the Purgatoire Mountains of today's Southern Colorado. These mountains bear older Native names which are Holy to all tribes.

Platica (pláh-tee-cah): Spanish for conversation. In New Mexico, and other parts of the Americas, *platica* can mean the distilled central meaning of what someone is trying to get across.

Proud flesh: when a horse experiences a gash, like cats, their bodies quickly self-bandage themselves and try to cover the exposed flesh by naturally producing a kind of thick, gooey, very frothy, white substance that seems to keep out flies and dirt, but sometimes solidifies and cracks. Though it's part of the natural healing process, we generally wash it off to keep the wound filling with real tissue, which if given a chance horses do admirably.

Questa (Spanish): signifies a steep slope, from the Spanish word for expenditure or the "difficult cost of energy it takes to climb up a Questa."

Quirt (Southwestern American English): cowboy fore-shortening of the Spanish word *cuarta*, signifying a short riding whip that can take any number of forms. The classic Mexican quirt has a wristband that attaches to a semi-stiff, tapered, braided shank about ten to fifteen inches long that has two, twelve to eighteen inch latigo lashes attached at the bottom. Usually very ornately braided leather over rawhide, but sometimes five multi-colored strands of rawhide braided over a rawhide core, or even different colors of sorted horsehair braided over a braided rawhide shank, quirts can be quite beautiful. Different Native American tribes in North America made extraordinary, customized quirts from pieces of moose antler and skin, elk antler, wood covered in brass tacks, buffalo or mountain sheep horn, all with lashes of stiff, brain-tanned neck leather or braided lashes and fancy beaded wristbands.

All over South America, particularly the Gauchos in Argentina, some Spaniards, various North African peoples, Turkmen nomads, Bashkir and Kyrgiz still make beautiful quirts covered in silver. Except for Gauchos, Chileanos, and American cowboys, who ride with quirts and spurs, most quirt-riding traditions don't use spurs to cue or motivate their horses, preferring the quirt to direct signals. The author is a quirt rider and quirt collector.

Rancho/Ranchito (New Mexican Spanish): though the word rancho has been introduced and adopted in modern English as the word ranch in Northern New Mexico a rancho and a ranch are not really the same thing. Originally like the Indigenous population, New Mexicans lived mostly in sedentary villages of side-by-side adobe houses that dotted the edges of the various springs and waterways of our area.

Though living communally, each family had a Rancho which was not located where they lived. The Rancho was land away from the village where their farms of Maize and vegetables were grown in fenced gardens generally with irrigation in the old North African-Middle Eastern pattern.

This "rancho" was also where people kept their milk cow, milk and meat goats, maybe their burro, their pigs and where they grew beautiful fruit orchards. Sometimes there was a little hut to get out of the sun or snow, or occasionally spend the night, though nobody really lived permanently at the "rancho," those members of the family or their employees in charge of herding their sheep, cows, horses might camp at the Rancho, but not with their animals. These were sheparded nomadically on open land grants in the style of Mestas even farther off.

What is now called a working ranch in English is called an "Hacienda" (a "making" place) in Spanish. A ranchito was where regular people had small landholdings away from their village houses.

In some old villages each house was placed so as to form a square of adobe houses around a central plaza.

From each house an extent of fenced land radiated like petals off a sunflower. These pieces of land were then the ranchitos of fruit, kitchen gardens and milk animals belonging to the families in the corresponding houses.

The ranchito or rancho then was never a prime residence for people, but where the barns, garden and animals lived.

The modern American nuclear family in a Ranch house on two acres, or the idea of "owning" a ranch as a place for the wealthy to go relax in the country has nothing to do with the word ranch or ranchito, which implies daily ranch work.

Even in the modern era most old New Mexican families living in far away cities still all have family ranchitos or ranchos in the mountains or out on the plains.

Rateros (Spanish American slang): means thieves or pick-pockets. From the word for rat.

Roan (Anglified medieval Spanish word): signifies a horse who is covered in two or more distinct colors of hair in tight formation, so as to appear as a single color from a distance, but changes in tonality at different angles of the sun. There are red roans (white and red mixed), yellow roans (yellow and white), blue roans (reflective gray black and white), and grulla (black and red and white tightly mixed). A lot of color variations occur in roan patterns, some horses sporting five or six different coat-colormoltings of roan annually. There are many local terms for these, like: coyote roan, strawberry roan, buttermilk roan, etc. The research is not all in on the real dynamics of roan coloration, because, in my own experience, a totally different follicle function happens in the old *Mesta* roans that has seemed to defy veterinary science to date.

Round pen: self-explanatory. Looks like a circular corral, about sixty five feet in diameter, but with no troughs or horse furniture, in which horses can be rather easily trained. The theory is that since horses run to get away from what scares them, if they flee from a person on the edge of the circle by running away, since the fencing is circular, the horse ends up right back where they started next to the person. In this way, when employed properly, a horse can be slowly made less wary and learn a number of rudimentary lessons on the ground, before being mounted to become a saddle horse. Round pens are very useful for helping rejuvenate convalescing horses, or taking the *sparks off* of an edgy animal: for exercising animals into a more reasonable mood.

Sabina (Spanish): the One-seed Juniper tree, whose very fragrant, durable presence covers most of the area of Northern New Mexico from five thousand to seven thousand feet. Most people from tall tree or forested parts of the world have no respect for our little New Mexico *Sabina* tree, but it forms a belt running the entire circumference of the Earth's land masses, all the way from Manchuria and

Mongolia, through parts of Northern Europe, into a lot of North America. Where it grows, it is universally considered very powerful good luck and health. The word *sabina* is also a modern horse color phrase.

Sacaton or **Zacaton** (Spanish from Nahuat, Sah-cah-tone): signifies a species of very tall thick-stalked Southwestern clump grass.

Side saddle: this is a pretty strange rig invented for European ladies, in that period when dress styles interfered with straddling a horse, and when a woman straddling a horse was considered too *barbarian* and unladylike. All nomadic tribes had incredible woman horse riders, none of whom were stuck riding side saddles. You have to see a side saddle in action to understand its function. But in short, it involves a rather bulky asymmetrical saddle with only one stirrup on the left, upon which a lady mounts by plopping her bottom into a tall side-facing cantle, after which she wraps her right leg around a kind of cushioned post protruding at about ten o'clock from the pommel, so that both legs are essentially hanging from the left side of the horse. Very hard on a horse's back and strange looking in motion, but I've seen women who can really ride in one. Running from the 12th century to the 20th, where along with the riding habit (a gentlewoman's riding *costume*), wasp-waisted-baleen-corseting, slave ownership and of course a crop, it's part of European gentry horse history.

Snaffle/snaffle bit (English) (*filete* in Spanish): a basic
bit used worldwide, in which pressure from the reins is
directly on the bars of the horse's mouth. Developed by
proto-Scythian, Indo-European pastoral nomads three
to four thousand years back, it was often the only metal
(bronze originally) part of all their horse's harness.
Composed mostly of two cheek-rings that are attached to
the headstall and reins, the rings are connected to each
other through the horse's mouth by two loose-sliding,
metal bars jointed in the middle that runs over the horse's
tongue. Considered the most gentle type of bit by most.

Saddle tree (English), or *fuste* (Spanish): as used in this book,
the core frame of a Southwestern saddle, upon which
are mounted successive layers of vegetable-tan leather,
rigging straps, cinches, stirrup leathers and stirrups.
Different cultures do it different ways. The Spanish use a
basket frame, the American Southwest a wood frame. The
saddles, as described herein, fit a horse only as good as its
tree fits. A bad fitting tree is a bad fitting saddle.

Sangre de Cristos (Spanish): literally Blood of Christ. The
main Northern New Mexico mountain range that is the
southernmost part of the Southern Rockies. Running
north to south, this beautiful range divides Northern New
Mexico ecosystems. To the east are the old-time buffalo
plains, and to the west are the Jemez mountains and
extensive canyon, desert, river land.

Strangely, the name was never originally used by New Mexican Spanish speakers, who called these mountains the *Sierra Nevadas*, or the *Snowy Saw*, or *Snowy Range*, as they called many ranges throughout their colonies.

It was a bunch of white Americans in the New Mexico Tourist Promotion Bureau trying to drum up business for New Mexico, who in the early 20th century, invented this romantic name and passed it off as an old Spanish settler term for the range, stating that New Mexico Spanish speaking Catholics likened the red glow that shone on the slopes during many of New Mexico's spectacular sunsets to the *Blood of Christ* on Good Friday! Of course every hill and mountain in our area is red at sunset. But these mountains really are wonderful, and the heart of all the land and people who lived around them, and now they are the Sangres.

Shinny: an Algonquin term used by Anglos for all the field hockey type games among all the Native tribes of the Americas. There are hundreds of styles and varieties. In New Mexico Pueblo culture, shinny is a ceremonial game played at only a certain time of year by two large teams, whose players each wield two curved sticks and a special stuffed hide ball. It's loud, rowdy, never ends, and a lot of fun. There are man-forms and lady-forms.

Shotgun house (rural New Mexico slang): for those adobe houses built when corrugated roofing tin and milled lumber became common place in the early 20th century. In those days all adobe buildings had flat roofs but when peaked tin roofs came in people just roofed over their flat roofs and created an attic.

Because all families built their own houses then, to simplify the carpentry necessary for the new peaked roofs, a large percentage of homes were built "shotgun" style: with all the rooms in a long row. Many old flat roof adobes had wild shapes as rooms were added on to accommodate growing children and grandkids and were difficult to roof "American" style.

Smokey withers: a Southwestern cowboy term for a horse with a dark, smokey patch of fur covering both sides of the withers, also called a smokey cross.

Sorrel (English), *alazán* (Spanish): horse coat color. Horse coat colors are impossible to describe accurately in short words and in the end are so thoroughly infused with the biases of the cultures of the people talking, the ambient light, which changes not only the horse's coat, but its appearance, that names of horse colors are vast. They totally change from climate and sun saturation and language. Plus, people are just as *racist* about how their horse colors equal their breeds, as they are about their fellow humans. The sorrel horse is a Western American term and signifies a beautiful red horse with no black points and maybe a blaze or a star. The Spanish equivalent for what is sorrel in the West, the word *alazán* is used. In both cases, the original meaning of either word refers to vegetation. *Alazán* refers to the color of a safflower plant at its different stages of color as it withers from a yellow to a beautiful red brown. Sorrel is an ancient Germanic word for the dry season color of certain coastal creeping grasses.

To me, a sorrel or an *alazán*, light, medium, dark or crayon red, just means a good red horse. This red color is the color that all feral horses assume when bred together for ages. Whole bands of red sorrel horses abound in the West. So sorrel mares are a veritable genetic seed bank of horse colors waiting to re-emerge when the right man finally shows up.

Spiderwebbing: wild, dark, squiggly lines along the forearms or withers of a horse's coat color, left over from early Pleistocene wild horse color.

Stallion: a sexually intact male horse or donkey who is capable of breeding mares. They are by nature very contentious, powerfully built, and a handful. It's rare to see people riding stallions without incident, but there are those that can and do.

Sunglaze: an imaginative term for a badly understood phenomena that takes place on the sleek summer coats of certain types of horses.

Seemingly holographic, this *sunglaze* is sometimes only apparent at certain angles, while others are visible in direct light, usually floating above the base color of the coat, as if the horse were emitting light.

A solid black horse may have a *red sunglaze* in dapples that floats at a certain angle of the sun, over the black. A light yellow buckskin might have an *orange sunglaze* at a certain angle, kind of opal like. A *blue sunglaze* on a roan will reflect the sky and give out an amazing, magical blue roan.

Old-time Native/Spanish/Mesta Barbs are famous for their opalescent sunglaze. Some people confuse this with the sunfade, which can be similar, but is only the bleaching of the tips of a dark horse's hair by the intense sun, giving a kind of *frosted* effect.

Taboon (Russian): used to describe the Central Asian and nomad custom of raising horses in large mare and foal herds with a single stallion in wide-open, unfenced territory. In taboon style, only geldings are ridden, and few stallions kept, and all mares are free to make more babies, and to be milked to make *kumiss* or fermented-milk liquor.

Ta'á Diné: see *Diné*.

Tie down (American cowboy English): a leather strap that clips to the base of a noseband, to a ring on the breast collar, or front cinch, that is adjusted so a horse can't toss his head or swing it about. I don't like tie downs. A lot of people use them.

Victorio: the non-Indian name of a very heroic and amazing Warm Springs Apache leader in the late 19th century, whose attempted friendship with whites in Southern New Mexico landed him and all his people, simultaneously, at war with both the US army and the Mexican army. The accounts of Victorio's multiple escapes from captivity on horseback are legendary throughout the Southwest. With a couple of his brave partisans he was killed in a rearguard, decoy-action between both armies, in a strategy that allowed the last remnants of his particular band to escape into a mountain of Northern Mexico, where they vaporized from view, but where everyone says they are living still, suspended in a happy, magical, aboriginal dimension.

Viga (Spanish): the visible beams crossing the ceiling of traditional Native and Spanish American adobe rooms that hold up the flat roof and latillas (see entry) made of whole peeled fir or spruce trunks. It is in these beams people kept their sacred items, weapons, land deeds etc.

A Small Note on the Language
in Stories of my Horses

Worldwide there are little pockets of unique ideas not thought of anywhere else, thriving in the wordology of people. People who in their particular dialects or vernacular-remakes of imposed national tongues or the modern patois-morphed version of their ancestral speech say the most brilliant, useful, beautifully intellectual things everyday; things not sayable in the so-called standard enforced English or German, Cantonese, French, Japanese, Spanish or any national identity language.

In these three books, *Stories of My Horses*, I have continued to try to cause "English" to flourish with some of the ironic humor, massive rhythmic diatribe, rich imagistic spark, elegant hard-headed speech patterns and talking-tones of the peoples and cultures from whence my own thinking, language and stories of my life have sprung. This is language that has not been sanitized in the boarding school, but it is smart and full of life.

Humans since forever have always kept their cultural distinctions, thoughts and hopes alive by the way they speak, not by storing them silently in written form. The language of these tales of mine, though written, have been deliberately created to be read out loud by you to your friends and family (not whispered, though that's better than nothing), to antidote the toxic mind-flattening algorithmic computerese of the hyper-abbreviating pseudo "written" language people have been coerced into by the modern need to homogenize all personal and cultural differences into user friendly *mush*. Though touted as such, this mush is not equality.

Equality cannot be achieved if all differences are erased. Equality doesn't mean you don't see a black man is black or a white man is pink, but that you love the blackness of the black man and dig the pink man his whiteness.

Equality is learning to hear, understand and then love the differences and then allowing these to all exist, *not* forcing everyone to speak, think and want the same mass-produced homogenized life polluting disposable existence.

So as incredible as it may seem if they are based in love, I want to keep all differences alive.

In keeping with that sentiment, any occurrences of wild punctuation, atypical sentence junctures, antique syntax or archaic vocabulary, capitalization of all live beings, cadences of repeated adjectives, paragraph-long rhythmic single-sentence diatribes where the subject or verb is the ultimate word are not mistakes, or bad copy-editing, but obstacles of beauty deliberately placed there in the stories of this series to force the reader to wade into the delicious stream of old-style indigenous village thinking without glossing over it all by the use of the "boring colonial bridge" of standard English.

Therefore, all perceived language inconsistencies are mine alone and are very consistent, purposeful ingredients in my private revolution of language in which words evolve like spoken flowers to summon bumblebees of never-thought-before-thinking in my sincere attempt to dethrone the homogenizing tyranny of the megabyte language over our natural born vernacular souls.

Acknowledgements

While this entire trilogy is my attempt to toast and acknowledge all the horses, one by one, whose companionship have always given me the life and vitality of the "wide open ride", it would be remiss not to remember all those people, places, and animals who made the series *Stories of My Horses* possible.

Firstly, of course, a great blessing and thanks to the mystic soul of the open land, the fabulous skies, varied terrain, plants, and animals of my native New Mexico—whose Native peoples, Spanish speaking peoples, and select Anglo ranchers and cowboys were the parent cultures that made me and the horses what we became—and where all the events revealed in the text took place.

Next, I would like to thank the spirits of all the horses themselves, both dead and still living, whose accounts appear in these three books. Without them there would have been nothing to tell.

But...

I would like to thank even more those horses both dead and alive, whose stories do not appear in these books and to apologize to those horses whose stories did for those descriptions of equally dramatic episodes of their lives that I chose to leave out.

For old wisdom insists that it is never a good idea to empty out your sack of life's hard-earned memories all the way. Because good powerful memories are special: like sourdough bread starter, where from every batch you have to keep back a fistful of dough to make the next down the line. In the same way, worthy memories retained re-start the next section of one's life, leavening the dull grind of the present into a life fully lived from where the sack of stories worth remembering is re-stocked! Always good to keep back just a pinch for the next round.

Next, I'd like to send a big, two person *abrazo* for Liz Dwyer and Curtis Weinrich of North Star Press for their courage, love of beautiful books, love of story, and unique willingness to bring forth the three volumes of the *Stories of My Horses* in such a friendly, professional way. The literary freedom that this willingness has afforded me, allowing me to write and publish books so dear to my life with my unique language use still intact and outside the assigned genre slots where all my previous books are forced to reside, is like letting my herd of words out for a good delicious gallop across the forgotten soul of the American West after years of being corralled and contained in the tiny neurotic pens of east coast urban categories.

Then for my typist Susannah Hall in the UK, in honor of the most well-done, patient typing of my hand-written manuscripts, I would like to send a ride in the King's carriage (without the King, unless of course he insists on coming along) filled to the roof with the best organic butter, with bars of gold, and crates of freshly baked crumpets, tea, and a samovar strapped on top, driven by Hugh and Kayode, to the best of times and a picnic on a revived English eel river to kiss the elvers with their poetry!

Like everything else I endorse, my books are written by hand, with a pen on real paper. But this handwriting of mine is extremely idiosyncratic and hard to decipher to say the least, so it takes a special talent to read my initial screed, then type it, as written, into a program, have me rewrite on a hard copy, scan it and return it to Britain to retype, adding all my amplifications, going back and forth in this way for as many as seven rounds, for every chapter, whilst the manuscript grows into a bigger and bigger, newer and different manifestation over the months, until Ms. Hall discovers that she's been actually typing four books that I'm working on simultaneously!

I know Ms. Hall has a magnifying glass and some other manual aids for deciphering my scrawl, but no doubt she's been blessed by some supernatural to magically pull it off.

In short,

Her typing has been indispensable.

I want to send a small south-facing springtime drumlin filled top to bottom with peace and Mariposa Lilies to my copy-editor Lisa Lawrence so she may sit inside them and drink the best Nahuat grown coffee surrounded by all the people who love her chatting about the word for golden fibulae in 6th century Alman to express my gratitude for her rare dedication to the integrity of my crazy language and her courage to smooth out my rambunctious comma pileups without killing the Native soul. All thanks and blessings.

The author as illustrator would like to thank and acknowledge the late Hoke Denetsosie. In the 1930's and 40's this Diné artist developed a black and white, crow-quill pen style of illustrating the most beautiful editions of what were intended as bilingual Navajo/English primers for Native school children to learn to write both Diné and English. The most unlikely publisher for these forgotten books was the Department of Education, in the Bureau of Indian Affairs, Department of Interior, in short the US Government! In a momentary flash of intelligent vision and good heartedness the government simultaneously put out similar bilingual language books in other Native languages throughout the country, illustrated by artists of the corresponding tribes.

Though Denetsosie's work later became associated with cartoonists and other less worthy endeavours, his illustrations for the *Na'nilkaadi Yazhi* (*Little Herder*) series was more than a brilliant achievement and has never been equalled in originality. Like everything else after WWII, the government numbed up, and anxious in the cold war lost the thread, and what began as an amazing hopeful trend was utterly forgotten. A lot of amazing artists of all types emerged from this trend but most melted away, swept back under the carpet of the craze of technological progress.

But to me the original solutions Hoke Denetsosie came up with on his own, without coaching, or tutoring to illustrate the land and his people of those times was not only so subtly ingenious, but always an inspiration to me, more so because his drawings correspond very well with some of the territory and the moods of the land in which *Stories of My Horses* takes place. He was great, lived to be a very old Native rancher, well loved by his people but largely overlooked as an artist. I had to say something, for as I drew I always thought about him.

And now I want to say thank you to my little family,

To my beautiful ten-year-old boy Gobi, who loves our *Mesteños* as much as I do, who writes stories and edits as much as I do. To my wonderous fourteen-year-old star-nebula loving daughter Tai, who also writes and edits as much as I do. And to their incredibly inspired teacher and beautiful determined mother, my wife, Johanna Keller Prechtel who using our special secret recipe of charred plants, mare, foal, and stallion manure compost has succeeded in growing a six-foot high broccoli thicket in December when even coyotes freeze solid like statues! (old time horses are good for lots of things besides riding!).

For their love for me and their patience with my barrage of humor and their tolerance of the overly fierce delivery of my vision regarding the need for a more substantial and beautiful culture that permeates my every word and action cannot be adequately rewarded with any words I could ever conjur.

And to you, gentle reader, for your love of the *wild open ride* over the wild open land and your willingness to eschew modern cynicism and ride with me in words, in ways and into places, where hardly any go anymore these days. But if we're not spiritually lazy, things can always change for the better and often do.

All blessings.

About the Author and Illustrator

As an avid student of indigenous eloquence, innovative language and thought, Martín Prechtel is a writer, artist, and teacher who, through his work both written and spoken, hopes to promote the subtlety, irony, and premodern vitality hidden in any living language. A half-blood Native American with a Pueblo Indian upbringing, he left New Mexico to live in the village of Santiago Atitlán, Guatemala, eventually becoming a full member of the Tzutujil Mayan community there. For many years he served as a principal in that body of village leaders responsible for piloting the young people through the meanings of their ancient stories in the rituals of adult rites of passage.

Once again, residing in his beloved New Mexico, Prechtel teaches at his international school, Bolad's Kitchen. Through an immersion into the world's lost seeds and sacred farming, forgotten music, magical architecture, ancient textile making, metalsmithing, the making and using of tools, musical instruments and food and the deeper meanings of the origins of all these things in the older stories, in ancient texts and by teaching through the traditional use of riddles, Prechtel hopes to inspire people of every mind and way to regrow and revitalize real culture and to find their own sense of place in the sacredness of a newly found daily existence in love with the natural world. Prechtel lives with his family and their Native *Mesta* horses in Northern New Mexico.

Martín Prechtel's previous works include: *Secrets of the Talking Jaguar*; *Long Life, Honey in the Heart*; *The Disobedience of the Daughter of the Sun*; *Stealing Benefacio's Roses*; *The Unlikely Peace at Cuchumaquic*; *The Smell of Rain on Dust: Grief and Praise; Rescuing the Light; The Mare and the Mouse;* and *The Wild Rose*.

Cover Painting, *Voice of the Giant*, by Martín Prechtel.